POLITICS AND THE
LEGAL PROCESS

Harper's American Political Behavior Series

Under the Editorship of David J. Danelski

POLITICS AND THE LEGAL PROCESS

JAMES EISENSTEIN

The Pennsylvania State University

HARPER & ROW, PUBLISHERS

New York, Evanston, San Francisco, London

Sponsoring Editor: Alvin A. Abbott.
Project Editor: David Nickol
Designer: Michel Craig
Production Supervisor: Stefania J. Taflinska

POLITICS AND THE LEGAL PROCESS Copyright © 1973 by James Eisenstein. All rights reserved. Printed in the United States of America. No part of this book may be used or reproduced in any manner whatsoever without written permission except in the case of brief quotations embodied in critical articles and reviews. For information address Harper & Row, Publishers, Inc., 10 East 53rd Street, New York, N.Y. 10022.

Library of Congress Cataloging in Publication Data

Eisenstein, James.
   Politics and the legal process.

   (Harper's American political behavior series)
   1. Judicial process—United States.   2. Law and politics.   I. Title.
KF380.E35   340.1'15   73-2704
ISBN 0-06-041883-4

CONTENTS

Preface vii

ONE: INTRODUCTION 1
1. A Political Approach to Law and the Legal Process 4

TWO: THE POLITICS OF RECRUITMENT IN THE LEGAL PROCESS 13
2. Elections in the Legal Process 15
3. The Politics of Appointment in the Legal Process 35
4. Politics, Recruitment, and Behavior 54

THREE: THE INFLUENCE OF THE STRATEGIC ENVIRONMENT OF MAJOR POSITIONS IN THE LEGAL PROCESS ON BEHAVIOR 81
5. The Strategic Environment of the Police 84
6. The Operating Reality of State Courts 98
7. The Operation of Federal District Courts 143
8. The Strategic Environment of Appellate Judges 176

FOUR: THE IMPACT OF THE LEGAL PROCESS 205
9. An Overview of the Impact of the Legal Process 206
10. The Impact of the Criminal Process 216
11. The Impact of the Civil Process 256
12. The Impact of Higher Courts 277

FIVE: CONCLUSION: THE LEGAL PROCESS IN THE POLITICAL SYSTEM 307
    13. Who Gets What in the Legal Process: Patterns of Output 309
    14. The Legal Process in the Political System: Explanation and Prospects 338

Index 353

PREFACE

MOST students entering introductory American government courses have only the vaguest notion of the nature and functioning of the legal process in our political system. Typically, even informed students know little about it beyond a recognition of the existence and importance of the U.S. Supreme Court. Unfortunately, they leave most such courses with little additional knowledge. It is a rare introductory text that goes much beyond the traditional discussion of the Supreme Court and judicial review.

This lack of information about the legal process is reflected in the discipline of political science generally. As interest in the traditional field of public law dwindled, it was replaced with commendable efforts to examine the question of why appellate judges decide cases as they do. But the study of appellate judicial behavior is no substitute for a comprehensive approach to the contributions made by the rest of the legal process to the functioning of the American political system.

This book is essentially directed at assisting in the task of rectifying these gaps. For the undergraduate student studying American government, it seeks to provide a reasonably comprehensive and explicitly political introduction to the operation and impact of the legal process. For the discipline of political science, it seeks to demonstrate the relevance of the legal process for the study of politics generally, to pull together research on a variety of components of the legal process from several disciplines, and to help speed the development and define the content of a new subfield devoted to the study of the legal process.

I owe a number of debts, both intellectual and personal, incurred in the writing of this book. Professor David J. Danelski offered general guidance and specific criticisms throughout. Professor Herbert Jacob offered a number of insightful criticisms on a later draft. Several of my colleagues, including Professors John Kingdon and Jack Walker, read earlier drafts. The 400 students who took my courses in the legal process at the undergraduate and graduate levels made innumerable helpful criticisms, comments, and suggestions. Like every author, I stubbornly refused to take many of the excellent suggestions of my critics. Finally, I would like to acknowledge the assistance of my wife. It extended far beyond the significant support, encouragement, and manuscript preparation that wives of authors typically provide. She served as an excellent critic, a demanding editor, and a frequent contributor of substantive ideas. My debt to her is greatest of all.

POLITICS AND THE LEGAL PROCESS

PART ONE
INTRODUCTION

FEW aspects of the American political system are as little understood as the legal process. Though most beginning students of political science know something about Congress, the president, and the federal bureaucracy, knowledge of the legal system rarely goes much beyond recognition of the Supreme Court as the third branch of government.

Ignorance of the American legal process cannot be justified on grounds of its irrelevance, lack of interest, or unimportance. Most of the major issues and events in American political life during the late 1960s and early 1970s directly involved the legal process. The riots in Watts, Newark, and Detroit, the street violence during the 1968 Democratic Convention in Chicago and the Chicago 7 conspiracy trial that followed, and the issues of "crime in the streets" and "law and order" which were featured in Richard Nixon's campaign for the presidency are prominent examples. Rioting and racism, violence and crime, the role of the police in assuring public safety and order are relevant in the eyes of almost everyone. Students are particularly interested in these and other topics related to the operation of the legal process. They are easily drawn into emotional and hotly contested discussions of the proper role of police or the degree to which law enforcement is prejudiced against the young, black, and poor.

While the highly visible events just mentioned demonstrate the importance of the legal process in dramatic fashion, they overshadow the significance of the low-visibility decisions made in great numbers daily in the legal process. These decisions have the most profound effects on the lives of millions of people each year. They involve questions of wealth, property, and ownership; the custody of children; the physical safety and security of private citizens; the dignity and attitudes of those arrested; even whether people spend a portion of their lives in prisons or mental institutions. But their cumulative significance extends beyond their impact on the lives of individuals to the heart of some of the basic questions of politics. What groups benefit and lose as a result of governmental action? How do political regimes invoke law and law enforcement to maintain themselves and the stability of the society which they govern? What obstacles do those forces promoting peaceful change (and violent change too) encounter in the legal process?

The fact that few people fully recognize the cumulative importance of these decisions does not make them irrelevant to the study of politics. In fact, it is all the more reason for studying them.

This book is about such decisions—who makes them, how they are made, what they are about, and what difference they make. Although they differ considerably in detail, these decisions share the common characteristics of being more or less directly related to the application of law. And all of them fall within the scope of what we will shortly identify as the legal process.

A major task of this book, then, is to provide the reader with a basic understanding of the importance of the legal process in the governing of American society. In part, this involves a description of the operation and impact of significant components of the legal process. Educational research has shown, however, that such information is usually forgotten rather quickly. It is far more important, therefore, to present to readers a way of looking at the legal process that increases their sensitivity to the significance of its operation, helping them to both understand and evaluate its functioning. In turn, this can contribute to their general knowledge and understanding of the American political process.

CHAPTER 1
A POLITICAL APPROACH TO LAW AND THE LEGAL PROCESS

THE perspective that shapes the entire approach and content of this book is that the legal process is an integral part of the political system. This perspective has profound consequences for the way in which the legal process will be defined, the aspects of it that will be studied and the techniques used to examine them, as well as the questions we seek to answer about it.

Politics is the process by which authoritative decisions about who gets what in society are made.[1] Ultimately, these decisions involve government, because it is through the participation of government that they are made authoritative and binding on society. The processes that surround the making of these decisions are composed of complex interactions among a variety of participants exerting influence in an attempt to further their own interests and goals.

If the legal process is but one of many components of the political system, it, too, must exhibit these interactions. What, then, is there about the legal process that allows us to distinguish it from other components?

---

[1] This definition draws upon the works of two political scientists. David Easton, in *The Political System* (New York: Knopf, 1960), Chapter V, defines politics as the process by which *values* (the things men desire) are authoritatively allocated for a society. Harold Lasswell has conceived of it as the process that determines who gets what, when, and how in society. See especially his *Politics: Who Gets What, When, How* (New York: McGraw Hill, 1936).

An obvious way to answer this question is to think of it as an analog of the legislative process. The primary function of the legislative process is to enact statutes that set general policy and to appropriate funds for their implementation. The legal process is concerned with the application and enforcement of law. Its association with *law* accounts for the use of the term *legal*. It is a *process* because the individuals and institutions constituting it interact regularly and repeatedly with one another and with other elements of the political system.

This definition leads to serious problems when examined closely because it relies on the terms *law enforcement* and *law*. It is difficult to find a more deceptively simple question than, What is law? Distinguished and venerable students of jurisprudence have struggled with this question for centuries. As anyone who has explored their work knows, the variety and complexity of the answers offered is overwhelming.[2]

If the use of the term *law* as the basis of a definition of the legal process creates problems, what alternatives exist? It is impossible to avoid all ambiguity. Any definition must use undefined terms. As Edwin W. Patterson explains in his book on jurisprudence:

Since any definition of a term must use other terms, and since any definition of those terms must use still others, any definition must consist ultimately of undefined terms; and the effectiveness of the definition in conveying meaning, at least initially, will depend upon the familiarity in conventional usage of the meaning of its constituent terms.[3]

---

[2] See, for example, Edwin W. Patterson, *Jurisprudence: Men and Ideas of the Law* (Brooklyn, New York: Foundation Press, 1953); M.P. Golding, ed., *The Nature of Law* (New York: Random House, 1966); H. L. A. Hart, *The Concept of Law* (Oxford: Clarendon Press, 1961); Hermann Kantorowicz, *The Definition of Law* (Cambridge: Cambridge University Press, 1958); Wilfrid E. Rumble, Jr., *American Legal Realism* (Ithaca, N. Y.: Cornell University Press, 1968).

[3] Patterson, *Jurisprudence*, p. 70.

We shall utilize the concept of a *court* as the undefined term at the basis of our definition of the legal process.[4] Most of us have a pretty good notion of what a court is.[5] Certainly its meaning is less muddled than that of *law*.

Thus, the legal process is defined as the sum total of the behavior of those individuals and positions that are more or less directly connected with the activities of courts. Both the traffic court in a small town and the U. S. Supreme Court are part of the legal process, since both fall within the meaning of the term *court*. The small town's city council and the United States Congress are not, since the relationship of each to courts is only indirect.

It is not necessary that participants in the legal process appear physically in a court for them to be connected with the activities that take place there. Many private attorneys and some criminal investigative personnel, for instance, never see the inside of a courtroom unless they are arrested themselves. Though they are less directly involved in courtroom activity than is a judge or juror, their behavior does affect what happens in court. In addition, their behavior is affected by their anticipations of what might happen in court. All behavior related to their job falls within the scope of the legal process under this definition, even if the likelihood of ending up in a courtroom is remote. The lawyer's routine advice to his clients, and the policeman's nonarrest activities on the beat are as much a part of the legal process as a judge's courtroom rulings.

A number of men holding official governmental positions are obviously part of the legal process. Judges and other

[4] Cf. Alf Ross, *On Law and Justice* (Berkeley, Calif.: University of California Press, 1959). He distinguishes law from other norms of conduct in that law involves directives to courts and judges.

[5] Familiar problems spring up the moment one forgets that some terms must remain undefined. It is tempting, for instance, to define courts as bodies that are at the center of the process of applying and enforcing law. But this only raises once again the question of what *law* is. A more fruitful approach is to consider courts as the formal institutions in which judges perform their official tasks. It is difficult to conceive of courts without judges.

court personnel such as probation and parole officers, clerks, stenographers, and bailiffs immediately come to mind. But a number of other governmental positions are closely linked to courts, including commissioners and referees, prosecutors, public defenders and legal aid attorneys, and the whole array of investigative agencies, from local and state police to the FBI and postal inspectors. Prison officials, parole boards, city attorneys, and state attorneys general are also participants in the legal process, although their involvement is not so direct.

Some positions are semiofficial. Though technically nongovernmental, they are extensively involved in the activities of courts. Private attorneys, bail bondsmen, and, in some jurisdictions, process servers, are good examples. Jurors can also be regarded as semiofficial participants. For the duration of their service, they are performing a public function and are paid with public funds.[6] Though paid from private sources, newspaper reporters covering courts and police perform quasi-public functions.

Finally, there are a number of people who sporadically become very actively involved in the legal process. The litigants in civil cases and private citizens who become defendants in criminal actions are particularly noteworthy. But representatives of interest groups and the mass media, leaders of political parties, bureaucrats, and elected officials in legislative and executive positions also have occasion to engage in direct interaction with personnel in the legal process. These occasional participants cannot be considered part of the legal process per se since only a small proportion of their total activity is more or less directly connected with the activities of courts. But their limited involvement is extremely significant since it is the primary link between the legal process and the rest of the political system.

There is a widely known and accepted view of law that, if adopted, would lead to a very different conception of the

---

[6] Private attorneys in some jurisdictions find themselves in an analogous position when they are appointed to represent a defendant who cannot afford to hire his own lawyer. In theory, of course, all members of the bar are "officers of the court."

legal process than the one adopted here. It will be referred to as the *traditional* view of law.[7] One of its principal opponents, Jerome Frank, nevertheless provided a good summary of it: "Law is a complete body of rules existing from time immemorial and unchangeable except to the limited extent that legislatures have changed the rules by enacted statutes. . . . Judges . . . are merely 'speaking the law.' Their function is purely passive."[8] In the traditional view, judges' decisions are not arbitrary. In fact, they have practically no discretion whatsoever. In the words of Sir William Blackstone: "The judgment, though pronounced or awarded by judges, is not their determination or sentence, but the determination and sentence of the law. It is the conclusion that naturally and regularly follows from the premises of law and fact. . . ."[9]

A study of the legal process based on the traditional view of law would emphasize the formal decision-making processes of courts from the perspective of how they ought to work if they conform to legal theory. Thus, it would examine the nature of legal reasoning, the use of statutes and constitutions as the basis of decisions, and the formal structures and procedures used in arriving at them (including jurisdictional rules, the nature of the adversary system, the role of the jury, rules of evidence and standards of proof, and so forth). Generally, the emphasis would be placed very heavily on courts to the near exclusion of prosecutors, police, plaintiffs, and other participants in the legal process.

The assumption that the legal process is intensely political

---

[7] Writers in the field of jurisprudence refer to this view by a variety of other terms: the conventional view; the classical view; the mechanical theory of law; legal fundamentalism; legal absolutism.

[8] In *Law and the Modern Mind* (Garden City, N.Y.: Anchor Books, 1963), p. 35, Frank describes the view of Professor Beale, a proponent of the traditional view, as follows: "Law, by definition, must have a noble aspect, a breath-taking sweep. Law must be, Beale asserts, "UNIFORM, GENERAL, CONTINUOUS, EQUAL, CERTAIN, PURE" [p. 53].

[9] Quoted by Rumble, *American Legal Realism*, pp. 49–50.

suggests the possibility that the behavior of judges and others in the legal process may not be solely determined by some abstract body of rules termed *law*. Indeed, the major rival to the traditional view of law in jurisprudence, legal realism, explicitly advocates such a possibility.[10] Although legal realists differ among themselves on a number of points, they share a profound skepticism of the traditional view, particularly in their "disbelief in the impact traditionally ascribed to established legal rules."[11] Legal realists speak derisively of the transcendental quality which traditionalists impart to law.[12] To the legal realist, law has no independent existence outside of society. It is the product of man in society, and changes as society changes. Discretion in the interpretation and application of statutes and legal precedents is inevitable and often desirable. Since decisions cannot be guided by a body of absolute principles that do not exist, factors other than legal rules (personal prejudices, attitudes, and values of the judge, for example) inevitably shape them.[13]

The basic approach taken to the nature of law in this book

---

[10] Rumble, in *American Legal Realism*, provides an excellent survey of the thought of American legal realists. Frank, in *Law and the Modern Mind*, has a lively and forceful presentation of his version of realism. For an excellent summary of major elements in legal realism, see Karl N. Llewellyn, "Some Realism About Realism—Responding to Dean Pound," *Harvard Law Review* 44 (1931), pp. 1222-1264; Charles G. Haines, in "General Observations on the Effects of Personal, Political, and Economic Influences in the Decisions of Judges," *Illinois Law Review* 17 (1922), pp. 96-116, contrasts the "mechanical theory" with the "theory of free legal decision."

[11] Rumble, *American Legal Realism*, p. 48.

[12] Oliver Wendell Holmes characterized it as a "Brooding omnipresence in the sky." Quoted by Frank, *Law and the Modern Mind*, p. 60.

[13] Alpheus Thomas Mason, in *Harlan Fisk Stone: Pillar of the Law* (New York: Viking, 1956), described the approach of Chief Justice Stone to these questions thusly: "Stone and his sophisticated associates alike realized that the harmonious application of eighteenth century generalizations to twentieth century existence, the perplexing search for 'legislative will,' calls for human sympathy, tact, curiosity, insight, intelligence—no automaton could do the job" [p. 784].

is entirely consistent with legal realism, though its genesis lies more in the work of political scientists than of the legal realists.[14] The emphasis is not on what the nature of some abstract conception of law is but rather on the *behavior* of the people we have identified as participants in the legal process.

It is difficult to escape entirely the notion that they are somehow involved in applying something known as law. To capture this notion while avoiding any implication that an adequate definition of law has been offered, the terms *law-as-applied* or *law-in-action* will be used throughout this book to refer to the consequences of the operation of the legal process.

The implications of this definition of the legal process can be seen in the way in which a specific problem is approached. We do not ask the same questions that one usually asks about law. We normally would ask what the law says about littering the sidewalk and expect an answer that describes the content of statutes and previous decisions of courts. Here, we would ask what the consequences are of littering the sidewalk. To answer the question of what the law-as-applied is, we must look at patterns of enforcement. If hippies, strangers, and Black Panthers are stopped, warned, or arrested by patrolmen when they are seen dropping something, for them it is against the law-as-applied. Some action of an official nature by law-enforcement personnel has been taken. The law-as-applied regarding littering may be quite different for the chief of police, the mini-skirted secretary, or the Marine captain.

Clearly, an emphasis on the law-as-applied cannot ignore

[14] I am referring especially to Arthur Bentley, *The Process of Government* (Chicago: University of Chicago Press, 1908); David Truman, *The Governmental Process* (New York: Knopf, 1951); and Harold Lasswell, *Politics*. Both Jack Peltason, *Federal Courts in the Political Process* (New York: Random House, 1955) and Herbert Jacob, *Justice in America* (Boston: Little, Brown, 1965) take a political approach to some aspects of the legal process. For a discussion of the political nature of local legal systems, see James Klonoski and Robert Mendelsohn, "The Allocation of Justice: A Political Approach," *Journal of Public Law* 14 (1966), pp. 326-342.

the content of statutes and case law. The behavior of patrolmen, prosecutors, judges, and private citizens is shaped significantly by them. But they need not be the determining factor. Imagine, for example, that there is no ordinance prohibiting littering the sidewalk. Now comes a member of the Black Panther party walking by a patrolman and littering. The officer may stop and warn him, or even arrest him, strip and search him at the station house, and release him without charge several hours later. He has been detained, temporarily deprived of his freedom, and searched just as if he had clearly violated an existing statute. For him, at that particular time, it was against the law-as-applied to litter the sidewalk. If the chief of police double-parks in front of a fruit stand, helps himself to a banana, and throws the peel on the sidewalk, the officer on the beat standing by just might not arrest him. Here, it is not against the law-as-applied for the chief to engage in such behavior.

There is another dimension to law-in-action that must be recognized. In addition to the behavior of participants in the legal process who enforce or fail to enforce statutes, a comprehensive survey of the law-in-action regarding littering must also examine the behavior of potential litterbugs. Some people refrain from littering because they wish to avoid official punishment, or because they feel it is morally wrong to violate an ordinance prohibiting such action. Others may deliberately litter because they know it is formally prohibited. In both instances, the behavior of private citizens is modified by perceptions of the legal process and law, and is an integral component of the law-in-action.

The emphasis of this book, then, is on <u>the behavior of participants in the legal process as they shape law-in-action and the consequences of their behavior. Its organization is based on four essential questions of politics: How are key decision-makers recruited?</u> Once recruited, <u>how and why do they behave as they do? What are the consequences of their behavior for who gets what? What conclusions can be drawn from the answers to the first three questions regarding the</u>

nature of the legal process and its relationship to the rest of the political system?

Part Two focuses on the recruitment process. What procedures are used to recruit which decision-makers? What factors shape the outcomes of these procedures? What sort of people are selected and what sort eliminated? What are some of the implications of the selection process for the behavior of those selected?

Part Three is concerned with the explanation of the behavior of many of the major participants as they perform their official duties. How much discretion do they have? What accounts for it? How is it exercised? How are they guided by (1) the demands of other significant position-holders with whom they deal; (2) by statutes and rules; (3) by superiors?

The ultimate justification for studying recruitment and behavior is impact. How are individuals affected by the operation of the legal process? What does it contribute to the formation of public policy? The chapters in Part Four survey the nature and extent of the impact of a variety of components of the legal process.

Finally, what general patterns can be identified in policy output? Which groups benefit from the operation of the legal process and which are hurt? How is the legal process used by groups and interests in society to further their goals? How can we explain the existence of the patterns found in outcomes? What can policy outcomes in the legal process tell us about how American politics operates generally? Finally, what are the prospects for reform? Part Five, "The Legal Process in the Political System," examines these questions.

PART TWO
THE POLITICS OF RECRUITMENT IN THE LEGAL PROCESS

THE politics of the legal process begins with the selection of personnel. This should not be surprising. Filling practically any position in our society involves at least some "politics" in the broad sense of that word. Students obtain summer employment because they or their fathers "know" someone. Sons of bosses whose advancement in their fathers' enterprises so amazes those passed over are notorious illustrations of the popular theory that it's not what you know but who you know that counts. Even avid sports fans may marvel at how successful professional athletes were in obtaining scarce places in National Guard units during the Vietnam war.

The politics of jobs is not confined exclusively to such medieval dealings between relatives and contacts. The establishment of allegedly objective criteria for selection (the use of high-school grades and standardized test scores for college admission is a good example) has profound effects on what types of people succeed. In fact, decisions on what objective criteria will be used and how they will be measured frequently generate considerable controversy. But even after ostensibly objective criteria are established, they may not always be objectively applied. Typing and shorthand skills may not be all that an executive looks over in hiring his personal secretary.

The politics of jobs does not stop at selection of personnel. Evaluations of performance for the purpose of promoting (or even deciding if someone will be retained) are also political. A variety of strategies are pursued by individuals to enhance their prospects of promotion. Giving an apple to the teacher, joining the "right" clubs, and marrying the boss's daughter are familiar examples.

When it comes to the political system, the politics of jobs is even more obvious. In addition to the factors just mentioned, characteristics acknowledged as *political* in the narrow sense of that term come into play. Candidates are nominated in primaries or conventions and run in general elections, executives appoint the party faithful, interest groups work for the selection of people favorable to their positions.

We routinely examine the recruitment process when we seek to understand the operation of any component of the political system. It is an excellent place to begin our treatment of the politics of the legal process.

Perhaps the most obvious questions to ask about recruitment are, what procedures are used and how do they operate? Most participants in the legal process are recruited either through election or some form of appointment.[1] The politics of elections in the legal process is described in Chapter 2. Chapter 3 looks at the forms of appointment found there.

There are, however, a number of other questions about recruitment processes. What kind of people are recruited? What are their career ambitions? What values, prejudices, and ideological convictions do they bring to their positions? To whom do they feel obligated for their selection? The answers to these questions can help unravel one of the most crucial questions of politics: Why do decision-makers behave as they do? In Chapter 4, we shall seek to describe some of the links between recruitment and the behavior of major participants in the legal process.

[1] Two other techniques for recruiting participants in the legal process—self-selection and coercive recruitment—are discussed in Chapter 4.

CHAPTER 2
ELECTIONS IN THE LEGAL·PROCESS

ELECTIONS appeal to Americans because of a widespread belief that they enhance the representativeness of government.[1] In theory, they encourage the operation of both direct and indirect mechanisms which insure that decisions reflect the values and wishes of the common man.

Direct control is exerted when voters choose candidates who represent their interests or defeat incumbents who have failed to do so. _Indirect control_ results when candidates and incumbents modify their policy stands and decisions to conform with what they think voters want.[2] Such "influence through anticipated reactions" rests on the belief that failure to make such

---

[1] Herbert Kaufman, in "Emerging Conflicts in the Doctrines of Public Administration," _American Political Science Review_ 50 (1956), pp. 1057-1073, has identified three competing core values in the organization and operation of American political institutions: representativeness, neutral competence, and executive leadership. Elections provide a major mechanism for achieving representativeness.

[2] For an extensive discussion of the role of elections in insuring representation and accountability, see Kenneth Prewitt, "Political Ambitions, Volunteerism, and Electoral Accountability," _American Political Science Review_ 64 (1970), pp. 5-17.

adjustments will mean electoral defeat. Several conditions must be met if these direct and indirect control mechanisms are to be effective in ensuring representativeness. Direct control of policy through elections requires:

1. Frequent elections in which there is at least some possibility that either candidate can win
2. At least two candidates competing for the same position
3. Clear enunciation by each candidate of the policies he will follow if elected
4. An informed electorate which has opinions about the policies it wants implemented by the officeholder, which knows the stands of the candidates and the past performance of incumbents seeking reelection, which supports the candidate coming closest to its views, and which actually votes in the election for this candidate.

The effectiveness of indirect control mechanisms, which must operate in conjunction with the direct mechanisms just described, assumes that:

1. Incumbents desire reelection or harbor career ambitions whose realization depends on acting in a representative way
2. Incumbents believe (whether correctly or not) that failure to propose and to act on acceptable policies will adversely affect success in the next election or in moving to another post
3. Incumbents have a reasonably accurate perception of what the electorate wants, will tolerate, and does not want.

To what extent are these conditions met for elections in the legal process? Enough information exists on three elective positions in the legal process to permit some tentative generalizations. They are state attorneys general, prosecuting attorneys, and judges.[3]

---

[3] County sheriffs are also elected. Despite their obvious importance, so little is known about them that they must largely be ignored.

ELECTION OF STATE ATTORNEYS GENERAL

The state attorney general probably has as much impact on state government as any other official with the exception of the governor.[4] As chief legal officer, he handles civil and criminal appellate litigation on behalf of the state and its agencies, and renders both formal and informal opinions on the legal status of administrative and legislative actions. The formal opinions, which set forth the limitations and requirements of state statutes and the state constitution, are regarded as authoritative until and unless they are overturned by a court. Requests for informal opinions and legal advice from legislators, local prosecutors, state administrative agencies, and even the governor inject the attorney general into the thick of policy formation in a wide variety of matters. His influence is also felt through investigations conducted by his staff and through his limited supervisory powers over local prosecutors. Because so many decision-makers rely upon him for advice and counsel, he probably knows more about what is occurring in state government than anyone else. Finally, his activities often place him in the center of public attention.

[4] There are only a limited number of published studies dealing with state attorneys general. For a recent comprehensive description of the history, powers, duties, and organization of the office in the various states, see *The Office of Attorney General*, National Association of Attorneys General, Committee on the Office of Attorneys General (February, 1971). Samuel Krislov has published one of the rare empirically based studies. See "Constituency vs. Constitutionalism: The Desegregation Issue and Tensions and Aspirations of Southern Attorneys General," *Midwest Journal of Political Science* 3 (1959), pp. 75-92. Studies of the office in a single state include "The Office of Attorney General in Kentucky: A Report of the Department of Law to the Committee on the Administration of Justice in the Commonwealth of Kentucky," *Kentucky Law Journal* 51 (1962-1963), pp. 1S-152S; and Richard A. Watson, *Office of Attorney General, Missouri Studies No. 1* (Columbia, Missouri: University of Missouri Research Center, 1962). See also Robert H. Gordon, *The Attorney General and Agency Counsels in New York State*, (Ph.D. diss., Syracuse University, 1966). Most other works deal with formal powers of the attorney general's office and prescriptions for reorganizing it. An unpublished paper by James Jordan, "Advisory Opinions: The Attorney General and His Environment" contains a summary of existing literature which I found very helpful.

The nationwide press coverage the attorney general of Kansas received when he personally led a drug raid on the University of Kansas in February 1971, to fulfill a campaign pledge is a good example.

All but a handful of state attorneys general are elected.[5] Two of the conditions for direct control of behavior by elections, frequent elections with competing candidates, are usually met. Candidates are nominated by the two parties and compete in a statewide, partisan general election in which other major officials (including the governor) are also selected. Although overshadowed by the race for governor, the contest for attorney general draws at least as much interest as other statewide offices. Since no one has studied these elections in detail, nothing is known about how clearly candidates enunciate their policy positions or how well informed the electorate is. However, enough research has been done on public opinion and electoral behavior to suggest that neither condition comes even close to being met. Compared to elections for other statewide posts like state auditor, state treasurer, and secretary of state, the race for attorney general draws about the same interest and attention.[6]

Data on the careers of attorneys general permit some speculation on one of the three conditions for indirect control through elections—the desire of incumbents for reelection or for some other political post. Because the office is important and visible, it attracts men who have already succumbed to the lure of high office. The fact that some move on to other posts suggests that many harbor further ambitions. Nearly one of every 20 governors serving between 1870 and 1950

---

[5] In seven states, he is appointed by the governor with legislative confirmation. The state supreme court appoints him in Tennessee. "The Office of Attorney General in Kentucky," p. 5S.

[6] One measure of their similarity is the frequency of changes in which party controls these offices. Joseph Schlesinger finds it is practically identical. *Ambition and Politics* (Chicago: Rand McNally, 1966), Table IV-1, p. 61.

had been his state's attorney general.[7] In some states, this is the usual pattern.[8] They may also move to the state supreme court. Krislov found that supreme courts in a third of the states had at least one former attorney general serving.[9] In Michigan, four of them were sitting on the court in 1969. Though they are not prominent in the federal judiciary or Congress, some do serve there. Six U.S. senators in the ninety-first Congress, for example, were former state attorneys general.[10]

On the basis of the available evidence, it appears that state attorneys general may be more concerned with obtaining some other post than being reelected. Historically, it has been a career post (i.e., held for an average of 12 years or more) in only two states.[11] A new man occupies the office in slightly over half of the instances in which a change is possible, but these changes involve a shift in the party affiliation of the incumbent less than a third of the time.[12] Although supporting evidence is spotty, a logical explanation is that many

---

[7] Joseph Schlesinger, *How They Became Governor* (East Lansing, Mich.: Governmental Research Bureau, 1957), Table XVI, p. 75. While the rate of one in 20 does not seem high at first glance, no single office was held by a high proportion of governors. The most frequently held prior post, lieutenant governor, was held by only 114 (about 11 percent) of the 995 governors studied (p. 23). A somewhat higher proportion of governors serving in 1957 were found by Krislov to be former attorneys general (five of 49) [Krislov, "Constituency vs. Constitutionalism," p. 88].

[8] Texas is the most notable example. Four governors between 1870 and 1950 served as attorney general. Schlesinger, *How They Became Governor*, pp. 83-87.

[9] Krislov, "Constituency vs. Constitutionalism," p. 88.

[10] They were: Bible (D.-Nev.); Brooke (R.-Mass.); Eagleton (D.-Mo.); Javits (R.-N.Y.); Mondale (D.-Minn.); and Saxbe (R.-Ohio).

[11] Schlesinger, *How They Became Governor*, Table III-2, p. 44. They were Oregon and South Carolina.

[12] *Ibid.*, Table IV-1, p. 61. The percentage of personnel change is 52.2 percent; party change is 15.29 percent, leaving 36.91 percent of personnel changes unaccounted for by partisan shifts.

incumbents voluntarily leave office to pursue other political ambitions. Lending support to this hypothesis is the fact that well over half of the attorneys general serving in 1927 and 1937 subsequently either ran for or actually held another important post.[13]

One thing is clear. The office can and does serve as a stepping-stone to other important posts. Certainly anyone who becomes attorney general must be aware of these possibilities. He has been elected by the same constituency that selects governors, senators, and, in some states, members of the state supreme court. His post puts him in the public eye. It would not be surprising to learn that his behavior is significantly shaped by calculations on how his chances for acquiring some other post will be affected.

ELECTION OF PROSECUTING ATTORNEYS

The responsibility for prosecuting violations of state law usually falls on a prosecuting attorney chosen in a countywide partisan election.[14] Most of his work is in the criminal area. City attorneys, corporation counsel, and the like handle much of the civil work of local governments.

Except for mayors of large cities, no locally elected officeholders are more visible to the public than prosecuting attorneys. Because crimes of violence are prominently featured in the mass media, prosecuting attorneys are assured of substantial exposure. Their participation in the investigation, arrest, and prosecution of murders, rapes, bombings, and other

---

[13] Krislov, "Constituency vs. Constitutionalism," p. 88. One in seven either remained in office 10 years or more or died in office. Only 14 of the 55 studied were found in private practice, corporation law, or business.

[14] About a third of the states have prosecutors whose jurisdiction is larger than one county. Prosecuting attorneys are known by a variety of titles, including district attorney, county attorney, circuit attorney, district attorney general, commonwealth attorney, circuit solicitor, states attorneys, and so on. See D.R. Nedrud, "The Career Prosecutor," *Journal of Criminal Law, Criminology, and Police Science* 51 (1960-1961), pp. 343-344.

crimes makes them local celebrities. The visibility of the office is enhanced by its depiction in courtroom scenes in books, movies, and television programs.

At election time, however, the office loses its distinctiveness. Unless it has been touched by scandal or has sustained attacks on its effectiveness, the race for prosecutor is buried by contests for the presidency, governorship, U.S. Senate, and other more important posts. Voters are swamped with literature and appeals from candidates for higher office and have little time or interest left to devote to the race for prosecutor. Many, in fact, fail to vote for either candidate for prosecutor.[15]

Herbert Jacob's study of elections of Wisconsin district attorneys notes several other features.[16] Nominees of the dominant party are often unopposed in the general election. Primary contests in such one-party counties are not very frequent either. Incumbents running in the primary and general elections are rarely defeated. In fact, only about 14 percent lost between 1944 and 1962. Sixty-five percent of the time they left office voluntarily. The average term in office for this period was four and one-half years.[17]

This description of elections for prosecuting attorney suggests the extent to which the four conditions for direct control through elections are met in Wisconsin. In absolute terms, several essential ones are missing, including frequently contested elections, meaningful campaigns, and high voter interest and participation. Relatively speaking, these elections fulfill the four conditions less well than contests for state

---

[15] This drop-off effect is commonly found in contests for lesser offices. See Jack L. Walker, "Ballot Forms and Voter Fatigue: An Analysis of the Office Block and Party Column Ballots," *Midwest Journal of Political Science* 10 (1966), pp. 448-463. In Washtenaw county, Michigan, one of every seven voting for president in 1968 did not vote for prosecutor.

[16] Herbert Jacob, "Judicial Insulation—Elections, Direct Participation, and Public Attention to the Courts in Wisconsin," *Wisconsin Law Review*, 1966 (1966), pp. 801-819.

[17] *Ibid.*, p. 810.

attorney general. But how do they compare to elections for other posts further down the ballot?

Information on elections to other offices in Wisconsin is not readily available, but we can examine existing data on elections for less important posts elsewhere. On one measure, frequency of contested elections, important differences do appear. A majority of Jacob's prosecutors were unopposed in the general election. This is probably unusually high. Only about 20 percent of the elections for the U.S. House of Representatives during the same general period, for example, were uncontested.[18]

But on the other measures, differences are not very pronounced. It is unusual for incumbents to be defeated in primaries in one-party areas. One study found that only 4 percent of U.S. congressmen from safe one-party districts were defeated in primaries.[19] The fact that only 14 percent of incumbent prosecutors lost reelection bids is also typical. About 18 percent of the members of the Connecticut House of Representatives lost reelection bids between 1946 and 1958.[20] About the same proportion of city councilmen (20 percent to be exact) in 87 San Francisco Bay area cities were defeated for reelection.[21] Between 1952 and 1960, only 5 percent of incumbent U.S. congressmen whose district boundaries were not changed were defeated.[22] Nor does the 65-percent voluntary retirement rate of Wisconsin prosecutors seem unusual. Over half of the San Francisco area councilmen, for example, leave office voluntarily.[23] Finally, high

---

[18] Data used for this calculation appear in the *Congressional Quarterly Almanac* XVII (1961), pp. 1028–1032.

[19] Julius Turner, "Primary Elections as the Alternative to Party Competition in 'Safe Districts,' " *Journal of Politics* 19 (1953), p. 209.

[20] James Barber, *The Lawmakers* (New Haven, Connecticut: Yale University Press, 1965), p. 286, n. 13 (paperback).

[21] Prewitt, "Political Ambitions," p. 9. Rates of electoral defeat for other offices fell in the same range. See Prewitt's discussion on p. 13.

[22] Unpublished research by the author.

[23] Prewitt, "Political Ambitions," p. 10.

turnover and short tenure characterize a number of other offices.[24]

With the important exception of frequent uncontested elections, elections for prosecutors are rather ordinary after all. If the opportunities they afford for direct control by the electorate are rather slim, so, too, are opportunities provided by election to many other positions.

In order to describe their degree of insulation from the electorate, however, it is also necessary to take into account the possibility of indirect controls. To what extent are county prosecutors sensitive to the effects of their behavior on future career ambitions? If we study the incumbents' desire for reelection as prosecutor, there are some significant limitations. Most prosecutors in Wisconsin seek reelection one or two times, since terms are for two years and the average tenure is more than four years.[25] But at any given time a number of prosecutors do not intend to seek reelection. As reported, 65 percent leave office voluntarily. Existing research on prosecutors suggests that few men seek to make a career of the office.[26]

This does not mean that behavior is not altered in anticipation of how one's future career will be affected. The fact that prosecutors come to office early in their professional lives suggests they quite naturally are concerned about what happens after they leave. In Indiana, 80 percent of incumbent prosecutors in 1963 entered office before the age of 40.[27]

[24] Barber, *The Lawmakers*, p. 8. A majority of state legislators, for example, must be replaced every other year.

[25] Jacob, "Judicial Insulation," p. 810.

[26] Herbert Jacob, *Justice in America* (Boston: Little, Brown, 1965), p. 78; Ken Ori, "The Politicized Nature of the County Prosecutor's Office, Fact or Fancy?—The Case in Indiana," *Notre Dame Lawyer* 40 (1964-1965), pp. 289-303, found only 3 percent of incumbents in 1963 in Indiana wanted to make a career of the office (p. 292). Exceptions do exist. The most notable is Frank Hogan, who has been Manhattan District Attorney since his election in 1942. See Richard H. Kuh, "Careers in Prosecuting Offices," *Journal of Legal Education* 14 (1961), pp. 175-190.

[27] Ori, "The Politicized Nature," p. 289.

Jacob found an almost identical figure for all Wisconsin prosecutors elected between 1942 and 1963.[28] Direct evidence from prosecutors confirms this. Four out of five Indiana prosecutors felt their service would help their careers along.[29] Nearly 60 percent of Wisconsin's prosecutors said they ran for the office because of the salary or to gain experience.[30]

Because our information on prosecutors is limited, there is a great danger we will forget that important differences may exist from state to state. In Oklahoma, for instance, 26 percent of its county prosecutors were over 60 years of age,[31] a very rare occurrence in Wisconsin or Indiana. Some had to be convinced to come out of retirement because nobody else was available for the job. It is unlikely that these men worried too much about their future careers.

The nature of career ambitions of prosecutors also varies from state to state. In Indiana, the office of prosecuting attorney serves as the first post for men with ambitions to hold other public offices. About 53 percent admitted to desires for another office, and another 14 percent were uncertain.[32]

In Indiana, "county prosecutors are young and inexperienced, and . . . are politically ambitious and tend to view their office as a means of political advancement."[33]

By contrast, Wisconsin prosecutors seem less interested in political advancement than in improving their prospects for a successful private law practice.[34] As mentioned before, they

[28] Jacob, "Judicial Insulation," p. 810.

[29] Ori, "The Politicized Nature," p. 293, Table 6.

[30] Jacob, "Judicial Insulation," p. 810.

[31] Hicks Epton, "Some Facts About County Attorneys in Oklahoma," *Oklahoma Bar Association Journal* 25 (1954), p. 1006.

[32] Ori, "The Politicized Nature," p. 293, Table 5.

[33] *Ibid.*, p. 303. Their perception was not entirely incorrect. Between 1900 and 1963, 25 percent of Indiana congressmen had been county prosecutor, over half of this number immediately prior to winning their House seats (*Ibid.*, p. 297).

[34] The description of characteristics of Wisconsin prosecutors in this paragraph is drawn from Jacob, "Judicial Insulation," pp. 810-811.

are relatively young when they become prosecutors; they seek the office for experience in trying cases, for making contacts, and for immediate financial reasons. Many leave when they feel that their position will no longer help or may even begin to hinder the growth of their future private practice. Two-thirds never hold an elective or appointive post again. Of course, just as some Indiana prosecutors undoubtedly seek to improve their legal careers, some of their Wisconsin brethren have political ambitions. About 22 percent became judges of one sort or another, while another 18 percent or so studied by Jacob held minor local positions.[35]

Thus, while prosecutors in both states are concerned about how their tenure will affect their future careers, the direction of their ambitions is somewhat different. It would be fascinating to know how a prosecutor seeking to build up his future private practice might differ in the way he acts in office from someone who will seek election or appointment to a higher position.

We shall have to await further research to learn just what prosecutors perceive to be the limits on their behavior beyond which they invite electoral retaliation. It is possible that a man in a small county who is normally unopposed for reelection is no less free from indirect control than a colleague who always faces a stiff race. He may feel (correctly) that if he steps beyond the bounds of permissible behavior, someone will be recruited to run against him. In a small county, a defeat of this sort can seriously hinder his success in private practice. One other possibility merits consideration: Elections in the four or five largest counties in a state may be more competitive, and the candidates more politically ambitious. In terms of the number of people affected by his decisions, the prosecutor in a populous urban area is disproportionately important.[36]

---

[35] Jacob, *Justice in America*, p. 78.

[36] For a discussion of how two consecutively elected district attorneys in New Orleans differed in behavior, see Herbert Jacob, "Politics and Criminal Prosecution in New Orleans," in Kenneth N. Vines and Herbert Jacob, eds., *Tulane Studies in Political Science* Vol. VIII (New Orleans: Tulane University, 1962) pp. 77–98.

ELECTION OF JUDGES

A dual controversy surrounds the question of how judges ought to be selected. The first concerns whether they should be appointed or chosen in some sort of an election. The second involves whether, if election is used, it should be partisan or nonpartisan.

Both elements of the controversy result from a clash between the competing values of representativeness and neutral competence. In the eyes of many, the characteristics, values, and especially the decisions of judges ought to be fairly representative of and responsive to the general population. As suggested at the outset of this chapter, the standard mechanism Americans have relied upon to insure representativeness has been the election. But the lingering hold of *traditional* views of law leads many to the belief that we ought to select competent, dispassionate men free from undue influence from the electorate to discover and apply abstract principles of law in neutral fashion. The hurly-burly of electoral politics is often deemed an inappropriate technique for recruiting such men. Proponents of neutral competence among judges usually prefer some form of appointment.

Nonpartisan elections represent something of a compromise between these two positions.[37] While retaining most features of elections, no party label appears on the ballot beside the names of candidates. Normally, the two parties are given no formal role in their selection and nomination.[38] Presumably, at least some of the hurly-burly, partisan passion, and irrationality thought by some to accompany partisan elections is eliminated.

The battle between proponents and opponents of these various techniques appears to be at a standoff at the state supreme court level. Fourteen states choose their justices in

---

[37] The most elaborate form of compromise, the *Missouri plan* or *merit plan* is discussed in Chapter 3.

[38] They may, however, covertly work for candidates. In Michigan, the parties each nominate candidates for the state supreme court, but they technically run on a nonpartisan ballot.

partisan elections, 15 under nonpartisan election plans, and 21 through some form of legislative or executive appointment.[39] Accurate statistics do not exist on exactly how many of the thousands of lower-level state judges and magistrates are elected. We do know that a variety of techniques are used to select judges even within the same state. Arizona, though perhaps an extreme example, elects supreme, appeals, and superior court judges in nonpartisan elections. Justices of the peace, however, run in partisan elections. City and town magistrates are selected according to local charter or ordinance (usually appointed by their local legislative bodies or the mayor).[40]

Until more research is conducted on the election of judges (and particularly lower-level judges), we must be content to hazard some tentative generalizations based on the limited information available. The six distinguishing characteristics of judicial elections described below point to two conclusions. First, the four conditions for direct control of behavior through elections appear to be largely absent. Second, they are even less evident than in elections for state attorneys general, prosecuting attorneys, or most other elected officials.

Infrequent elections

Many judges come up for reelection only infrequently. Supreme court justices in Mississippi are required to face the electorate every 14 years.[41] This is an extreme case, of course. But the shortest term for elected state supreme court judges is six years, matched only by U.S. senators among

---

[39] Information on method of selection for major judicial posts in the various states is drawn from the Council of State Governments' *State Court Systems: A Statistical Summary* (Chicago: Council of State Governments, 1970 revised edition), Table II. The highest court in most states is called the supreme court. In New York, the highest court is the court of appeals, while lower-level trial courts are called supreme courts. Few opportunities to confuse are missed.

[40] *Ibid.*

[41] Council of State Governments, *State Court Systems*, Table IV.

major officials. The average term is 8.3 years.[42] Lower court judges also enjoy longer terms of office than do most other officials. The median term of office for judges in the major trial courts of 47 states is 6 years, and the mean is 6.36 years.[43]

Noncompetitive Elections

In some regions of the country, judicial candidates are often unopposed, particularly in races for lesser judgeships. Only 40 percent of the races for Wisconsin circuit judgeships were contested between 1940 and 1963, and the figure was considerably lower (about 20 percent) when an incumbent judge was running.[44] Very nearly the same proportion of Louisiana judges serving between 1945 and 1960—41.1 percent to be exact—faced opposition.[45] In Texas, 86 percent of the judicial elections were found to be uncontested.[46] Several students of New York politics report that in New York City and its environs, it is customary for both parties to nominate incumbent trial-level judges if they seek reelection. In fact, it is not unusual for the parties to strike a bargain on the division of judicial posts made available by the creation of addi-

---

[42] *Ibid.*, calculated from Table IV and excluding three states with life terms.

[43] *Ibid.* In New York City, less than 2 percent of all judges have terms of less than 10 years. Wallace Sayre and Herbert Kaufman, *Governing New York City* (New York: Russell Sage, 1960), p. 534.

[44] Jacob, "Judicial Insulation," p. 806. When contested, the elections were often won by lopsided margins. Over 40 percent of them were won by more than 60 percent of the vote.

[45] Kenneth N. Vines, "The Selection of Judges in Lousiana," in Vines and Jacob, *Tulane Studies*, p. 115.

[46] Bancroft C. Henderson and T.C. Sinclair, *The Selection of Judges In Texas: An Exploratory Study* (Houston: Public Affairs Research Center, University of Houston, 1965), p. 20. Similar patterns in the characteristics of judicial elections described in this section are also found in California. See Beverly Blair Cook, *The Judicial Process in California* (Belmont, Calif.: Dickenson, 1967), pp. 46–54.

tional judgeships or retirements. The parties come up with a single slate which both endorse.[47]

Elections are also noncompetitive in the sense that incumbent judges are rarely defeated when they are challenged.[48] Of the 20 circuit court judges seeking reelection in Wisconsin between 1940 and 1963, not one lost. Only four incumbent justices of the Wisconsin Supreme Court were defeated between 1853 and 1949.[49] Only one out of 19 supreme court and court of appeals judges in Louisiana sitting between 1945 and 1960 left office due to their defeat at the polls.[50] In Minnesota, less than 5 percent of district judges were beaten in reelection tries between 1912 and 1941.[51] Less than 10 percent of Louisiana district court judges left the bench due to defeat.[52] Similar rates are found in Texas.[53]

Low Voter Turnout

Fewer persons vote in judicial elections than in most other elections. Even when we would expect participation to be high—in November elections involving governors, senators, and the like—significant numbers fail to vote. In the November 1966 elections in Detroit, for example, 48 percent of

---

[47] Sayre and Kaufman, *Governing New York City*, p. 534. See also Kenneth Dolbeare, *Trial Courts in Urban Politics* (New York: Wiley, 1967), p. 30.

[48] Again, important differences between states are found. A study of partisan elections of circuit judges in Missouri found higher levels of both competition and more frequent defeat of incumbents than studies of other states have shown. See Richard A. Watson and Rondal G. Downing, *The Politics of the Bench and the Bar* (New York: Wiley, 1969), p. 233 and Table 6.5, p. 232. However, the trend has been toward less competition in recent years.

[49] These figures are reported in Jacob, *Justice in America*, p. 98.

[50] Vines, "The Selection of Judges in Louisiana," p. 114, Table 10.

[51] Jacob, *Justice in America*, p. 98.

[52] Vines, "The Selection of Judges in Louisiana," p. 114, Table 10.

[53] Henderson and Sinclair, *The Selection of Judges in Texas*, p. 20. Between 1952 and 1962, 4.9 percent of trial judges suffered electoral defeat in a primary or general election.

those voting for governor did not cast a ballot in the nonpartisan race for recorder's court.[54] In contrast, only 9.7 percent failed to vote for attorney general in this election. And in November 1968, only about 12 percent of those who voted for president did not vote for county prosecutor.[55]

When judicial elections do not coincide with races for other important offices, turnout is generally even lower. A hotly contested election in 1965 for justice of the Wisconsin Supreme Court drew but 30 percent of the electorate.[56]

Low Voter Interest and Lack of Information

A fairly direct measure of lack of interest in judicial elections can be found in the statistics just presented on the failure of voters to cast ballots. A poll taken in New York City confirmed low voter interest and their lack of information about judicial elections. Less than half of those voting in the November 1966 election cast a ballot in the judicial races; less than 15 percent of those who did vote for judges could correctly name even one man who was running.[57] It is not necessary to belabor the point. In most judicial elections, voters are uninterested, uninformed, and unlikely to vote.

Issueless Campaigns

Another distinctive feature of judicial elections can be found in the nature of the campaigns waged. Although few elections produce rational dialogue on the issues between candidates, most do give the electorate some clue as to how each candidate might behave once in office. Promises are made and stands are taken on at least some issues. This is not so when it

---

[54] Data from Wayne County, Michigan, director of elections.

[55] The drop-off from the top of the ticket to the lowest statewide office generally seems to range from a few percent to 10 percent. See Jack L. Walker, "Ballot Forms and Voter Fatigue," pp. 452–455.

[56] Jack Ladinsky and Allan Silver, "Popular Democracy and Judicial Independence," *Wisconsin Law Review* 1967 (1967), p. 154.

[57] "Poll Finds Voters Apathetic on Judges," *The New York Times*, January 29, 1967.

comes to judges. Judicial candidates do not normally promise how they will decide certain types of cases. If they take any stands at all, it is on such themes as "respect for law," "efficiency," and "reform of court organization."

Usually, the existence of formal restrictions and the knowledge that violations might bring criticism from the press and bar succeed in keeping judicial elections quiet, boring, and without real debate on issues of substance. The Canons of Judicial Ethics of the American Bar Association place severe restrictions on a candidate. Both political activity and the taking of stands on issues before the court are prohibited. Members of the legal profession, particularly the leaders of the organized bar, support and wield informal and formal sanctions to enforce these ethical limitations. Furthermore, newspapers and other media may criticize a judicial candidate who strays from observance of these norms.[58]

The Impact of Nonpartisan Elections

For most voters, the most important piece of information about a candidate is his party. In nonpartisan judicial elections, lack of a party cue forces voters to rely upon other cues, which, as we have seen, cannot very often be the policy stands of the candidates. This leaves only a few alternatives: whether the candidate is an incumbent; whether his name is recognized; whether he is endorsed by various groups (such as the local bar association). The absence of party labels also may reduce the electorate's interest in the contest. Thus, nonpartisan elections make meaningful voter control even more difficult to attain.

As Professor Jacob has concluded, judicial elections usually resemble plebicites more than meaningful contests between competing candidates. They do not normally afford even the

---

[58] For a description of a judicial election where one of the candidates waged an issue-filled campaign that attacked the incumbent and the state supreme court for its decisions, see Ladinsky and Silver, "Popular Democracy and Judicial Independence." This candidate did draw the criticism of the press and the bar for his tactics, and was narrowly defeated.

nominal opportunities for direct control that elections for prosecutor and attorney general do. Once in office, judges face reelection only infrequently, are often unopposed, and are even more often victorious.

Under special circumstances, however, judicial elections do more closely resemble other elections. When an incumbent chooses not to run for reelection, the ensuing election is more likely to see two competing candidates.[59] Of course, if the election is partisan, the opportunities for a meaningful choice are enhanced. Voters who are otherwise uninformed have at least the party cue to help them choose between the candidates. But even nonpartisan primaries and elections generate political activity that meets some of the conditions for direct control. A nonpartisan candidate's friends and law partners may utilize personal and organizational contacts to mobilize support (votes, public endorsements, contributions). In part, this effort can have ideological and policy overtones. Sometimes, party organizations will covertly work for one of the candidates, giving him access to mailing lists, lists of potential contributors, workers, and publicity.

The politics involved in securing a nomination or an appointment to fill a vacancy also provide opportunities for representation of popular attitudes. In some areas (New York City is a prominent example), nominations serve as a reward to lawyers who have worked for and contributed heavily to their parties. Elsewhere, parties emphasize other qualities (legal ability, probable behavior in office, etc.).

Finally, where judges are elected on a partisan ticket during a general election in November, and where both parties run candidates who stand a chance of winning, the outcome is influenced considerably by how the top of the ticket fares. To the extent that judges reflect the general orientation of their parties, and to the extent that shifts in voter sentiment reflect approval or disapproval of that orientation, a crude form of voter control operates.

[59] Jacob, in "Judicial Insulation," (pp. 806-807), shows that competition in Wisconsin is far more likely to occur if no incumbent runs. The margins of victory are also cut when no elected incumbent is running.

But these three special circumstances are merely that—special. When we look at the sum total of judicial elections, few of them exhibit any one of them. If effective control exists, it is through indirect rather than direct mechanisms.

Our information about the conditions for indirect control is limited but suggests some basic conclusions. Judges are elected somewhat later in their careers than prosecutors. Where more than 80 percent of Wisconsin prosecutors were less than 40 years old when they assumed office, less than 20 percent of circuit and supreme court justices were.[60] Similar findings emerged from a study of Louisiana judges.[61] Judges also have more experience in government prior to becoming judges. Slightly over half of the judges chosen in partisan elections in one study had held a prior public office, while 30 percent of those in nonpartisan elections had been officeholders previously.[62] In Texas, over 94 percent of those state trial judges who were initially elected had held at least one prior post.[63]

Some elected judges, particularly in lower courts, move on to other positions. In Louisiana, nearly 30 percent of district court judges between 1945 and 1960 left office for other governmental positions.[64] But for many, an elected judgeship is the terminal position of their careers. Fully 90 percent of Louisiana's elected judges who are on the bench at age 45 remain there until they reach retirement.[65]

---

[60] Ibid., p. 811.

[61] Vines, "The Selection of Judges in Louisiana," p. 104, Table 1.

[62] Once again, the study was conducted by Herbert Jacob. See Jacob, "The Effect of Institutional Differences in the Recruitment Process: The Case of State Judges," Journal of Public Law 13 (1964), p. 110. Interestingly, where men chosen in either type of election had held a previous office, it was likely to be prosecuting attorney (roughly 75 percent of the time).

[63] Henderson and Sinclair, The Selection of Judges in Texas, p. 62. Here too, a high proportion (53 percent) had been county or district attorneys. See p. 69.

[64] Vines, "The Selection of Judges in Louisiana," p. 114, Table 10.

[65] Ibid., p. 105.

To the extent that indirect controls operate, it is probably due to the judge's desire for reelection to the same post. Several obvious limitations on their effectiveness have already been described. Long terms make it necessary to seek reelection infrequently. Often nobody will run against the incumbent; when they do, they rarely defeat him. Nevertheless, the prospect of having to face the electorate, particularly as election time approaches, may cause judges to modify their behavior in order to reduce their chances of becoming an exception.

CHAPTER 3
THE POLITICS OF APPOINTMENT IN THE LEGAL PROCESS

MORE positions in the legal process are filled by appointment than by any other method. Furthermore, they tend to be the more important ones. The whole federal legal establishment—judges, attorneys, and investigators—is appointed. With the exception of sheriffs, all police personnel are appointed as well. A number of lower-level state judges and justices on 21 state supreme courts are selected by this method.

Earlier, it was noted that elections are valued because they contribute to representativeness. Appointment can be used to further other goals, including neutral competence and executive leadership.[1] Civil service systems, which allegedly remove political considerations from appointment decisions, are thought by their supporters to locate qualified and competent men. Permitting executives to pick key decision-

---

[1] A third is the maintenance and strengthening of political party organizations. For a fascinating and perceptive discussion of the role judicial positions play in a local party structure, see Wallace Sayre and Herbert Kaufman, *Governing New York City* (New York: Russell Sage, 1960), Chapter XIV.

makers is thought to enhance their ability to exert vigorous and centralized leadership.[2]

A comprehensive analysis of the politics surrounding the appointment of hundreds of officials throughout the legal process is neither possible nor necessary. But it is important to convey in general terms how the appointment process works. We shall examine four types of appointment: by an elected executive such as the president, a governor, a mayor; bureaucratic appointment (e.g., civil service); by state legislatures; and the Missouri plan, a mixture of executive appointment, nonpartisanship, and referendum elections used to select judges in 11 states.[3]

EXECUTIVE APPOINTMENT—THE FEDERAL CASE

U.S. Attorneys

The best way to capture the complexity of the federal appointment process is to describe one aspect of it in some detail.[4] Since most existing literature focuses on judges, it might be interesting to examine appointments to another federal legal post, that of the office of U.S. attorney.[5] We

---

[2] Herbert Kaufman, "Emerging Conflicts in the Doctrines of Public Administration," *American Political Science Review* 50 (1956). Since representativeness is thought to emerge through the election process, the appointments made by elected executives may be shaped by some of the same forces that affect who is nominated and elected.

[3] Sheldon Goldman, "American Judges: Their Selection, Tenure, Variety, and Quality," *Current History* 61 (July, 1971), p. 3. Executive appointment is the principal means of choosing judges in 8 states, legislative appointment in 4, partisan election in 14, and nonpartisan election in 13.

[4] For an interesting discussion of the governor's role in the selection of state judges, see Bancroft C. Henderson and T.C. Sinclair, *The Selection of Judges in Texas: An Exploratory Study* (Houston: Public Affairs Research Center, University of Houston, 1965), Chapter III.

[5] The discussion is based on research conducted by the author in 1965. Over 200 interviews were conducted throughout the country with U.S. attorneys and those with whom they deal in the course of their work. See James Eisenstein, *Counsel for the United States: An Empirical Analysis of the Office of United States Attorney* (Ph.D. diss., Yale University, 1968), Chapter II.

shall then contrast these appointments with those for federal judgeships.

U.S. attorneys represent the federal government in 93 judicial districts throughout the United States and its territories. They prosecute violations of federal law and represent the government in most civil actions in U.S. district courts. Formally, they are part of the Department of Justice, subject to the authority and control of the attorney general. Unlike the field personnel of most federal agencies, however, they are neither appointed nor removed by the central agency. The president nominates U.S. attorneys, and they are confirmed by the Senate in the same way that ambassadors, cabinet officers, and judges are. Only a president can remove a U.S. attorney from office.

Although not widely recognized as important decision-makers, U.S. attorneys have a profound impact on the nature and direction of federal law enforcement in their districts. They play a crucial part in implementing the policies of the Department of Justice. Beyond that, they are in a strategic position to affect the administration of other federal governmental policies and the operation of state and local law enforcement. They also serve as sources of information to policy-makers and politicians. Finally, the position is an important stepping-stone to higher posts, particularly the federal judiciary.

Although U.S. attorneys are nominated by the president, he rarely plays a direct role. Instead, their selection is usually delegated to the deputy attorney general and his staff, though White House aides handling patronage also participate on occasion. This is logical, since U.S. attorneys are under the direct supervision of the Department of Justice. The department has a keen interest in selecting men who are both competent and capable of being controlled.

When senators of the president's party represent states where vacancies exist, the custom of *senatorial courtesy* applies. By tradition, these senators have the right to veto appointments to federal posts in their states by declaring the appointees "personally obnoxious." Courtesy thus transforms the procedural requirement of Senate confirmation into a potent resource for senators of the president's party.[6] Other senators, particularly members of the Judiciary Committee, play a role in those few appointments that become controversial.

A number of other actors also participate. Local and state political party officials are active, working either through the senator or directly with the Department of Justice. Their importance increases (as does that of U.S. representatives) when there is no senator from the president's party. Prominent members of the bar who practice in federal court sometimes participate. So do federal judges. It is extremely important both to the future U.S. attorney and to the department that judges get on well with the appointee. Hence, when judges make direct appeals on behalf of prospective nominees, their recommendations carry a good deal of weight. But even if nothing is heard from the judges, their probable reactions to possible nominees are taken into account. Bar associations seem to pay almost no attention to these appointments. This is somewhat surprising since, as we shall see, they take a keen interest in the appointment of federal district judges.

U.S. attorneys themselves are sometimes active in the selection process. When U.S. attorneys leave office before the president's term expires, they sometimes work on behalf of their chief assistant U.S. attorney. In almost every instance where a vacancy occurs, there are aspirants for the job actively seeking support from members of the bar, party officials, and elected officials. However, the eventual appointee may have been drafted without doing anything to further his own cause.

It is difficult to generalize about the appointment of U.S. attorneys because there are so many circumstances that can

---

[6] Senators from the "out" party are not consulted and do not invoke courtesy. A variety of interesting practices exist for avoiding conflict when both are in the president's party (taking turns, splitting responsibility geographically if more than one district exists in the state, bargaining on each nomination). Nevertheless, deadlocks between them do sometimes arise.

affect the outcome. The more important factors include: (1) whether there is a senator from the president's party in the state where the vacancy exists; (2) whether the senator insists on his own candidate or is willing to leave the choice up to the Department of Justice after its consultation with him; (3) the political influence the senator enjoys, both within the Senate and in his state; (4) the quality of the men suggested by senators and other local political figures; (5) the importance of the office where the vacancy exists to the department's law enforcement program; (6) the "tradition" of the office in the district (is it regarded as "political" or "nonpolitical," are appointees normally more distinguished by their legal or political qualifications, do politically ambitious men seek it as a stepping-stone or shun it as a dead end); (7) the extent of various candidates' efforts on their own behalf; (8) the reaction of local federal court participants to prospective appointees; (9) the point during the term of a president that the vacancy occurs; and (10) special circumstances such as scandal in the office or pending politically sensitive cases.

These and other variables affect the patterns of influence that result in the selection of an appointee. It is obvious that there are practically an infinite number of combinations possible.

Despite the variety and complexity of circumstances that shape appointments of U.S. attorneys, a few general characteristics emerge. Appointees must be attorneys and residents of the judicial district where the vacancy occurs. With only rare exceptions, they are at least nominal members of the president's party. More often than not, they have been rather active politically.

Despite the fact that U.S. attorneys are presidential appointees, any notion that the president essentially makes the choice himself is, as we have seen, oversimplified and naïve. Nor is the senatorial courtesy model, which assumes that local federal officers are appointed by a state's senators if they belong to the president's party, accurate and valid in the case of U.S. attorneys. One problem is that it tells us nothing about what happens when there is no senator from the president's party.[7] This model is also mistaken in other ways.

First, it assumes that every senator in a position to invoke courtesy has the desire to pick the U.S. attorney himself. In practice, this does not always happen. An official closely involved in these appointments during the Kennedy administration reported that in only about 15 to 20 percent of the appointments did a senator submit the name of one man as *the* appointee. The usual procedure was for the senator to submit the names of four or five candidates, all of whom he indicated would be acceptable to him. This permitted the senator to say that each of the candidates had been recommended by him, but shifted the burden of making the final choice to someone else.[8]

The second problem with the senatorial model is the assumption that the senator can succeed in getting his candidate nominated and approved. Some senators may find they are so dependent on local politicians that they not only have no hand in selecting the nominee, but also are unable to invoke courtesy for fear of the repercussions at home. Even when free to recommend a candidate, senators cannot always see that their men are appointed. The ability to block any appointment through the use of courtesy is not the same as actually controlling who receives the post. The president (or more accurately, the Department of Justice acting on his behalf) possesses a key resource—the ability to select who will be proposed to the Senate. If the department refuses to name the senator's man, he can only play "dog in the manger" by refusing to approve anyone else and retaliating

---

[7] For the years 1953 and 1961, when a new administration was faced with 172 appointments where senators could be a factor, 55 of them were in states where neither of the senators was from the president's party.

[8] According to department officials in the Nixon administration, GOP senators have taken a more active role in selecting nominees.

by opposing the president on other matters before the Senate.[9]

A few senators are able to wield such great influence over the fate of a president's program that the possibility of alienating them over who will be U.S. attorney is just not worth the price. These men, if they so choose, are able to live up to the influence attributed to all senators in the senatorial model. But there are not many of them. Nor do they always insist on a particular candidate. And even if they do so, the department may find the candidate perfectly acceptable.[10]

In most cases, however, the department can pursue a number of strategies to avoid nominating someone a senator insists upon whom the department finds unacceptable. One is to convince him to back down by emphasizing the weaknesses of his candidate and proposing a highly qualified and politically unopposable alternate. Another is to permit the incumbent from the previous administration to remain in office. Or, the department can inspire a judge to appoint its candidate to serve as acting U.S. attorney until his replacement is confirmed. It then does nothing. The court appointee is U.S. attorney and the senator has been frustrated. Alternatively, the department can dispatch an acting U.S. attorney or can wait until Congress is not in session and make a *recess* appointment. There is always the danger that a recess appointment will be vetoed by the senator at a later date, of course. But these interim appointees are often able to gain

---

[9] Some senators have been held in such low esteem by their colleagues that their attempts to invoke courtesy have been rejected. We should also remember that even if he can convince the administration to nominate his candidate, a senator's problems are not necessarily solved. Sen. Edward Kennedy got President Johnson to nominate Francis X. Morrisey for a federal judgeship in 1965. But there was such a reaction against the nomination that Kennedy was forced to request that it be withdrawn. An account of the episode can be found in *The New York Times* articles of Sept. 28, Oct. 17, 19, 20, 21, 22, and Nov. 6, 1965.

[10] Those who are familiar with the power of the late Senator Kerr of Oklahoma in the Senate can appreciate the comment of a Kennedy administration official: "It so happened that Senator Kerr had three fine U.S. attorneys."

support for their permanent appointments once they are functioning as U.S. attorneys.

Thus, neither the senatorial nor presidential models accurately describe the reality of these appointments. If we modify the presidential model to substitute the Department of Justice, we are somewhat closer to the truth. But perhaps the best way to describe the process is by the term *bargaining*. Appointments result from negotiations between the Department of Justice on the one hand, and senators and other local political and legal figures on the other. The relative strength of the various participants varies as the circumstances described earlier change. Overall, the department is probably the single most important force. If a guess had to be made as to which was the most common outcome, however, it would be that the department and key political figures (usually including a senator) arrive at a compromise acceptable to each but perhaps the first choice of neither.

Other Federal Appointments: Judges

How do appointments of U.S. attorneys compare to federal judicial appointments? Several fine pieces of original research into the process exist, and the results of these studies have been summarized elsewhere. [11]

Harold Chase's excellent description of the appointment of federal district judges reveals a process very much like that followed for U.S. attorneys. The deputy attorney general and his staff, senators from the president's party where the vacancy exists, local and state political figures, sitting judges,

---

[11] Joel Grossman, *Lawyers and Judges: The ABA and the Politics of Judicial Selection* (New York: Wiley, 1965); Sheldon Goldman, "Judicial Appointments to the U.S. Courts of Appeals," *Wisconsin Law Review* (1967), pp. 186-214; Harold W. Chase, "Federal Judges: The Appointing Process," *Minnesota Law Review* 51 (1966), pp. 185-218; David J. Danelski, *A Supreme Court Justice is Appointed* (New York: Random House, 1964); Richard J. Richardson and Kenneth N. Vines, *The Politics of Federal Courts* (Boston: Little, Brown, 1970), Chapter 4; Thomas Jahnige and Sheldon Goldman, *The Federal Courts as a Political System* (New York: Harper & Row, 1971), Chapter 3; Herbert Jacob, *Justice in America* (Boston: Little, Brown, 1965), pp. 89-97.

members of the bar, the Senate Judiciary Committee, and the FBI (through its background investigation) all play much the same roles in appointments to district judgeships. The same formal procedures are used. The geographical area affected, that is, the judicial district, is identical. The relative influence of the various actors is roughly equivalent also. Chase found senators were important but hardly the determining force many once thought them to be. Within the limits of set procedures and the interaction of the same participants, Chase also found considerable variety in the specifics of individual appointments.

One significant difference is the increased participation of the organized bar. The American Bar Association's Standing Committee on Federal Judiciary is routinely asked to assess all nominees. They are rated as "exceptionally well-qualified," "well-qualified," or "not qualified." The impact of the committee's ratings, however, has varied considerably over the years. [12]

Several other differences are found. The level of interest in district judgeships is generally higher, reflecting the belief that the post is more important than a U.S. attorneyship. Consequently, the activity surrounding these appointments is somewhat more intense. More people are involved, and more people are interested in getting the appointment. Senators also seem to pay more attention to the selection process. Like U.S. attorneys, nearly all judicial candidates are at least nominal members of the president's party, [13] and quite often very active members. But there appears to be more concern over the legal competence of prospective nominees, reflecting perhaps the lifetime tenure of appointees.

Appointments to the U.S. Courts of Appeals differ only in degree. If anything, qualifications of appointees are even

---

[12] For the complete story of the ABA Committee's role in the selection of judges, see Grossman, *Lawyers and Judges*.

[13] From Roosevelt on, over 90 percent of the district judges appointed shared the president's partisan affiliation. Richardson and Vines, *The Politics of Federal Courts*, p. 68.

more carefully scrutinized. But along with legal ability and intelligence, ideological considerations weigh more heavily. Those involved in the appointment process are concerned with how prospective nominees will decide cases involving important matters of policy.

Although U.S. Courts of Appeals have jurisdiction over cases arising from a number of districts in several states, usually one state will successfully claim the right to have one of its residents fill the vacancy. This results in consultations with senators and other leaders of the president's party from that state. But such senators are not able to invoke senatorial courtesy to block a court of appeals appointment as easily as for district court appointments. Consequently, their influence is not as great as in district court appointments. The Department of Justice and the president have considerably more leeway here.

Appointments to the U.S. Supreme Court are the most familiar to the general public. Anyone who pays even casual attention to current events is aware that political considerations shape them. The dominant criterion seems to be an appointee's expected conformity with the ideological and policy stances of the president. President Johnson looked for men with liberal inclinations. Nixon turned to middle-of-the-road or conservative men for his first appointments, and made no secret of that fact. "If Judge Haynsworth's philosophy leans to the conservative side," observed Nixon, "in my view that recommends him to me." [14] Of course, this does not mean the president will always predict accurately. The conservative President Eisenhower, reflecting on his appointment of Earl Warren as chief justice (a man whose decisions were almost consistently liberal), is reported to have said that Warren's appointment was "the biggest damn fool mistake I ever made."

Throughout our history, intense political controversy has from time to time surrounded the appointment and confir-

[14] "Nixon Vows Help For Haynsworth Till Senate Vote," *The New York Times*, Oct. 21, 1969.

mation of justices.[15] The political character of Senate debates on the confirmation of presidential nominees to the Court is obvious to even the casual observer. Although the rhetoric of such debates contains references to "judicial integrity," "cronyism," and "qualifications," the driving force behind much of the politics of confirmation is policy. Most opposition and support of nominees rests on guesses as to how the individuals will decide important questions. Although other elements may influence a senator's evaluation, nominees attacked on other than policy grounds very often appear to disagree with their Senate opponents on major points of policy.

Clearly, the president and his advisors have more influence on Supreme Court appointments than the other positions we have been discussing.[16] Senators (along with sitting justices and the attorney general) have sought to influence the president's choice, but their efforts are rarely decisive.[17] Normally, the best an individual senator can do is to take a leading role in attempting to block an appointment. Despite President Nixon's unhappy experience with the Haynsworth and Carswell[18] appointments (and President Johnson's with Justice Fortas), presidents have usually been able to win approval of their Supreme Court nominees.

Of course, a number of factors other than ideological considerations enter into these appointments. A fascinating and detailed examination of their complexity and variety can be found in Danelski's study of the appointment of Pierce Butler in 1922. In addition to intense activity by senators

[15] President Johnson's proposed elevation of Justice Fortas to the chief justiceship toward the end of his term, and the denial of confirmation of Clement Haynsworth and G. Harrold Carswell at the beginning of Nixon's are recent examples.

[16] Robert Scigliano, *The Supreme Court and the Presidency* (New York: Free Press, 1971), p. 91, reaches the same conclusion.

[17] *Ibid.*, p. 92.

[18] For an interesting if somewhat one-sided journalistic account of the successful effort to block the confirmation of Carswell, see Richard Harris, *Decision* (New York: Dutton, 1971).

and the attorney general, the nomination involved the chief justice, the president, prominent members of the bar and lower-level federal judiciary, and the hierarchy of the Roman Catholic church among others. Other considerations that enter into these appointments include the geographical balance on the court and the ethnic, religious, and racial characteristics of prospective nominees.

Patterns of Federal Appointment

Several recurring themes and trends implicit in the foregoing discussion can be explicitly stated. Six general characteristics and hypotheses are offered to illustrate the sort of generalizations we ultimately need to generate about all aspects of the legal process:

1. With the exception of the U.S. Supreme Court, nearly all appointments to posts in the legal process are of low visibility to the general public. Most people neither know about nor care very much about such appointments.
2. The low visibility of most appointments has several significant consequences. The general public has little direct influence. Those individuals and groups that are directly affected by such appointments, who know when vacancies exist, and who have the necessary political skills and resources have a disproportionate impact on the final selection. In a sense, appointive politics are "closed politics" where relatively few, well-informed, interested actors play the predominant roles.
3. Through the participation of elected officials (both executive and legislative), limited, though indirect and tenuous, representation of the general electorate is provided.
4. The actual appointment process is infinitely more complex than the formal selection procedures suggest.
5. The most significant element shaping executive appointment is the level of the post. The higher the post, the more likely it is:
   a. That there will be competing candidates who attempt to mobilize support for their candidacies.
   b. That there will be substantial pressures directed to the individ-

ual who has the formal authority to designate the nominee, and from a greater number of sources.[19]
   c. That there will be extensive "checking out" of potential nominees with important actors. This increases the number of actors who are able to exercise an effective "veto." In turn, this makes it more likely that controversial candidates—that is, ones who take a strong stand one way or another or who belong to minority groups—will be eliminated from consideration.
   d. That the primary criterion of judgment used by significant actors will be their assessments of the behavior of potential nominees once in office rather than their qualifications (i.e., formal competence, training, or party loyalty). Possible appointees to important posts will be scrutinized to determine how they will decide questions involving important policy issues.
6. Regardless of the importance of the post, partisan politics plays an important role in most appointments.

Characteristics and Careers of Federal Legal Appointees

Information about the characteristics and careers of these men, though it is limited, provides a few clues about the potential impact that career ambitions might have on their behavior. U.S. attorneys historically serve an average of 5.5 years.[20] Only 7 percent served more than 10 years, and another 14 percent held the post toward the end of their active professional lives. Most, then, hold the post for several years and move on to something else. Many hope to improve the quality and financial returns of their private practice, much as local prosecutors do. But three out of four come to the office with experience in another governmental post, and it is only natural that many of them have further ambitions.

---

[19] If the appointing executive moves very quickly to fill a vacancy, there may not be time for competing candidates to emerge and build up pressure for their selection.

[20] Information on the careers of U.S. attorneys is drawn from Eisenstein, *Counsel for the United States*, Chapter VII.

Most are young enough when appointed to anticipate a subsequent career in government or private practice.[21]

Partial evidence of the political ambitions of U.S. attorneys rests on the success they have had. Nearly one out of four has gone on to another governmental post. Nearly half of this group became federal judges. My research in 1965 indicated that a far larger proportion have political ambitions. It is likely that well over a majority of U.S. attorneys desire appointment to the federal bench.

Thus, U.S. attorneys expect to do something else after leaving office, and they recognize that their actions will affect what happens to them. As with all public officials, they recognize that scandal or a universal reputation for incompetence and corruption would be disasterous to their future career ambitions. Having a reputation as someone who frequently loses cases or makes the judges furious is not likely to help in obtaining a partnership in the local prestigious law firm. Difficult cases may consequently be avoided where possible, and special pains taken to accommodate the judges. Those desiring appointment to the bench must impress their senators, the Department of Justice, and the local judges; the implacable opposition of any one of them is likely to doom the attorney's future chances for a judicial appointment. Whether the realization of this fact significantly alters the behavior of a given U.S. attorney, of course, depends both upon the nature of the man and the expectations of his senators and judges, and the department. Finally, men who aspire to elective office may seek to keep their names before the public as much as possible.

With judges, it is a very different matter. They are seldom worried about moving up to another post.[22] The judgeship is

---

[21] *Ibid.*, p. VII-9, Table VII-2. The average age at appointment is just over 45. Nearly a third are under 40 and but 14 percent are over 55.

[22] Some district judges aspire to elevation to the court of appeals, and with good reason. One third of the appeals judges sitting in 1963 had served on the district bench (Richardson and Vines, *The Politics of Federal Courts*, p. 77). It is interesting to note that both G. Harrold Carswell and Clement Haynsworth were serving on courts of appeals when nominated by Nixon to the Supreme Court.

the high point and end-point of their careers. They only have to avoid behavior that could lead to impeachment; otherwise they are in office for as long as they care to be. Federal judges are about as isolated from pressures related to their futures as political decision-makers can be.

CIVIL SERVICE OR "BUREAUCRATIC" APPOINTMENT

Policemen, federal investigative agents, probation officers, assistant prosecutors, and other lower-level personnel in the legal process obviously go through some hiring procedure. For lack of a better term, we shall call it *bureaucratic appointment.*

Selection of assistant district attorneys, probation officers, judges' clerks, and policemen [23] in smaller departments is often handled directly by the "boss" (be he prosecuting attorney, judge, or chief of police). There are few formal restraints on who he can pick if certain obvious qualifications are met. Thus, prosecutors must pick members of the legal profession as assistants. Chiefs of police usually don't hire women for road-patrol work. Some may apply rather strict criteria to determine who is qualified; others may rely upon whim or the individual's political credentials. The selection of such personnel is so unstructured that it is a natural place to look for all sorts of factors—personal friendship, nepotism, recommendations from politicians and other influential persons, the prospective employee's ability, and so on.

Sometimes, bureacratic appointment is much more formalized. This is particularly true of the larger police departments. Both hiring and promotion are covered by civil service regulations. General entrance requirements, including competitive examinations, and a training course must be successfully passed by the individual.

Civil service is generally regarded as being nonpolitical. Presumably, civil service procedures screen all candidates on the basis of their abilities. Race, political connections, and

[23] The characteristics and attitudes of police officers are examined in Chapter 5.

other irrelevant attributes are theoretically disregarded. This assumes, of course, that the criteria established in civil service regulations are both neutral in themselves and applied in an evenhanded fashion. As we will see in Chapter 4, such assumptions cannot always be made.

The criteria used to evaluate performance and promote individuals in bureaucratic organizations such as police departments are important in shaping behavior as well as in determining who occupies what position. For the most part, this area is largely unexplored. It does appear that assistant prosecutors feel winning most of their cases is important to their careers. Patrolmen seek the "good pinch," that is, the clean arrest of someone suspected of committing a serious felony.

One good example of the impact which evaluation procedures can have comes from Jerome Skolnick's study of the behavior of police detectives in a West Coast city.[24] Like most police departments, this one evaluates detectives on their "clearance rate," the percentage of reported crimes that are "solved." One way to solve crimes such as burglaries is to get arrested suspects to confess to previously unsolved thefts. The more crimes the suspect admits committing, the better for the detective's and the department's clearance rate. The result is detectives become as interested in clearing unsolved crimes to boost their performance scores as in obtaining convictions. The suspect willing to admit to a number of previous burglaries can exchange his confessions for favorable treatment (prosecution on only a few of many provable counts, a light sentence, a promise of no future prosecution on crimes already committed). This may lead to what Skolnick calls the "reversal of penalties" where a burglar willing to confess to a number of crimes receives a lighter sentence than his less active (or less imaginative) fellow criminal.

---

[24] Jerome Skolnick, "The Clearance Rate and the Penalty Structure," in *Justice Without Trial* (New York: Wiley, 1966), Chapter 8.

LEGISLATIVE APPOINTMENT

In four states, judges are selected by the state legislature rather than by the governor or the voters. Legislative appointment is used for all but the lowest-level judges in Connecticut and Virginia, for most (but not all) major judicial positions in South Carolina, and for appellate judges only in Rhode Island.[25] Although it is not one of the more important techniques of judicial recruitment nationwide, several interesting characteristics deserve brief mention here.

All four of these states were among the original thirteen colonies. The procedure survives from early colonial times. Although the dynamics of the process have not been studied, it must be intensely political. Undoubtedly the patterns of partisan politics shaping other decisions of the legislature intrude into the selection of judges as well.

The characteristics of the men chosen provide some clues about the process. Nearly all (95 percent in one study) have held prior public office.[26] But even more striking is the fact that they are likely to be members or former members of the legislature.[27] In addition to partisan politics, then, the politics of personal relationships in the legislatures of these states probably plays a major role in judicial selection.

Legislative appointment presents several interesting questions for future research. Do men seek seats in the legislature with the intent of securing judicial appointments? Do legislators with judicial ambitions pursue particular strategies of behavior in an attempt to maximize their chances of selection

---

[25] Goldman, "Judicial Appointments," p. 3.

[26] Herbert Jacob, "The Effect of Institutional Differences in the Recruitment Process: The Case of State Judges," *Journal of Public Law* 13 (1964), p. 110. Nearly half attended law school in the state, a somewhat lower figure than Jacob found for all but the executive appointment method of recruitment. However, nearly 70 percent had a college degree, higher than for any other method.

[27] *Ibid.* Slightly more than 80 percent of the judges selected by the state legislature in Jacob's sample had served in the legislature.

by their fellows? If so, how does their behavior affect the legislative process? Finally, do judges chosen from state legislatures differ in their behavior on the bench from men with different backgrounds?

THE MISSOURI PLAN

In eight states, a selection process unique to the legal system has been adopted for choosing judges that combines elements of both appointment and election. This "nonpartisan court plan" (also referred to as the Missouri plan because it was first adopted in Missouri) eliminates, according to its proponents, much of the politics from the selection process. Partisan political considerations—a man's party affiliation, his prior service to his party, his loyalty to a particular faction—all allegedly will be submerged in order to obtain distinguished members of the bar who display true judicial impartiality, ability, and integrity.

In Missouri, the plan for selection of justices of the state supreme court and the three appeals courts works as follows: The governor appoints one of three men on a list submitted by a special nominating commission. The appointee then runs unopposed after serving a year in office, and may be retained or rejected by the electorate. The nominating commission is composed of three lawyers elected by the state bar association, three laymen appointed by the governor, and the chief justice of the Missouri Supreme Court. Political parties are formally eliminated from the process. Cronies of the governor and loyal but incompentent party hacks are presumably rejected by the nominating commission in favor of distinguished members of the bar who lack the political connections and desire to compete successfully for a strictly appointive or elective post. [28]

Two professors at the University of Missouri have now

---

[28] Trial-level judges (circuit courts) in St. Louis and the Kansas City area are also chosen under the plan. The nominating commissions are composed of local laymen appointed by the governor and lawyers elected by members of the bar in each area.

completed an extensive survey of the plan's operation in their state.[29] Not surprisingly, they found that politics had not been eliminated at all. The Missouri plan in operation retains many elements found in regular appointive and elective recruitment systems. This is particularly true in Kansas City (Jackson County). A presiding judge of the court of appeals there used his influence when he was on the nominating commission to select men on the basis of friendship, past association, and family background. He disregarded all Republicans.

Generally, the panels of three nominees sent to the governor were balanced on a partisan basis—two men from the governor's party and one from the other party. Members of the commission engaged in *logrolling*—they voted to place some men on the panel because other commissioners agreed to support their candidates. Furthermore, the panels submitted to the governor could be *stacked* in several ways. One was to *rig* the panel—accomplished by nominating a friend of the governor, a political enemy of his, and someone from the other party. Sometimes the panels were *wired*—the governor made explicit efforts to get the man he wanted to appoint to be among the three nominees. Finally, the governor was sometimes confronted with panels that were *loaded*—none of the nominees was acceptable to him.

The failure of the Missouri plan to eliminate politics from judicial selection calls into question the degree of success it has in attaining some of its other aims. Proponents have long argued that the Missouri plan will result in the selection of better judges who will make better decisions. Opponents have charged that it makes more probable the selection of higher-status, large-firm attorneys with more conservative attitudes.

The debate raises a number of more general significant questions. Which groups and interests are favored by what types of recruitment processes? How does the method of recruitment affect the behavior of incumbents? These and related questions are examined in Chapter 4.

[29] Richard A. Watson and Rondal G. Downing, *The Politics of the Bench and the Bar* (New York: Wiley, 1969).

CHAPTER 4
POLITICS, RECRUITMENT, AND BEHAVIOR

THE study of recruitment processes is interesting and significant in its own right. But the primary justification for studying them lies in the link between recruitment and the behavior of major participants in the legal process. Recruitment processes affect who the participants will be; who the participants are affects decisions; how they are selected affects who will have access to them and the types of influence to which they will respond.

THE CHARACTERISTICS OF THOSE RECRUITED

Most of the positions in the legal process discussed in this book are attractive ones. Men desire and compete for judgeships, openings on the prosecutor's staff, the office of sheriff, and even many of the lesser jobs (patrolman, court clerk, probation officer). If "Who gets what" is a central question of politics, part of the answer is found in the patterns of recruitment to these positions. This suggests a need to examine which social groups, economic interests, and political ideologies are most and least successful in securing these positions.

Donald Matthews, who examined the backgrounds of decision-makers in a variety of positions, reached a conclusion that accurately describes the legal process: ". . . the more important the office, the higher the social status of its normal incumbent. Thus incumbents in the top offices are mostly upper and upper middle-class people."[1] Most important positions in the legal process can be filled only by attorneys. The financial and social barriers to becoming a member of the legal profession restrict the pool of available candidates for these positions significantly. A degree from a recognized law school is now required for entry into the profession. Most states also insist upon a state bar examination. Part of the examination process typically calls for the candidate to pass certain fitness requirements. Convicted felons, members of alleged subversive organizations, and those whose principles prevent them from swearing to bear arms in defense of the state government are prime candidates for being declared "unfit."[2] In order to attend law school, it is usually necessary to have an undergraduate degree. Since scholarships in law school are scarce, most law students must obtain the necessary funds themselves. The result is that all of the social, economic, and cultural factors that limit the opportunities of the poor and minority group members in our society to obtain a college education operate to restrict access to the legal profession. It should not be surprising to learn that members of the bar are disproportionately drawn from the middle and upper-middle class, or that in 1960, only one lawyer in a hundred in New York City was black.[3]

---

[1] Donald Matthews, *The Social Background of Political Decision-Makers* (New York: Random House, 1954), p. 32.

[2] The politics surrounding the establishment and administration of bar examinations is fascinating. In some states, the examination is written by lower-status members of the legal profession, and requires detailed knowledge of state law and procedure. Lower-status law schools devote most of their efforts toward prepping students for the examination. Graduates of prestige law schools sometimes have much trouble passing it. This is particularly true of New York's.

[3] Jerome Carlin, *Lawyers' Ethics* (New York: Russell Sage, 1966), p. 21. The national average that year was not substantially different.

The specific characteristics of U.S. attorneys and federal judges confirm these generalizations. Socially, they have been representatives of "upper-middle America." They are overwhelmingly white. Religious affiliation, disproportionately higher-status Protestant, is summarized in Table 1. On other standard sociological measures—family background, father's occupation, social class, ethnic origin, and education—federal judges and U.S. attorneys also emerge as high-status individuals.[4]

Although hard information is not available, state attorneys general are probably comparable to U.S. attorneys and federal judges. State judges and prosecutors most likely come from somewhat more humble but still considerably above-average backgrounds since all have successfully overcome the barriers to entering the legal profession.

Two additional characteristics of important decision-makers are noteworthy. The first is their tendency to be "local boys"—born, raised, and educated in the state (and sometimes even the specific community) in which they serve. Half of the Wisconsin prosecutors studied by Jacob were born in the county that elected them; five out of six were Wisconsin-born.[5] They also tended to remain in Wisconsin for their undergraduate and legal education. Over 90 percent of Louisiana judges were born and raised in the state; 75 percent attended college there, and most of the rest went to a Southern school.[6] Two-thirds of Louisiana's district judges

---

[4] This is most pronounced in the case of Supreme Court justices. See John Schmidhauser, "The Background Characteristics of U.S. Supreme Court Justices," *Midwest Journal of Political Science* 3 (1959), pp. 2-49. See also James Eisenstein, *Counsel for the United States: An Empirical Analysis of the Office of United States Attorney* (Ph.D. diss., Yale University, 1968), Chapter VII; and Thomas Jahnige and Sheldon Goldman, *The Federal Courts as a Political System* (New York: Harper & Row, 1971), pp. 64-70.

[5] Jacob, *Justice in America* (Boston: Little, Brown, 1965), p. 77.

[6] Kenneth N. Vines, "The Selection of Judges in Louisiana," in Vines and Jacob, eds., *Tulane Studies in Political Science* Vol. VIII (New Orleans: Tulane University, 1962), p. 105.

Table 1. Religious affiliation of federal legal appointees and other selected decision-makers

Religious affiliation	U.S. attorneys[a] (%)	Supreme Court[b] (%)	U.S. Courts of Appeals[c] (%)	U.S. District Courts[d] (%)	U.S. House eighty-first Congress[e] (%)	U.S. Senate eighty-first Congress[e] (%)	1950 U.S. Population[e] (%)
High-status Protestant[f]	40	69	42	?	29	29	13
Low-status Protestant[g]	37	20	30	?	55	57	46
Total Protestant	(77%)	(89%)	(72%)	(76%)	(84%)	(86%)	(59%)
Catholic	21	7	18	18	16	12	34
Jewish	2	3	6	6	1	1	6
None; unknown	—	1	3	—	0	0	—

[a] James Eisenstein, *Counsel for the United States: An Empirical Analysis of the Office of United States Attorney* (Ph.D. diss., Yale University, 1968), Chapter II. Based on 57 percent of sample of U.S. attorneys serving between 1896 and 1960 who were located in *Who's Who in America*. No information on religion for 43 percent of the sample was found.

[b] For period 1889 to 1957, adapted from John Schmidhauser, "The Justices of the Supreme Court: A Collective Portrait," *Midwest Journal of Political Science* 3 (1959), Table 6, p. 22.

[c] Eisenhower and Kennedy appointees, based on Table 2, p. 70 of Thomas Jahnige and Sheldon Goldman, *The Federal Courts as a Political System* (New York: Harper & Row, 1971). The "other Protestant (unspecified)" category has been combined with "Low-status Protestant" category.

[d] Harding through Eisenhower appointees (1920–1960). Figures calculated on basis of Table 1, p. 69, in Jahnige and Goldman.

[e] Derived from Donald Matthews, *The Social Background of Political Decision-Makers* (New York: Random House, 1954), p. 27. Figures are total claimed membership.

[f] Episcopal, Presbyterian, Congregational, Unitarian.

[g] Methodist, Baptist, Lutheran, all others.

Columns may not add up to 100 percent due to rounding error.

were born and raised within the confines of their districts.[7] Nearly 70 percent of U.S. attorneys were born in the states where they served, and 60 percent attended college or law school there.[8] Similar figures have been cited for federal judges.[9]

Second, the men who obtain the most important positions are not newcomers to public life. Eighty percent of federal district judges sitting in 1961 had prior governmental experience.[10] Nearly as many U.S. attorneys (76 percent) had held a public position prior to assuming office.[11] As already noted in Chapter 2, state judges are also likely to have had previous governmental experience. Limited evidence confirms the expectation that state attorneys general have also served previously.[12]

Although the similarities in the backgrounds of the men who occupy these positions are pronounced, some differences can be found. As Donald Matthews suggested, their characteristics vary with the level of the position. A study which compared the characteristics of appellate and trial judges in 12 states where both were chosen by the same procedure confirms this. It found appellate judges had higher

[7] *Ibid.*, p. 107. Bancroft C. Henderson and T.C. Sinclair, *The Selection of Judges in Texas: An Exploratory Study* (Houston: Public Affairs Center, University of Houston, 1965), find a similar pattern in Texas (see pp. 56-58). In Missouri, the same trend is found, though not so pronounced. See Richard Watson and Rondal Downing, *The Politics of the Bench and the Bar* (New York: Wiley, 1969), p. 218.

[8] Eisenstein, *Counsel for the United States*, Chapter VII.

[9] Richard J. Richardson and Kenneth N. Vines, *The Politics of the Federal Courts* (Boston: Little, Brown, 1970), pp. 70-73.

[10] Jacob, *Justice in America*, p. 95. Eisenstein (*Counsel for the United States*, Chapter VII) found in a spot check of the careers of 187 federal judges sitting in 1916, 1936, and 1959 that 15 percent were former U.S. attorneys and another 7 percent had been assistant U.S. attorneys.

[11] Eisenstein, *Counsel for the United States*, Chapter VII.

[12] Prior experience of attorneys who later became governor confirms this. Thirty-four of the 41 men in this category who served as governor between 1870 and 1950 had law-enforcement experience before becoming attorney general. Joseph Schlesinger, *How They Became Governor* (East Lansing, Mich.: Governmental Research Bureau, 1957), Table XVI, p. 75.

levels of education.[13] The age of position-incumbents also varies with level. Generally, the more important the post, the older the incumbent is when he assumes it. For instance, in Chapter 2 we noted that Wisconsin prosecutors are usually under 40 years of age whereas trial judges seldom are. Seventy percent of U.S. attorneys are appointed before age 50.[14] Only 36 percent of federal judges are that young when appointed.[15] Geographical location also accounts for some differences; Missouri circuit judges chosen by the same procedure differ both in their age at appointment and the nature of their legal education in different parts of the state.[16]

The most interesting variations, however, are associated with selection procedure. Judges chosen in partisan elections, for instance, are more likely to have been born and educated in their home states than those chosen in nonpartisan elections, but the quality of their education is somewhat lower.[17] They are more likely to have held political office prior to their election to the bench and to be identified with a political party.[18] Judges chosen by state legislatures are

[13] Herbert Jacob, "The Effect of Institutional Differences in the Recruitment Process: The Case of State Judges," *Journal of Public Law* 13 (1964), p. 115. Watson and Downing found the same pattern when they compared supreme court with lower-level judges in Missouri (*The Politics of the Bench and the Bar*, p. 218, Table 6.4).

[14] Eisenstein, *Counsel for the United States*, Chapter VII.

[15] Jacob, *Justice in America*, p. 96, citing unpublished data on district judges sitting in 1961.

[16] Watson and Downing, *The Politics of the Bench and the Bar*, p. 208, Table 6.1.

[17] Jacob, "The Effect of Institutional Differences," p. 107.

[18] A summary of the differences between judges chosen by these two methods, drawn from several tables in the Jacob article noted above, follows:

	Percentage chosen in partisan election (N=321)	Percentage chosen in nonpartisan election (N=329)
Born in district	53.6	9.4
Attended law school in state	62.9	54.7
Attended sub-standard law school	19.6	1.5
Held prior public office	53.6	30.4
No party identification	31.5	50.4

most likely to have a partisan identification and prior experience.[19] In Missouri, the substitution of the nonpartisan court plan for elections had two effects: It raised the average age of the judges from the forties to the fifties and it increased the number of appellate judges who had served previously in lower courts.[20]

RECRUITMENT AND THE BEHAVIOR OF INCUMBENTS

There are two general ways in which recruitment could affect the behavior of incumbents. One is through the direct and indirect control mechanisms described in Chapter 2 that theoretically operate in elections. The second is by affecting the susceptibility of decision-makers to particular arguments, values, and pressures. The assumption is that men who come to office with certain values, experiences, contacts, and obligations will be predisposed to weigh the arguments and pressures they encounter in their decision-making in particular and consistent ways.

Direct and Indirect Controls Through Recruitment Processes

Two questions must be considered in order to ascertain the impact of direct and indirect controls through recruitment. How effective are such controls? To the extent they are effective, just *who* is doing the controlling?

The description of elections for positions in the legal process in Chapter 2 leads to several obvious generalizations about their effectiveness. The legal process is no exception to the general proposition that the conditions necessary for direct control of policy through elections are rarely met for any position. Compared to the control actually exercised

---

[19] *Ibid.*, p. 112. Ninety-five percent have held another office. The figure for appointed judges is 57 percent. There is some question about the frequency of prior political experience among Missouri plan judges in Missouri. Jacob cites 17 percent; Watson and Downing, *The Politics of the Bench and the Bar* on p. 214 report that it is about 50 percent.

[20] Watson and Downing, *The Politics of the Bench and the Bar*, p. 344.

through elections for executive and legislative posts, there is considerable variance by position, with attorneys general most likely to be controlled and judges least likely. The specific election procedures utilized (whether elections are partisan or nonpartisan, whether nomination and renomination is controlled by a strong party organization) also influence the amount of control possible. Finally, there are a variety of special circumstances that affect the level of control achieved across time (a scandal, an aggressive and unorthodox candidate, a lopsided contest for a higher office on the same ballot).

The effectiveness of indirect control through elections is even more difficult to evaluate, particularly since we have little information on the career ambitions and perceptions of the relevant decision-makers. As noted in Chapter 2, attorneys general and local prosecutors meet several of the requirements: They are relatively young, anticipate an active career subsequent to leaving office, and frequently go on to hold higher public office. The long terms, low probability of defeat, and reduced career mobility of elected state judges do not produce conditions that maximize possibilities for indirect control.

Appointed officials, of course, are not free from similar controls, particularly when they can easily be dismissed by a superior. [21] Although there are limits to the ability of any superior to control the behavior of his appointed subordinates, considerable influence is possible. Appointed officials are also affected by criteria used for evaluation and promotion, as the description of the clearance rate and its impact on detectives' behavior in Chapter 3 suggests.

To the extent that control does exist, how does it affect

---

[21] One of the major explanations for the difficulties the Department of Justice has in controlling the behavior of U.S. attorneys is that the department neither can hire nor fire them by itself despite the fact it is given formal supervisory authority over them. See Eisenstein, *Counsel for the United States*, Chapter IV. Relations between U.S. attorneys and the department are described briefly in Chapter 7 of this volume.

behavior? To answer this question, we need to know *who* is doing the controlling. The initial impulse of many is to answer, "the electorate." In practice, this is rarely true, particularly with respect to judges. Their actions are directly visible to only a small portion of the electorate. When their decisions become known to any substantial number of people, it is through the actions of specialized groups and interests—newspaper reporters and editors, spokesmen for police organizations, bar associations, political party organizations, and occasionally civic groups (for example, the League of Women Voters). It is more likely that judges will respond to these groups rather than to the electorate directly. Where partisan elections are held, judges may be particularly anxious to avoid any actions which might jeopardize their chances for renomination. Perhaps the most likely source of control, however, comes from other participants in the legal process. Prosecutors, defense attorneys, and courtroom personnel have a continuing exposure to and interest in their decisions. Ironically, these individuals are also rather unlikely to make efforts to control judges' behavior except in the most extreme circumstances. They are too dependent upon the judges. Few attorneys relish the thought of appearing before a judge he has opposed for reelection.

Similar circumstances affect control over other appointed and elected officials. Police chiefs must worry about city council members and mayors. These officials normally receive pressure from specialized groups within the community about police practices, but not from the general electorate. Prosecutors, too, may be more concerned about the reactions of the elites to whom their decisions are visible. If his behavior is acceptable to the police, judges, other elected officials, and party organizations, the prosecutor will have little to fear from the electorate.

To the extent that recruitment processes result in direct and indirect controls over the behavior of decision-makers in the legal process, then, they are likely to be exerted by elements within the local political elites and not the broader community.

Recruitment and Decisional Predispositions

Recruitment processes inevitably select some individuals and reject others. If the characteristics of those chosen lead directly or indirectly to particular decision tendencies, the link between recruitment and behavior is established.

A very serious problem arises in trying to establish this link. The specific characteristics in question, whatever they may be (social status, party affiliation, attitudes and values), must be the direct cause of distinctive decisional characteristics. For instance, we know that some prosecutors are Democrats and others Republicans. But unless we can show that this makes a difference in their decisions, this does not help us to explain their behavior.

What do we know about the relationship between various personal charateristics and decision patterns? A limited number of studies have established a relationship between certain background characteristics and decisions of judges. The most notable of these characteristics is party affiliation. [22] Stuart Nagel found Democratic appeals judges were consistently more liberal than Republican judges in 15 types of cases. [23] He also found that this relationship was strengthened when the method of recruitment was examined. Appointed judges were more likely to vote contrary to the pattern their party affiliation would predict than were elected judges. [24] A study of the decisions of southern federal judges in race-relations cases by Kenneth Vines found Democrats were more likely to display segregationist tendencies in their decisions and Re-

---

[22] Joel Grossman, "Social Backgrounds and Judicial Decision-Making," *Harvard Law Review* 79 (1966), pp. 1551–1564, summarizes the major findings of research on judicial backgrounds and behavior up to 1966.

[23] Stuart Nagel, "Political Party Affiliation and Judges' Decisions," *American Political Science Review* 55 (1961), p. 845. For example, Democratic judges were more likely to favor the defense in criminal cases, the tenant in landlord-tenant cases, the debtor in creditor-debtor cases, and the employee in employee injury cases.

[24] *Ibid.*

publicans more likely to be integrationists.[25] But party differences do not consistently emerge. Missouri attorneys who ranked the quality of state judges found no difference between Republicans and Democrats.[26] More significantly, however, even when differences have been found they have not been very large.

This is true of nearly all relationships between judges' decisions and their social characteristics tested. Missouri judges who represented plaintiffs while in private practice were ranked more proplaintiff than those who represented defendants.[27] Judges who were formerly prosecutors were found to be less likely to decide in favor of defendants in criminal cases than judges who had not been prosecutors.[28] Judges who scored on the liberal side of an attitude questionnaire tended to be on the liberal side in their decisions when compared to conservative judges.[29] Protestant judges less often ruled for criminal defendants than Catholic judges; among the Protestants, those associated with high-status denominations were found to be less favorably disposed to defendants.[30] But none of these relationships were statistically very strong.

The difficulty in predicting decisional tendencies from such background characteristics was confirmed by a study which specifically examined the degree to which differences in appellate judges' decisions could be explained by them.[31]

[25] Kenneth Vines, "Federal District Judges and Race Relations Cases in the South," *Journal of Politics* 26 (May, 1964), reprinted in Theodore Becker, ed., *The Impact of Supreme Court Decisions* (New York: Oxford University Press, 1969), in Table 4, p. 84.

[26] Watson and Downing, *The Politics of the Bench and the Bar*, Table 8.12, p. 303.

[27] *Ibid.*, p. 318.

[28] Stuart Nagel, *The Legal Process From a Behavioral Perspective* (Homewood, Ill.: Dorsey, 1969), Table 18.1, pp. 230–231.

[29] *Ibid.*, p. 213.

[30] *Ibid.*, Table 18.1, pp. 230–231.

[31] Donald Bowen, *The Explanation of Judicial Voting Behavior From Sociological Characteristics of Judges* (Ph.D. diss., Yale University, 1965).

Generally, the background variables tested explained less than 10 percent of the variance.

Background characteristics affect behavior in a broader sense, however, for they help to determine a judge's contacts and acquaintances. If he has been active in a party organization, he will know people in politics. It will be easier for lawyers with political ties and party officials to obtain access to him. The significance of the "local boy" phenomenon is probably similar. Those born, raised, and educated in the community will generally have intimate ties with the local political and legal elite. They are both better able to determine local sentiment and are more susceptible to a variety of local pressures than newcomers.[32]

The predominance of upper middle-class white males most likely has similar consequences. Such people are naturally able to empathize with those who come from similar origins. Their contacts and social lives are with people of similar background. Their attitudes and values are likely to be representative of their social circles. This does not mean that their values inevitably determine their decisions. In fact, many cases involve disputes between people with these same social characteristics. But it does mean at a minimum that they are likely to have difficulty in understanding the speech, life styles, and attitudes of many other citizens who appear before them.

This suggests another way in which recruitment can affect the behavior of decision-makers in the legal process. We have been speaking of the relationship between individual characteristics and the behavior of individual judges. But the behavior of the legal process as a whole may be significantly affected if people with certain attitudes and outlooks are systematically excluded from decision-making roles while others are favored.

The recruitment process does appear to screen out effectively those whose opinions and life styles are unusual. Few

---

[32] The behavior of federal judges in the South dealing with school-desegregation cases tends to confirm this. For a fuller account, see Chapter 7 of this volume.

militant homosexuals, black separatists, or revolutionary anarchists are sitting on the bench. Furthermore, the more important the post, the less likely that anyone holding unusual social and political views will occupy it. Individuals recruited for higher posts generally are selected from among those who have previously held less important ones. When an incumbent of a lesser post displays unusual behavior or deviant attitudes, he is usually eliminated from consideration for a higher office. Thus, <u>the breadth of political and social attitudes represented on the bench is narrower than that found in society generally.</u>

THE POLITICAL SYSTEM, RECRUITMENT, AND THE LEGAL PROCESS

To what extent does the legal process operate as an autonomous unit applying its own principles and decision-rules, and to what extent does it mirror the social forces, politics, and values of society? The answer in part depends upon the nature of the relationship between the legal process and the larger political and social system.

In screening out individuals with deviant political and social views from important positions, the recruitment process acts as the vehicle which transmits some of society's preferences to the legal process. There are several other significant ways, however, in which recruitment accomplishes this.

The Participation of Political Forces in Recruitment

In attempting to influence the selection of personnel in the legal process, a number of organized political and social interests become directly involved. Most of the same groups that we expect to find active in the recruitment of executive and legislative decision-makers can be found seeking to influence recruitment in the legal process.

This is best illustrated in the case of judges. No matter what the level of the judgeship is, we usually find elected officials, professional politicians, party organizations, lawyers and bar associations, and various interest groups (civil rights, labor, business, finance) participating.[33] The ties established between these participants and the legal process are not limited to the effect their activity has on who is selected. Sources of information, contacts, and lines of communication are renewed, strengthened, and created. They remain after particular positions are filled, facilitating continuing interaction between the legal process and other participants in the political system.

Earlier we noted that although the men chosen for important posts generally resembled one another, some differences were associated with various selection procedures. An analogous phenomenon is found with respect to the participants in the selection of judges. Although the same groups are usually involved, their relative influence on the outcome varies according to the procedure used.

Elected officials such as a governor have far more say in an appointive system than when some form of election or the Missouri plan is used. He may only seek to influence who the nominating commission puts on its list of three under the Missouri plan. He may be able to determine who will be nominated for statewide partisan judicial contests, but this depends upon his influence within his political party.

Lawyers and judges, on the other hand, fare best under the Missouri plan. Presiding judges serving on the nominating commissions apparently are the most influential participants in shaping their decisions.[34] Lawyers and their bar associa-

---

[33] This point is nicely illustrated by an unpublished study of the nonpartisan primary and general election of 12 recorder's court (criminal trial) judges in Detroit in 1966. Eighty candidates filed for 24 positions on the final ballot. A number of groups entered the contest by endorsing and working for candidates, including local political party organizations, good-government groups, homeowners associations, and the bar association. At least some links between voting patterns and policy positions of the candidates emerged. White middle-class areas gave greater support to law-and-order candidates. Black sections supported black candidates. Though voter interest was low, many characteristics of partisan elections were present despite its official nonpartisan status. See Thomas Payette, "Judicial Elections in Detroit: Candidates, Interest Groups, and Voters," unpublished paper, 1968.

[34] Watson and Downing, *The Politics of the Bench and the Bar*, p. 339.

tions may endorse candidates in partisan and nonpartisan judicial elections, as well as seek to influence the governor in appointive systems. But with the possible exception of federal judicial appointments, they are not likely to have as much impact as when their elected representatives serve on nominating commissions under the Missouri plan.

Interest groups probably find it difficult to swing much weight under Missouri plan schemes, though they undoubtedly try. They can participate in elections through endorsements, contributions, and the like. But their access is best under appointive schemes, particularly where legislative concurrence is required. [35]

Finally, party officials have few opportunities to participate in Missouri plan appointments, though they may do so indirectly if they have access to the governor or some member of the nominating commission. But they can participate fully in attempts to influence the choice of an appointing executive of their own party. Their greatest influence, naturally, comes when partisan elections are held. Their participation in nomination and election procedures is open and direct. Nonpartisan elections do not freeze them out entirely, but such elections do make things more difficult. Their activities must be covert and indirect, such as making available to favored candidates sources of funds, mailing lists, campaign workers, and precinct files. In some areas, such covert help is common. Although running without party labels and explicit appeals based on party loyalty, the candidates are recruited by one party and generally known to be candidates of that party.

There are several explanations for the partial convergence found in the politics surrounding judicial recruitment. One is that these procedures do not really differ as much as one

---

[35] Wallace Sayre and Herbert Kaufman, *Governing New York City* (New York: Russell Sage, 1960), p. 550, found interest groups exerted little influence in judicial nominations and elections in New York City.

would think.[36] In elective systems, midterm vacancies are filled by interim appointments. Vacancies arise so frequently that formal elective systems of recruitment become de facto appointive systems.[37] Of the 434 judges serving on the high courts of the 36 states which provided for the election of these judges between 1948 and 1957, over 55 percent (242) initially gained their posts by appointment to vacancies.[38] Although these men eventually must face the electorate, they run as incumbents. Defeat of incumbent judges is so infrequent that as a practical matter, they can be thought of as appointees.

But even if the actual procedures used in different selection techniques did not converge, we would still find similar patterns of influence in all of them. Judicial positions are desirable. Individuals want them and they will make efforts to secure them regardless of the formal procedure. Furthermore, various groups and interests in society recognize the importance of these positions and hope to exert some influence over which men will exercise the power that they possess. Differences in selection procedures can affect how influential these various groups and interests will be in a particular instance. They can also shape the manner in which

---

[36] A.A. Berle, in a provocative article, essentially argued that election and appointment are ultimately almost identical because party leaders really make the choices in both. He was referring primarily to New York State, and while there is a good deal of validity to his argument, it does not apply universally ("Elected Judges—Or Appointed," *The New York Times Magazine* Dec. 11, 1955, p. 26). However, there is some evidence that the same is true for other posts as well. See Kenneth Prewitt, "Political Ambitions, Volunteerism, and Electoral Accountability," *American Political Science Review* 64 (1970), pp. 8-9, for data on San Francisco area city councilmen.

[37] This is not entirely accidental. Some judges will resign before their term expires so a governor from their party can appoint his successor. The successor then can run for election as an incumbent.

[38] James Hearndon, "Appointment as a Means of Initial Access to Elective State Courts of Last Resort," *North Dakota Law Review* 38 (1962), p. 64.

they go about trying to exert influence. But they cannot and do not diminish their desire to affect who is selected. Given the desire, ways and means to exert such influence will be found.

Self-selection and the Representation of Social Forces

Self-selection plays a part in recruiting nearly all participants in the legal process. But it is particularly important for two: lawyers and plaintiffs in civil matters. No matter how vigorous their own efforts are, men seeking available appointive or elective posts must be chosen over their competitors by the appointing officials or the voters. There are also a limited number of positions open. Self-selection differs in that the individual's desire and ability determine whether he is recruited or not. Furthermore, no set limits exist on the number of people who can become plaintiffs or attorneys. In general, lawyers and plaintiffs attain their status because they want to. Of course, as we have seen, the formal requirements for admission to the bar may prevent many who would like to become attorneys from realizing their goal. The resulting biases introduced result in an unrepresentative social composition of the bar that reflects the distribution of status and wealth in society generally.

These same factors affect the internal structure of the bar. Recruitment to various positions within the legal profession, particularly to the highly coveted positions within large firms, depends on two factors—the law school attended and the individual's grades. Large firms recruit at the elite law schools. Since entry into these schools was for years strongly affected by one's social standing, parents' income, religion, race, and similar socioeconomic factors, sharp differences in the social status of large-firm lawyers and individual practitioners exist.[39]

---

[39] Carlin, *Lawyers' Ethics*, pp. 22-36, documents consistent differences between large-firm lawyers and solo practitioners on a number of variables, including client status, type of practice, level of courts practiced in, social background, and education. See also Jack Ladinsky, "Careers of Lawyers, Law Practice, and Legal Institutions," *American Sociological Review* 28 (1963), pp. 47-54.

But other aspects of broad social processes are reflected in the recruitment of lawyers as well. The desire for social mobility and prestige helps account in part for the attractiveness of the legal profession to certain groups in the recent past. This is illustrated by the old story of the two Jewish grandmothers who met one day on the street. "My," observed one, looking at the two grandsons accompanying the other, "what nice grandchildren. Tell me, how old are they?" The other eagerly answered: "The doctor is seven and the lawyer is five." Jerome Carlin has some empirical evidence for this. He found that the solo practitioners in Chicago he studied typically entered the profession in hopes of rising above their immigrant parents' status. [40]

Today this motivation is probably less important. Low-tuition night law schools, which were readily accessible to the children of the immigrant poor, have either disappeared or raised both their entrance requirements and fees. [41] Now that a college degree is normally a prerequisite for studying law, the legal profession is only one of a number of options open to those among the disadvantaged who manage to acquire a college degree. Law students today claim they were attracted to law school by general interest in the law, the desire for independence in their work life, and intellectual stimulation more than by the expectation of good incomes and high prestige. [42]

Potential plaintiffs cannot realize benefits from the legal process unless the initiative of bringing a lawsuit is taken. In this sense, plaintiffs are self-selected. The distribution of

---

[40] Jerome Carlin, *Lawyers on their Own* (New Brunswick, N.J.: Rutgers University Press, 1962), pp. 3-4.

[41] Carlin, in *Lawyers' Ethics*, pp. 20-22, reports that a majority of lawyers admitted to the bar in New York today attended full-time rather than "mixed" (i.e., with night classes, part-time students as well as full-time students) law schools. Before 1920, over half had two years or less of college; today, only 4 percent are in that category.

[42] Based on a research paper of a Michigan undergraduate which examined the reasons students at three Michigan law schools gave for going to law school. James Graff, "Factors in the Decision to Enter Law School," unpublished paper, 1968.

plaintiffs' benefits to members of society therefore depends on the social characteristics of those who bring suit. Here too, then, broad social forces have an opportunity to structure outcomes.

As with the recruitment of attorneys, formal requirements are also important in the recruitment of civil litigants. Most civil litigation entails hiring an attorney and paying a variety of legal fees.[43] This effectively eliminates many poorer citizens as civil plaintiffs. A study done in Detroit found only 17 percent of those with incomes over $15,000 had never seen an attorney; 44 percent making less than $7,000 had not.[44] Another study found that the very poor are not likely to go into legal bankruptcy.[45] Obviously, those without adequate financial resources are frequently excluded from filing suit. This introduces a significant bias at the onset of the civil litigation process.

Aside from the monetary requirement, however, there are not many significant restraints on filing a lawsuit. In fact, if everyone with the money to afford litigation actually went to court whenever he could, the civil courts would be overwhelmed. To the regret of many lawyers, only a fraction of all matters that could be brought to the attention of a lawyer result in someone collecting a fee. In fact, the Detroit survey mentioned above revealed that 30 percent of the city's citizens had never seen a lawyer about anything.[46] Interviews with a sample of New Yorkers sustaining the mildest form of injury in auto accidents (slight shock, contusions) showed that 13 percent made no attempt to recover for their injuries at all, and another 21 percent tried to recover without seeing a lawyer.[47] In Wisconsin, most creditors with delinquent

[43] The major exception is personal injury litigation, where the attorney receives a proportion of the award (25 to 40 percent) if there is one.

[44] Leon Mayhew and Albert J. Reiss, "The Social Organization of Legal Contacts," *American Sociological Review* 34 (1969), pp. 310-311.

[45] Herbert Jacob, *Debtors in Court* (Chicago: Rand McNally, 1969), p. 72.

[46] Mayhew and Reiss, "The Social Organization," p. 310.

[47] Roger B. Hunting and Gloria S. Neuwirth, *Who Sues in New York City* (New York: Columbia University Press, 1962), p. 8.

debtors who could go to court do not; many delinquent debtors in turn do not choose to begin bankruptcy proceedings.[48]

Why do some people see a lawyer, file a suit, or go bankrupt when others do not? Which people are most likely to do each? Now that some research has been done, we can at least identify some of the factors that appear to play some role.

The *resources theory* is one explanation.[49] It holds that people with money to meet the cost, the education to recognize the need, and the knowledge of how to proceed will be more likely to see a lawyer and initiate a suit. The resources theory does not explain everything, however, because not everyone with the income and general educational level sufficient to support litigation actually goes to court. Other factors must be at work.

One such factor appears to be the degree of social integration of the potential litigant. People with wide networks of supportive relationships—the kind who will talk over problems with other sympathetic persons—are more likely to wind up in court.[50] Not surprisingly, the chances of going to court are enhanced when their contacts include such authority figures as doctors or employers who recommend that a lawyer be contacted.[51] Another factor is the nature of the dispute—the greater the damage caused by an accident, or the more in debt a person is, the more likely he is to institute court proceedings. Prior experience with the legal process is also important. Accident victims who had recovered money in a previous accident were naturally more likely to try to do so again than those who had failed to recover in the past.[52]

[48] Jacob, *Debtors in Court*, p. 130.

[49] Mayhew and Reiss, "The Social Organization," p. 311, briefly state the *resources theory* and critique it.

[50] Hunting and Neuwirth, *Who Sues*, p. 11.

[51] *Ibid.*; see also Jacob, *Debtors in Court*, pp. 61-62.

[52] Interestingly enough, any contact with the legal system in New York City as a witness, juror, or party to a suit reduced the accident victim's propensity to file a claim, suggesting a general disillusionment with the legal process there (Hunting and Neuwirth, *Who Sues*, p. 12).

Two other factors of considerable interest have been suggested. Jacob found that the political culture of a community affected bankruptcy and garnishment rates.[53] In traditional or conservative communities, creditors hesitate to turn delinquent accounts over to a lawyer, and lawyers are prone to make more informal efforts to collect before they resort to a garnishment. Likewise, delinquent debtors are less likely to resort to bankruptcy there. The other variable that affects who uses lawyers and the courts has been called "the social organization of legal institutions."[54] The argument here is that the legal profession is organized to handle some types of problems better than others. Problems arising from the sale, transfer, and protection of property, personal injuries, and divorces are handled by specialists whose experience and organization make them effective and efficient. But consumer matters, landlord-tenant relations, and welfare problems are not so easily handled by the current structure. Thus, the problems encountered by some segments of the population (welfare recipients, tenants) are not as readily handled by the legal profession as problems arising from ownership of property. There is no doubt some validity to this theory. But if we move back one step farther to examine why legal institutions are organized as they are, it is likely we will discover that they arise to meet the needs of those with the money available to hire legal talent.

Other Forms of Recruitment and the Reflection of Social Forces

As noted earlier, civil service procedures are designed to screen candidates for positions on the basis of their ability. Political considerations, social origins, and other criteria not deemed relevant to the employee's performance on the job presumably are ignored.

---

[53] Jacob, *Debtors in Court*. A garnishment is a court order served on an employer directing him to withhold all or part of an employee's salary. Creditors use it to enforce collection of alleged debts.

[54] The argument presented here is drawn from Mayhew and Reiss, "The Social Organization."

In practice, this is not always the case. Some of the same factors that affect other recruitment techniques operate in civil service as well.

If civil service is to function in an unbiased fashion, the criteria established in civil service regulations must be applied neutrally. There is nothing magical in civil service procedures, however, that guarantees such neutrality. If there is a strong desire to circumvent such regulations, the human mind is usually ingenious enough to learn how to do it. In Albany, New York, a local civil service system determines entry and promotion in the police department. Yet, according to one study, "Entry to and promotion within the police department are controlled by the Democratic party."[55]

Even if civil service regulations are applied in a neutral manner, there is still room for politics. The criteria used in entrance requirements and examinations profoundly affect who gets hired and promoted and who does not. Much has been written about the middle-class bias of many such tests. But other requirements can affect recruitment too. Most departments have minimum height requirements. Since police are often called upon to restrain excited and sometimes dangerous citizens, this makes sense. But height requirements effectively eliminate most Puerto Ricans from consideration. Another reasonable requirement is that a man have a clean arrest record. Yet many young black males in urban ghettos find it is nearly impossible to avoid arrest for one reason or another.

Thus, most general requirements, no matter how fairly applied to individuals, increase the chances of some groups in society of being hired and hinder other groups. No requirements are neutral in this sense. It is not surprising, then, that standards for entry often become the center of political disputes.

Finally, no matter how closely a civil service recruitment procedure approximates the ideal of fairness and impartiality,

---

[55] James Q. Wilson, *Varieties of Police Behavior* (Cambridge, Mass.: Harvard University Press, 1968), p. 24.

it can only select from the pool of candidates who actually apply for positions. A variety of social factors operate to induce certain segments of society to seek particular positions and discourage others. The predominance of the Irish in the police forces of many urban communities is not merely a reflection of their political power. Traditionally, police work has been attractive to the urban Irish. A reverse situation exists with respect to blacks and state highway police. Even when outright discrimination and discriminatory requirements are eliminated, it is difficult to find many blacks who are interested in applying.

There is another important way in which political and social values of society affect the legal process through recruitment. Some who find themselves in the legal process are less than cheerful volunteers. If given the choice, most criminal suspects would prefer to have been ignored rather than "recruited" by the police. Many called to jury duty or brought to court as defendants in civil actions participate not because they want to but because they have to. For these actors, recruitment into the legal process involves a strong element of coercion. The politics involved is not immediately obvious; but it is both significant and interesting.

Generally, if someone called for jury duty really wants to avoid serving, it is possible to do so. But those called at least have to tell the court the reasons why they do not wish to serve. It is not unreasonable to predict that many who are initially unhappy at being chosen nevertheless end up sitting.[56] Other factors serve to exclude persons from the process. Most experienced trial lawyers have very definite notions about the types of people they want to keep off juries in the cases they try.[57] Perhaps the most interesting political aspect of jury selection, however, is the fact that

---

[56] In fact, some people become so interested in serving that they lie during the jury selection process so that they may serve. See Dale W. Broeder, "Voir Dire Examinations: An Empirical Study," *Southern California Law Review* 38 (1965), pp. 503-528.

[57] Unpublished research by the author.

procedures for selecting the panels of prospective jury members often systematically and deliberately exclude certain types of people. The exclusion of blacks from juries in the South, of course, is the most notable example. However, working-class people, blacks, and other minority group members are less likely to be called than the middle class and the elderly in most jurisdictions. And in Detroit, it was discovered in early 1970 that jury commission members were eliminating men with long hair, beards, and other characteristics which they felt were unbecoming of prospective jurors.

In terms of the number of people involved, the arrest of citizens is the most significant component of coercive recruitment. If it were always clear when a violation of law occurred, and if the violator were detected, arrested, and prosecuted in each instance, there would be no discretion and no politics in the recruitment of criminal defendants. In reality neither condition is met. We shall examine police behavior in some detail later. Here, it is sufficient to mention the discretionary decisions made that result in the differential selection of criminals. It is not always clear when a law has been violated, particularly *order-maintenance* statutes dealing with disturbing the peace, vagrancy, and drunkenness. Decisions have to be made in allocating investigative resources among clear-cut violations, meaning that some types of crime are virtually ignored. Police on patrol can and do decide to ignore some acts and treat others harshly, and little can be done to stop them. Different arrest patterns exist. The ones that are found in any given locality result from conscious and unconscious decisions on the part of the police.

Local Political Systems, Recruitment, and Behavior: An Illustration
Recruitment injects the values of the larger political system directly into the legal process when

1. The nature of the recruitment process reflects and is shaped by the local political system and its values.
2. The men recruited by this system also share the dominant values of the local political system.

③ These men, because of their values and socialization, behave in ways consistent with the values of the larger political system.

Up until recently, we had little hard evidence that these conditions were actually being met. Now, however, a study conducted by Martin A. Levin presents the first systematic evidence that this linkage indeed appears to operate.[58]

The study compares the recruitment and behavior of criminal court judges in two major cities, Pittsburgh and Minneapolis. Pittsburgh has a *traditional* political system: City elections are partisan; the party organizations, especially that of the Democrats, exhibit most of the characteristics associated with machines—strong leadership, patronage, apprenticeship, and advancement up the line in political jobs for the faithful. As in New York, the parties regard judicial positions as important incentives for attracting the active support of politically oriented attorneys.[59] Minneapolis, on the other hand, is an example of the *good-government* model of local political systems. City elections are nonpartisan. The parties are weak and play a relatively minor role in governing the city. Political patronage is not prevalent.

In both cities, there appears to be widespread public support or at least acceptance of the existing political patterns. It is not surprising that the procedures for selecting judges are consistent with these patterns. Minneapolis has nonpartisan judicial elections in which the political parties play no active part. When midterm vacancies occur, the governor typically appoints someone who has won the endorsement of the local bar association. Pittsburgh elects its judges on a partisan ballot. Nominations are controlled by the parties. When the governor must fill a vacancy, he relies upon the local parties to make the selection.

The selection procedures recruit judges in the two cities whose characteristics differ in the expected direction. They are summarized in Table 2.

[58] Martin A. Levin, "Urban Politics and Judicial Behavior," *The Journal of Legal Studies* 1 (1972), p. 193. The following discussion draws heavily on this article.

[59] Sayre and Kaufman, *Governing New York City*, Table 2, p. 538.

Table 2. Characteristics of Minneapolis and Pittsburgh judges[a]

City	Position prior to assuming office	Partisan affiliation and activity
Pittsburgh	Appointed or partisan elected governmental position	Active party member
Minneapolis	Business-oriented private practice	Inactive politically

[a]Martin A. Levin, "Urban Politics and Judicial Behavior," *The Journal of Legal Studies* 1 (January 1972), pp. 196-197.

Professor Levin has described the attitudes of the judges in the two cities as follows:

[W]e find that the Minneapolis judges tend to be more oriented towards "society" and its needs and protection, and towards the goals of their professional peers, than towards the defendant. Their decision-making is also formalistic in character. The Pittsburgh judges typically are oriented towards the defendant rather than towards punishment or deterrence. Their decision-making is particularistic and pragmatic.[60]

These attitudes are congruent with and reflect the general political and social values of their communities.

Finally, there are important and substantial differences in behavior that appear consistent with these attitudes. In particular, the sentences of Pittsburgh judges are more lenient. Holding prior criminal record and race constant, Pittsburgh judges give probation more often in 22 types of offenses, Minneapolis judges in only two.[61] Their sentences are shorter than those of Minneapolis judges in 13 of 16 offense categories.[62] Also, proceedings in Pittsburgh courtrooms are more informal.

The analysis of recruitment in Part II of this book suggests that the links between the legal process and the rest of the political system are significant and varied. There appear to be

[60] Levin, "Urban Politics," p. 203.
[61] *Ibid.*, p. 198.
[62] *Ibid.*, p. 200.

some direct relationships between recruitment, the characteristics of those selected, and the nature of the decisions that they make. But it is important to emphasize the limited value of these personal characteristics in explaining behavior. Most of the relationships found are not very strong. Recruitment affects behavior, but it does not absolutely determine it. To understand fully the operation of the legal process and the decisions made there, we must look beyond the characteristics and processes that result from recruitment to examine the pressures, values, and strategic situations that confront its major participants. Part III seeks to describe the politics internal to the legal process that shape the behavior of its central decision-makers.

PART THREE
THE INFLUENCE OF THE STRATEGIC ENVIRONMENT OF MAJOR POSITIONS IN THE LEGAL PROCESS ON BEHAVIOR

ALL of us are shaped by the situational context in which we find ourselves. Our behavior is influenced according to the pressures, demands, and opportunities we encounter. As we are shaped, so do we try to shape the behavior of others.

This is true for participants in the legal process as well. Each is located in a network of recurring social relationships and responsibilities that affect behavior. We will refer to this network as the *strategic environment*. If we are to understand how the legal process actually works, we have to know something about the strategic environment of the people who comprise it.

Part Three, then, serves as a bridge between the preceding three chapters, which examined how people are recruited into positions in the legal process, and the four chapters in Part Four, which look at the consequences flowing from their actions. Specifically, it examines the forces that help to explain why prosecutors, judges, police, and others behave the ways in which they do.

Those filling a particular position have specific duties or tasks that are imposed upon them. They are given tools and resources and are expected to perform certain tasks in specific circumstances. Bricklayers are supposed to lay bricks, prosecutors prosecute, Ping-Pong players paddle.

For the most part, people at least make an effort at performing their tasks. Job duties are sometimes internalized as personal obligations. The bricklayer may feel he ought to lay bricks, and the prosecutor that he ought to do what a prosecutor is supposed to do. They find that others with whom they come into contact expect them to do so as well. Failure leads to a loss of respect, unpleasant interpersonal relations, and other sanctions. Conformity brings rewards.

Filling a particular position does more than impose a specific set of duties and expectations, however. It also brings its incumbents into contact with a limited set of other individuals on a regular basis. Furthermore, the types of decisions or responses required as a result of this contact recur again and again. Bricks, mortar, and the foreman appear; scheduled preliminary hearings and arraignments require that a prosecutor be present and that decisions be made; appellate judges are confronted with briefs, oral arguments, and decisional conferences with their brethren.

Group norms and customs enforced by coworkers can also shape the *way* tasks are performed. In other words, interaction with other people holding the same position is an important component of the strategic environment. How many bricks should be laid in a day, and how well? Which cases should be prosecuted vigorously? What percentage of them should be won? How should prosecutors treat the police officers they encounter? What types of arguments may be legitimately made to a fellow appellate judge?

For the most part, everyone in a given position will be enmeshed in very similar strategic environments. But other factors that affect behavior are also present, and their impact is less uniform. The personal characteristics of the individual is one such factor. Whether someone is stubborn or accommodating, a happy extrovert or withdrawn sourpuss affects how he does his job. His personal values do too, especially when they clash with what his job requires of him. Another such factor we might call the *situational context*. It consists of the personal characteristics of other participants, physical arrangements, and a number of unusual circumstances. Whether the judge is tyrannical or pleasant, the police competent or incompetent in gathering evidence, and whether the papers are crusading about a crime wave and lax prosecution or generally ignoring the crime beat, are all possible factors in a prosecutor's strategic situation. Whatever its specific content, the situational context has a definite impact on how an individual behaves.

In Chapter 5, we will examine the strategic environment of the police in a systematic fashion. For the positions discussed in Chapters 6 through 8, a much less-structured format will be used.

CHAPTER 5
THE STRATEGIC ENVIRONMENT OF THE POLICE

ALL of us have our own stories to tell about the police. One of the few popular songs ever to be made into a movie, "Alice's Restaurant," describes the apprehension and conviction of a litterbug. If you are at a loss for something to talk about in a bull session or during an encounter with the opposite sex, try the police.

The police are the object of a good deal of public rhetoric, although for the most part it is not too enlightening. From the right of the public stage, we are exhorted to support our local police in efforts to stamp out disrespect for the flag, crime, and subversives; from the left, we hear such thoughtful slogans as "pig," "fascist pig," "racist pig," and "oppressive tool of the establishment."

The police are too interesting and too important to leave to those who make the most noise. Fortunately, we know a good deal about the politics of police work.

THE FORMAL TASKS OF THE POLICE

Examine your attitudes and the attitudes of those around you toward the police. Most people view them with a rich mixture of conflicting feelings—respect, grudging recognition of the importance of their function, fear, and apprehension. Most of us are, in a word, ambivalent.

Ultimately, attitudes toward the police stem from the fact that they embody two attributes that go to the heart of our existence in society: authority and force. They are formally delegated by society the authority to use force on behalf of common goals. The fact that we forcefully prevent people from doing some things, that we deprive people of their liberty, their property, and sometimes their lives in the name of the common good is both reassuring and frightening. It is reassuring to know there is someone to protect us from violent criminals, even when the likelihood of encountering them is small. But the fact that *we* might become the object of police action frightens most of us.

Any political regime must deal with the problem of controlling agencies to which it delegates the use of force. Democratic regimes, however, are faced with a particularly difficult problem. On one hand, the police must effectively perform two basic tasks—the enforcement of laws and the maintenance of order. On the other hand, we expect them to perform these tasks while adhering strictly to the requirements of legality. Legality implies: (1) that the police ought not to make rules of conduct, but only enforce those made by democratic law-making institutions; and (2) that the rules ought to be enforced in a neutral, dispassionate manner with a minimum of force.

We require legality if democratic ideals are to be realized. But we also require effective law enforcement and order maintenance. These two goals pose a serious dilemma, for meeting the demand of legality often interferes with effectiveness. Since neither can be achieved completely without partly sacrificing the other, hard choices must be made. The ways these two competing goals are balanced has important implications for society. Police play a major part in determining what sort of balance between them is achieved.[1]

---

[1] Jerome Skolnick has a stimulating discussion of the concept of legality and its relation to the police function in his excellent study of police behavior, *Justice Without Trial* (New York: Wiley, 1966). For Skolnick, the "essential element [of legality] is the reduction of arbitrariness by officials" (p. 8).

When we think of police work, the apprehension of dangerous felons is likely to come to mind. Dick Tracy and "Dragnet" notwithstanding, however, a significant proportion of police activity involves quite different tasks. Some involves "housekeeping," the internal administration and record-keeping found in any bureaucratic organization. But much involves keeping the peace (or maintaining order) and providing various services (traffic control, delivering babies, and so forth). These are as much a part of the activity of police departments as hunting armed robbers.[2]

The distinction between *law enforcement* and *order maintenance* is not legal but practical.[3] Except for service activities, all proper police actions have to do with enforcing statutes. But to the officer in the field, the differences are quite real. Order-maintenance situations are ambiguous. It is not always clear if disorder exists (is the drunk too loud, is the spectator too enthusiastic, is the wolf merely friendly). Nor is it always clear which party in a fight or argument is at fault and ought to be arrested. The ambiguity is compounded by the vagueness of statutes dealing with loitering, creating a nuisance, and disturbing the peace. Law-enforcement situations involve much less ambiguity. The statutes are clearer and require little interpretation. When an armed robbery has occurred, it is easier to recognize it than when someone is disturbing the peace. There is little doubt that a crime has been committed in law-enforcement situations, and general support for apprehension of the culprit exists. The question of who is guilty remains, but the question of blame is not a

---

[2] Most studies of police stress that patrolmen in particular are more involved with peace-keeping than law enforcement. See, for example, Michael Banton, *The Policeman in the Community* (London: Tavistock Publications, 1964). James Q. Wilson, *Varieties of Police Behavior* (Cambridge, Mass.: Harvard University Press, 1968), analyzed a sample of citizen complaints radioed to patrol cars in Syracuse and found three times as many involved order maintenance as law enforcement (Table 1, p. 18).

[3] This discussion is based on Wilson, *Varieties of Police Behavior*, pp. 16–17.

problem. Store owners rarely start armed robberies of their own establishments. But it often is difficult to know who started a brawl.

Several additional features of police work are noteworthy. First, much of society's unpleasant dirty work falls to them.[4] They take the dead to the morgue, assist at the scene of serious automobile accidents, subdue the beserk, pick up filthy drunks. Second, police are not likely to be popular. Many citizens coming into contact with the police are distinctly unhappy about it. No matter how correct and professional their behavior is, the police are unpopular for the same reason that high-school assistant principals are disliked: They enforce rules. Third, it is difficult to evaluate their performance. Measures of crime rates and police performance (such as clearance rates) are notoriously unreliable.[5] Often they are manipulated to bolster the case for increased budgets or to demonstrate how effectively crime is being battled. Furthermore, we cannot rely on the reports of the "clients" of police. Few bank robbers or forgers write letters to the editor complimenting their arresting officers for diligence, good police work, and politeness. Complaints about police behavior from arrestees are heavily suspect since they are usually people with low credibility in the eyes of society. Ordinary citizens can also encounter the police in circumstances that give rise to distorted and unflattering views of their work. The question of how well the police perform their job is very often difficult to answer accurately.[6]

---

[4] William A. Westley, *Violence and the Police* (Cambridge, Mass.: Harvard University Press, 1970), p. 19.

[5] The President's Commission on Law Enforcement and Administration of Justice found actual crime is more than double that reported in the Uniform Crime Reports. See their *Task Force Report: Crime and Its Impact—An Assessment* (Washington, D.C.: U.S. Government Printing Office, 1969).

[6] For a discussion of the difficulties of citizen evaluations of police performance, see Wilson, *Varieties of Police Behavior*, pp. 25-27.

THE BACKGROUND, PERSONALITY, AND VALUES OF THE POLICE [7]

Police are recruited from a narrow segment of society. They are generally white and come from lower-middle class or working-class families. Their values are the values of their class background—traditional and conventional. God, country, the flag, hard work, self-reliance, and "toughness" are valued. Open promiscuity, messiness, unconventional dress, drugs, and public drunkenness are viewed with hostility. They like to look at braless women, but would disapprove if their wives adopted the no-bra look. They are for order, for the system, for America. Most simply do not like blacks; in fact, most cultural and racial minorities are disliked.[8] Many policemen supported Barry Goldwater in 1964 and George Wallace in 1968.

The working personalities of police (i.e., the attitudes reflected in and shaped by their work) exhibit three distinctive

---

[7] It is likely that most federal investigative agents and some state police units differ markedly from local police units, but if we restrict our discussion to local police forces, we can begin to generalize without distorting reality too drastically. A number of studies of local police converge rather nicely in their findings. The composite description presented in this section is drawn from Skolnick, *Justice Without Trial*, especially from Chapter 3, "A Sketch of the Policeman's 'Working Personality' "; Wilson, *Varieties of Police Behavior*, Chapter 2, "The Patrolman"; Arthur Niederhoffer, *Behind the Shield: The Police in Urban Society* (New York: Anchor Books, 1969), especially Chapters 3, 4, and 5; Daniel Swett, "Cultural Bias in the American Legal System," *Law and Society Review* 4 (1969), pp. 79–110; Westley, *Violence and the Police*, especially Chapters 3 and 4; David H. Bayley and Harold Mendelsohn, *Minorities and the Police* (New York: Free Press, 1969), Chapters 1 and 2. For a journalistic description of several individual policemen, see L. H. Whitmore, *Cop!* (New York: Holt, Rinehart and Winston, 1969).

[8] A systematic description of the value systems of police is provided by Swett, "Cultural Bias," pp. 87–88. Westley's findings on attitudes toward blacks in the department he studied in 1950 are chilling: "... no white policeman with whom the author has had contact failed to mock the Negro, to use some type of stereotyped categorization, and to refer to interaction with the Negro in exaggerated dialect when the subject arose" [*Violence and the Police*, p. 99].

characteristics that cannot be attributed solely to their social origins. These are suspiciousness, apprehensiveness, and cynicism. Police learn to be suspicious both from training manuals and by talking to more experienced men.[9] Suspiciousness learned during training is reinforced by experience. Police soon learn that people they encounter often lie outright, bend the truth, and cajole. They also find that suspiciousness often pays off handsomely: A fugitive felon is captured after a routine stop for questioning because he "looked suspicious." A false arrest is avoided because the alleged victim's concocted story was not accepted.

Police are apprehensive about their safety, and their awareness of danger is constantly reinforced. Ocasionally they are attacked themselves. More often they learn that another member of the department has been attacked and perhaps wounded. Whenever a policeman is killed anywhere in the country, it becomes a topic of conversation and renews anxiety among his fellows.[10] Their apprehensiveness is also nourished by their exposure to humans at their worst—agitated, tense, violent. Seeing bloodied victims of accidents and assaults contributes further to their uneasiness.

Two characteristics of the dangers police face are unusual. Unlike coal miners, construction workers, and steeplejacks, the source of danger doesn't come from accidents or inanimate objects. It comes from other human beings. To make matters worse, danger seems to erupt suddenly. The lead

[9] In an article (Thomas F. Adams, "Field Interrogation," *Police* 7 (1963), p. 28, cited by Skolnick, *Justice Without Trial*, pp. 45-46.) on choosing whom to question, one police expert offered the following: "A. Be suspicious. This is a healthy police attitude, but it should be controlled and not too obvious; B. Look for the unusual." He then listed some 20 items illustrating the "unusual," including "automobiles which do not look right," "hitchhikers," "solicitors or peddlers in a residential neighborhood," and "persons wearing coats on hot days."

[10] In 1969, 86 law enforcement officers were killed and more than 35,000 assaulted. The assault rate was 16.9 for every 100 officers. U.S. Federal Bureau of Investigation, *Uniform Crime Reports: 1969* (Washington, D.C.: U.S. Government Printing Office, 1970), p. 46 and Table 51, p. 150.

paragraph of a *New York Times* story tells a chilling tale that illustrates the unexpected nature violence against the police can assume: "A prisoner who was being fingerprinted yesterday in a Bronx police station grabbed a detective's revolver, killed him with two shots and sprayed the squad room with the remaining bullets." [11]

A third distinctive element in their working personalities is cynicism. Study after study reports that police take a dim view of human nature. Some people are just no good. They lie. They're violent. They break the law. Social reformers and other do-gooders are naive and doomed to failure. You can never rely on good intentions. The cynicism of police is pervasive, affecting even their views of the nature of police work itself. Experienced patrolmen in particular are likely to hold cynical and disparaging views of the department, their superiors, and police work in general. [12] It also extends to the perceptions they have of the general public. The public is regarded more as an enemy than a supporter or friend. If not outright hostile and dangerous, the people they encounter are apt to be complaining, critical, indignant, condescending, or unappreciative. [13]

The feeling that the public does not appreciate them is particularly painful. Police believe they provide an essential service to the community at considerable risk to themselves and for low pay. They aspire to middle-class, professional status and the respect that goes with it. They do not feel they get it. Consequently, they crave and even demand respect.

[11] "Detective Slain by a Prisoner Who is Then Shot Dead," *The New York Times*, Feb. 16, 1971.

[12] Neiderhoffer, *Behind the Shield*, Chapter 4, and Appendix. One question Neiderhoffer asked was: "Testifying in court, (a) policemen receive real cooperation and are treated fairly by court personnel; (b) police witnesses are treated no differently from civilian witnesses; (c) too often the policemen are treated as criminals when they take the witness stand." Half of a sample of men with from two to 12 years' experience picked the third choice (p. 235).

[13] Police tend to overestimate public hostility toward them and underestimate the frequency of favorable attitudes. See Wilson, *Varieties of Police Behavior*, p. 28.

Other major attributes of police culture, particularly secrecy and police solidarity, are logical consequences of the three characteristics just mentioned. If the public is hostile and critical, then outsiders must be excluded from the internal working of the department. Information that might lower police prestige and discourage respect must remain inside the department. Norms of secrecy even extend into the department. Men who are too free in revealing what their partners did while on patrol become identified as "stoolies" and are ostracized. [14]

Similarly, criticism of any police officer is taken as a blow to the standing of everyone in the department. As a result, solidarity is high. Police stick together. Fellow officers are rarely criticized and normally defended regardless of the charge. Even former Attorney General John Mitchell, who is certainly identified as being strongly propolice, was criticized by police organizations for federal indictments brought in early 1971 against several Los Angeles policemen involved in the fatal shooting of Mexican-Americans.

Although secretiveness and solidarity are exhibited by most bureaucratic organizations, these qualities are especially pronounced with the police. [15] They are reluctant to rely upon other agencies encountered in their work and even avoid contact with them. Even though cases involve matters that should properly be brought to the attention of social workers, police hesitate to contact them. Social workers reciprocate in kind. This mutual reluctance to interact characterizes their relations with most agencies and individuals routinely encountered. [16]

---

[14] Westley, in *Violence and the Police*, particularly found this to be true in the department he studied. See especially Chapter 4. See also Skolnick, *Justice Without Trial*, pp. 52–53.

[15] In part, this accounts for the difficulties encountered in trying to study them.

[16] For a discussion of police isolation, see John P. Clark, "Isolation of the Police: A Comparison of the British and American Situations," *The Journal of Criminal Law, Criminology and Police Science* 56 (1965), pp. 307–319.

The isolation of the police also extends to their social life. Their social activities are largely confined to other policemen and their wives. When they are with nonpolice, their occupation often leads to unfriendly comments and embarrassing situations. Naturally, everyone has a little less fun if a policeman attends a party with nonpolice. Getting good and drunk, bragging about shady deals, complaining about disputes with others, or sharing a little pot are less fun when you know one of the group is a cop.

All these major elements of police culture—conventional morality and values, suspiciousness, apprehensiveness, cynicism, secrecy, and solidarity—are consistent and mutually supportive. Their stability and strength are constantly renewed through interaction with fellow officers and the sordid, corrupt, and brutal aspects of society that they repeatedly encounter.

THE WORKING ENVIRONMENT OF THE POLICE [17]

The patrolman's primary task is maintaining order rather than apprehending suspected felons. Inevitably, he is confronted with very difficult choices. Should he look the other way or intervene when order is apparently violated? If he decides to intervene, what precisely should he do? Only the naïve rookie is likely to answer, "Arrest 'em!" Experienced men have learned that arrests involve considerable bother. It takes time and effort to go down to the station house, fill out reports, and perhaps testify in court. When cases are dismissed or convicted defendants receive probation, the incentive to make arrests in the future is diminished. Then, in a number of situations, arrest is not the best way to maintain order. Arrests are and should be resorted to selectively.

When a patrolman encounters a situation involving public order (a vagrant, a drunk, a minor scuffle, rowdy teen-agers, a

---

[17] The environment of detectives differs in important respects from men on patrol. However, nearly all detectives began their careers as patrolmen. For a discussion of differences between foot patrol and radio-car patrol, see Westley, *Violence and the Police*, pp. 34–36.

petty dice game), he is on his own. Statutes dealing with the situation are often ambiguous. Furthermore, he cannot question everyone carefully and ponder what to do for 30 minutes. He must act immediately, and on the basis of scanty information given by agitated, frightened, hostile, or sullen individuals, who tell him conflicting, confused stories or nothing at all. With it all is the ever-present possibility he will become the target of physical attack.

Another distinctive feature of a policeman's decisions is their low visibility.[18] Whether he "looks the other way," gives a warning or lecture, or perhaps resorts to physical violence, his superiors usually have no independent way of knowing what happened. Norms of secrecy, which suggest that the "best policy is to go along in the car and forget about it when you get out,"[19] contribute to low visibility of a policeman's decisions.

The point is perhaps so simple that we lose sight of its significance. Given low visibility, it is impossible to force patrolmen to adhere strictly to specific standards of behavior. Much of what an officer on patrol does he does on his own with tremendous discretion. Even when an arrest is made, it is generally a low-visibility event. With a few exceptions involving serious and noteworthy crimes or notorious individuals, hardly anyone really pays much attention to arrests.

The hostility between blacks and police has received wide attention, but encounters with the white poor, teen-agers (particularly gang members), and other minority groups are no less antagonistic. Relations with other actors in the legal process itself are strained over the disposition of arrested individuals. Many police resent it deeply when the prosecutor dismisses a case or a judge grants low bail, a suspended sentence, or probation. They believe the people they arrest deserve punishment. If they have not violated some specific

---

[18] This concept is discussed by Joseph Goldstein, "Police Discretion Not to Invoke the Criminal Process: Low Visibility Decisions in the Administration of Justice." *Yale Law Journal* 39 (1960), pp. 543-594.

[19] These words of a rookie describing what he was taught during his first few patrols are quoted by Westley, *Violence and the Police*, p. 165.

statute, then they have behaved in some reprehensible manner. Police are fond of telling how they will see someone they regard as dangerous, criminal, and a troublemaker back on the street within hours of an arrest. It is not surprising some policemen feel that if those deserving punishment are actually to receive it, it has to be administered by them or not at all.

Despite police solidarity, the relationship between patrolmen and detectives is not always smooth. College students yearn for really interesting courses and satisfying relationships with the opposite sex. The police seek the clean felony arrest, a "good pinch." Here there is no ambiguity. Prosecutors and judges approve and follow up with appropriate action. The officer's reputation within the department is enhanced and the likelihood of promotion increased. Even some degree of public praise and recognition may follow. But apprehension of an armed robber, rapist, or fugitive murderer is difficult. Good pinches are scarce, and there is a great deal of competition for them. Unfortunately, the patrolman finds detectives take over as soon as possible when a serious felony occurs. He soon finds himself guarding the door while detectives question suspects or witnesses and gather evidence. If they possibly can, the detectives see to it that they themselves make the felony arrest. Since detectives generally receive higher pay and have more interesting and prestigious work, it is easy to understand why patrolmen envy and even resent them.[20]

The major elements in the working environment of detectives can be presented only in summary fashion here.[21] First,

---

[20] See Neiderhoffer, *Behind the Shield*, Chapter 3, especially pp. 62, 77, 82–83. See also Westley, *Violence and the Police*, p. 43. Westley reports that the desire of patrolmen to make a good pinch before the detectives arrive to snatch the credit sometimes prompts them to rough up suspects in order to get quick confessions (p. 129).

[21] Skolnick, in *Justice Without Trial*, has the best description of detectives to date. See especially Chapters 5 through 8. See also Neiderhoffer, *Behind the Shield*, pp. 81–85; and Westley, *Violence and the Police*, pp. 36–43.

like patrolmen, they seek the good pinch. Unlike patrolmen, however, their opportunities for making them are more numerous. Second, as suggested in Chapter 3, their performance is often evaluated on their *clearance rate*, the proportion of all reported crimes "solved." This leads to several interesting consequences. It is often more important to a detective to solve reported crimes by having a suspect confess to a whole series of them than to obtain a conviction and stiff sentence. As a result, suspects can bargain with detectives. In return for the suspect's confession to a series of unsolved crimes, the detective works to lessen the sentence imposed for the crime for which the suspect has been indicted. [22]

Third, the work of narcotics, gambling, and vice-squad detectives requires that they set up and administer informer systems. [23] Since these crimes normally do not have victims, the police themselves must act as complaining witnesses. To locate bookies or dope peddlers and to win their confidence so bets will be accepted or sales made, information, introductions, and other forms of assistance are needed. Inevitably, these detectives are brought into close association with the petty criminals who are involved in such practices. They must overlook (and sometimes encourage and finance) minor violations in hopes of developing big cases. Thus, a dope addict or prostitute may be released without prosecution in return for an agreement to provide information about the narcotics trade. Often, detectives are forced to make small payments to their informers. The result is a fascinating and complex pattern of mutual interaction and dependence.

THE POLICE IN POLITICS

Police are frustrated and angry. They are angry about their low status, the danger they face, lack of public respect and appreciation, and what they see as the disintegration of society. Ironically, they increasingly borrow tactics from

---

[22] See especially Skolnick, *Justice Without Trial*, Chapter 8.

[23] *Ibid.*, Chapters 6 and 7.

some of the groups they meet in violent confrontation. They, too, have begun to demonstrate, protest, and even strike.

Militant police organizations like the Detroit Police Officer's Association and the New York City Patrolman's Benevolent Association have escalated their tactics rapidly. Unofficial strikes in the form of "blue flu" epidemics (caused by a sharp pain in the wallet which simultaneously leads police to call in sick) are giving way to outright strikes. Twenty-five thousand patrolmen struck for six days in New York City over a back-pay dispute in January of 1971.[24] Attempts to limit the control of command officers have begun and are likely to increase.[25] They have engaged in active and frequently successful campaigns against civilian review boards. In New York City, they abolished the newly created review board through initiative petition and referendum.[26] In a few instances, militant splinter groups of police have been implicated in physical beatings of members of disliked groups (such as the Black Panthers) and have sent observers to monitor the courtroom behavior of judges they feel are too soft on defendants.[27]

CONCLUSION

One student of the police summed up the predicament of the policeman quite well when he observed that he faces the danger of the soldier, the authority problems of the teacher, and the demands for production of the industrial worker.[28]

---

[24] For an account of the strike, see *The New York Times*, Jan. 16 through 21, 1971.

[25] An impressionistic survey of the rising militancy of police can be found in Chapter 7, "The Police in Protest," of Jerome Skolnick's *The Politics of Protest* (Washington, D.C.: National Commission on the Causes and Prevention of Violence, 1969).

[26] *Ibid.*, pp. 278-280 (Clarion book edition).

[27] *Ibid.*, p. 285.

[28] Skolnick, *Justice Without Trial*, p. 42.

He is asked to be a professional—to handle difficult matters on a routine basis that for others are emergencies. Yet he lacks the social status, income, support facilities, and training that most professionals enjoy. As Wilson observes, the patrolman's role is "one in which subprofessionals, working alone, exercise wide discretion in matters of utmost importance (life and death, honor and dishonor) in an environment that is apprehensive and perhaps hostile." [29]

It should come as no surprise, then, to learn that police have a profound impact on the content of law-as-applied. They have both the opportunity and motivation to make countless decisions that have a direct bearing on who gets what from the legal process. The nature of their impact will be examined in considerable detail in Chapter 10.

[29] Wilson, *Varieties of Police Behavior*, p. 30.

CHAPTER 6
THE OPERATING REALITY OF STATE COURTS

STATE FELONY COURTS: ADVERSARY IDEAL AND BUREAUCRATIC REALITY

PUBLIC attention is normally drawn to the more serious crimes—major thefts, robberies, and crimes of violence. Most defendants charged with them are brought to state felony courts.[1] These courts usually have original juridiction over crimes punishable by imprisonment for a year or more. They are the highest courts of original jurisdiction in state judicial systems.

The Adversary Ideal

Most of us form images of how criminal courts work from high school civics texts, news reports of Supreme Court decisions, fictional depictions in plays, novels, and television series like "Perry Mason," Law Day speeches, and press reports of newsworthy trials. The adversary ideal or due process model that emerges from these descriptions contains four major tenets.

---

[1] One estimate places the number of defendants in state felony courts at about 300,000. See Lee Silverstein, *Defense of the Poor in Criminal Cases in American State Courts* (Chicago: American Bar Foundation, 1965), p. 7. About 41,000 defendants appeared in federal criminal cases at the time Silverstein's estimate was made. See the *Annual Report of the Attorney General of the United States: 1963* (Washington, D.C.: U.S. Government Printing Office, 1963), p. 84. Thus, federal district courts account for only between 10 and 15 percent of all felony cases.

The first holds that accused persons have their fates decided by juries of 12 fellow citizens. Although cases may legitimately be disposed of by a dismissal of charges, a trial before a judge without a jury, or a voluntary plea of guilty, the jury trial is considered the major mechanism.

Second, the accused is assured of fair treatment through adherence to procedures and values which taken together afford him due process. They include informing the defendant of the charges brought against him, the right to counsel, the right to call defense witnesses and to cross-examine prosecution witnesses, impartial application of specialized rules of procedure and evidence, and the open and public nature of the proceedings.

Third, everyone accused of a crime receives individual consideration of his case on its own merits. The specific nature of the evidence, the circumstances of the alleged offense, indeed, all aspects of the case are given careful attention in an unbiased fashion.

Finally, no one person is permitted to act simultaneously as prosecutor, judge, and jury. Objectivity and fairness are supposedly guaranteed by having independent decisionmakers perform the tasks of prosecuting, defending, determining guilt, and judging. The antagonistic relationship between prosecutor and defense attorney in the adversary proceeding of the trial is supposed to insure a just outcome.[2]

The Bureaucratic Reality

Because it is not totally inaccurate, the due process model presents an especially misleading picture of how criminal courts operate. Most of the widely publicized criminal cases we know about come close to meeting the requirements of the adversary ideal. The problem lies in the fact that it

---

[2] For a more complete treatment of the major components of due process, see Abraham Blumberg, *Criminal Justice* (Chicago: Quadrangle, 1967), pp. 21-25. He includes, among other things, speedy arraignment before a magistrate, the privilege against self-incrimination, the prohibition against unreasonable searches and seizures, the right to counsel, and the right to reasonable bail.

accurately describes how the criminal process works only a very small proportion of the time. The adversary ideal is nothing like what happens to the overwhelming majority of people (on the order of 90 percent) who find themselves in a state felony court. Rather, they encounter what we shall call the *bureaucratic reality* of state felony courts.[3]

The contrast between the adversary ideal and the bureaucratic reality is sharp on all four points. Jury trials are rare exceptions, not routine events. About 90 percent of all convictions (felonies and misdemeanors) come from guilty pleas.[4] For felonies alone, the figure is probably about 70 percent, though it may dip as low as 32 percent in some

---

[3] The term *bureaucratic reality* is suggested by Blumberg's "bureaucratic due process," a phrase he uses to describe the operation of a state felony court in New York. See Blumberg, *ibid.*, p. 4. The discussion that follows is based on Blumberg and the following additional sources, all of which more or less agree in their descriptions of state felony courts. David Sudnow, "Normal Crimes: Sociological Features of the Penal Code in a Public Defender Office," *Social Problems* 12 (1965), pp. 255-276, reprinted in Richard Quinney, *Crime and Justice in Society* (Boston: Little, Brown, 1969), pp. 308-335; Jerome Skolnick, "Social Control in the Adversary System," *Journal of Conflict Resolution* 11 (1967), pp. 52-70; Donald J. Newman, *Conviction: The Determination of Guilt or Innocence Without Trial* (Boston: Little, Brown, 1966); Frank W. Miller, *Prosecution: The Decision to Charge a Suspect with a Crime* (Boston: Little, Brown, 1969); George Cole, "The Decision to Prosecute," unpublished paper delivered at the 1968 American Political Science Association Convention; Brian A. Grosman, *The Prosecutor: An Inquiry into the Exercise of Discretion* (Toronto: University of Toronto Press, 1969); Dominick R. Veltri, "Plea Bargaining: Compromises by Prosecutors to Secure Guilty Pleas," *University of Pennsylvania Law Review* 112 (1964), pp. 865-895.

[4] Robert W. Winslow, ed., *Crime in a Free Society: Selections from the President's Commission on Law Enforcement and Administration of Justice* (Belmont, Calif.: Dickenson, 1968), p. 290. The President's Commission collected statistics from 11 jurisdictions involving 123,000 convictions. Eighty-seven percent were by guilty pleas (p. 294). This same source cites an American Bar Foundation study that estimates the rate of 90 percent (p. 293). In Stuart Nagel, "Disparities in Criminal Procedure," *UCLA Law Review* 14 (1967), the rate was found to be 83 percent.

states and reach over 90 percent in others.[5] Full-fledged jury trials are literally deviant cases.

In theory, guilty pleas should be made voluntarily, with full knowledge of the penalties that can be imposed, and without any threats or promises made to induce the plea. Typically, the judge will ask those pleading guilty a series of questions, including: "Has anyone promised you anything if you plead guilty?" "Have you been threatened in any way?" "Are you making this plea voluntarily?" "Did you really commit the crime?" But these questions serve different purposes from those assigned to them in the adversary ideal. In most cases, these formal courtroom proceedings are little more than public ritual ratifying and sanctifying private bargains to obtain guilty pleas. Adherence to constitutional requirements in accepting guilty pleas is more facade than safeguard, conveying the illusion of substance to the defendant and outside observers.

Individualized consideration of cases is unusual. Typically, cases are categorized and routinely processed like others falling into the same category. Police, public defenders, prosecutors, and judges have set images of *normal crimes* in which the facts of the case, the nature of the offense, and the characteristics of the defendant fall into a familiar pattern.[6] Certain charges are lodged and the usual bargains reached: counts are dropped or reduced and the usual sentence recommended in return for a guilty plea. In other words, cases are processed in a routine bureaucratic manner.

[5] Lee Silverstein, in his *Defense of the Poor in Criminal Cases in American State Courts* (Chicago: American Bar Foundation, 1965), found this range among the various states. The median figure was 67 percent (see Table 27, pp. 92-93). Newman, *Conviction*, on p. 3, n. 1, estimates that guilty pleas account for between 70 and 85 percent of felony convictions. Blumberg, *Criminal Justice*, p. 29, found that over 90 percent pleaded guilty in felony cases in every year between 1950 and 1964 in the court he studied.

[6] *Normal crimes* is a concept discussed by Sudnow in his article of the same title.

Finally, in place of independence of key participants, we typically find strong interdependence among them. Prosecutors, defense attorneys, and judges share interests and are mutually dependent on each other. As a result, none can act wholly independently. Each shapes his behavior in particular cases in anticipation of its affect on the willingness of others to cooperate with him in the future. Some elements of conflict remain, but they are overshadowed by mutual understandings and cooperation. This may be difficult to believe in light of the courtroom conflict witnessed in the Chicago 7 conspiracy trial or in "Perry Mason" reruns, but it's true nonetheless.

The bureaucratic reality of state felony courts can best be explained by examining specifically how prosecutors, defense attorneys, and judges depend upon one another to meet the demands placed on them by their respective positions.[7] But we need to describe the nature of each of these positions before we can understand how they depend upon each other.

The Strategic Situation of Prosecutors

Prosecutors make decisions of crucial importance for arrested individuals. Until recently, they made decisions affecting life and death. Should a suspect be charged with murder punishable by death? Should the death penalty be sought? If efforts to restore the death penalty succeed, prosecutors will once again have this awesome power. But even if they do not, prosecutors will retain control over decisions that can lead to life imprisonment.

The stakes are not as high in their routine decisions, but they are nonetheless significant. Prosecutors everywhere have the formal authority to decide:

---

[7] It should be noted that while state felony courts display many characteristics normally associated with bureaucracies, they lack an important one: hierarchical authority relationships among the major participants.

① Whether arrested individuals will be prosecuted or dismissed without charges being pressed
② How much bail should be recommended
③ What charges will be brought
④ How many counts of each charge will be brought
⑤ What will be offered in return for a guilty plea.[8]

No list can fully capture the full human impact of these decisions. The bail recommendation often determines whether a defendant will be free awaiting trial or languish in pretrial detention. The nature of the bargain he agrees to in accepting a guilty plea affects whether a man will go to prison and for how long.

Prosecutors also have a significant say as to the direction of law enforcement in their communities. Through the use of grand juries, their own investigators, and their influence over the police, they can launch investigations into previously ignored areas. By declining prosecutions, they can discourage enforcement of certain statutes. On the other hand, vigorous prosecution of some crimes may deter others from committing them. Their willingness to pursue and develop police brutality and political corruption cases can shape the political climate of the community.

Prosecutors encounter few restrictions in making these decisions. No superiors exist to dictate policy to them.[9] Most of their decisions are barely visible to the press or public. The only people who really observe them—police, judges, and defense attorneys—are rarely in a position to dictate what

---

[8] For a similar list of the prosecutor's powers, see Blumberg, *Criminal Justice*, p. 58.

[9] Although some state attorneys general have limited supervisory powers over local prosecutors, these powers are rarely exercised. Judges have limited supervision over them, particularly with regard to their courtroom behavior.

they should do.[10] Prosecutors may be subjected to pressures from political party leaders, but they are important elected officials themselves, and are not without leverage of their own.

A prosecutor's discretion is not unlimited, however. Several practical considerations arising from his strategic environment constrain his behavior. If a crime, such as rape, murder, or public corruption attracts great publicity, he has little choice but to prosecute. Moreover, if many of these cases are lost, his reputation will be badly damaged.

He must also cultivate an image of general competence and effectiveness on routine cases by maintaining a high conviction rate. Police, judges, newspaper reporters, the legal community, political leaders, and even segments of the general public expect a prosecutor to convict about the same number of people as his predecessor, and to lose only a small proportion of his cases. The fact that he *thinks* everyone is watching his conviction rate (whether they are or not) raises fears that a drop in the number or proportion of convictions would lead to a public outcry, a ruined reputation, and damage to his future prospects in both law and politics. For most prosecutors, the conviction rate is of prime concern.[11] It consequently becomes more important not to lose than to

---

[10] As the foregoing pages suggest, however, the interdependence among court regulars does open the way for influence. Federal judges, for instance, sometimes affect prosecutors' decisions on what cases to bring. See James Eisenstein, *Counsel for the United States: An Empirical Analysis of the Office of United States Attorney* (Ph.D. diss., Yale University, 1968), Chapter III.

[11] This attitude extends throughout prosecutors' offices. Assistant prosecutors kid one another about losing cases, but the joshing does not conceal implicit judgments that losers are somehow not up to snuff and are letting the office down. Few want to acquire an office reputation as a loser. For a description of the operation of norms concerning winning in a prosecutor's office, see John Kaplan, "The Prosecutorial Discretion: A Comment," *Northwestern Law Review* 6 (1965), p. 180.

win. Many prosecutors prefer to dismiss the case or to plea bargain generously rather than to chance losing.[12]

In more serious and well-publicized cases the charges must bear some reasonable relationship to the crime.[13] Normally, murderers cannot be convicted of simple assault or rapists of indecent exposure without undesirable repercussions for the prosecutor.

The Strategic Situation of Defense Counsel

All cases in state felony courts are brought by the prosecutor's office. The attorneys representing the accused, however, come from several sources. They can be privately retained by the defendant or provided by and paid by the government. Privately retained lawyers fall into three groups. There are a very few skilled trial specialists, often with national reputations, who normally charge substantial fees. Men like F. Lee Bailey and Edward Bennett Williams and their somewhat less well-known counterparts are the elite of criminal defense work. In populous areas, there are small groups of less prominent men who also specialize in criminal work. They account for a high proportion of all cases with retained counsel, and

---

[12] Simple mathematics can illustrate why this is so. If a prosecutor is presented with 100 cases, 50 of which are very good and 50 so-so, he can insure a high conviction rate by dismissing the second 50. Even if he loses one or two of the remaining 50 cases, he will have over a 95 percent conviction rate. His zealous counterpart who goes ahead on all 100 cases may succeed in getting convictions on 30 of these 50 extra cases. He has convicted nearly 80 people, not just under 50. But his conviction rate is less than 80 percent. Two things prevent the prosecutor from becoming overly cautious and dismissing too many cases: (1) the need to get a respectable number of convictions; and (2) the pressures from the police who want weak but important cases prosecuted regardless of the likelihood of conviction.

[13] Sudnow, in "Normal Crimes," p. 317, reports that both prosecutor and public defender are concerned that defendants "receive their due," that is, that their punishment be somehow commensurate with their criminal behavior.

charge considerably less than their better-known brethren.[14] A larger group of general practitioners and small-firm attorneys will occasionally take a criminal case, but the bulk of their practice is civil law. In urban areas, they handle only a small proportion of the criminal work. In smaller communities where there are not enough criminal cases to support specialists, this group may handle most of them.

Several techniques are used to meet the Supreme Court's requirement that defendants in felony cases who cannot afford to hire lawyers are entitled to representation.[15] In some jurisdictions, all such cases are given to the public defender's office. Like the prosecutor, the public defender is a government employee, though he is usually appointed rather than elected. Elsewhere, private attorneys are appointed by the presiding judge. The details of the various techniques used to select appointed counsel are largely irrelevant to our discussion. One aspect of the method used is significant, however. In some jurisdictions, most appointments are made from a group of *hangers-on*, attorneys who spend all of their time waiting in court for appointments. Their entire livelihood depends on such appointments. The alternative is to select attorneys in general practice who appear in criminal court only when appointed. For them, such appointments are infrequent, financially unrewarding, and a general drain on their time.

[14] For example, six criminal specialists handle 90 percent of the cases with retained counsel in Baltimore [The President's Commission on Law Enforcement and Administration of Justice, *Task Force Report: The Courts* (Washington, D.C.: U.S. Government Printing Office, 1967), p. 126]. Cole, in "The Decision to Prosecute," reports a similar situation in Seattle, where there are eight criminal specialists. Skolnick, "Social Control," p. 59, found five or six criminal lawyers took most cases in a California city.

[15] The most important case in this area is Gideon v. Wainwright, 372 U.S. 335, 83 S. Ct. 792, 9 L. Ed. 2d 799 (1963). The story behind it is told in Anthony Lewis's *Gideon's Trumpet* (New York: Random House, 1964). For a detailed account of how the poor obtain counsel, see Silverstein, *Defense of the Poor*, Chapter 2 (assigned counsel systems) and Chapter 3 (defender systems).

We are mostly interested here in the attorneys who handle the bulk of criminal cases—public defenders, the hangers-on, and local criminal specialists. Although all three constantly interact with prosecutors, defendants, judges, and other courtroom participants, there are important differences in their situations. Public defenders are faced with a dual responsibility. As public employees, they must represent every defendant who cannot afford counsel. In doing so, they must fulfill vague but nonetheless compelling standards of adequate representation. Local judges, the bar, groups representing the interests of the poor, the local governmental unit appointing and paying them, and to some extent the press and general public all expect the public defender to see that his clients' right to adequate representation is met. In particular, he does not want appeals courts to reverse convictions of his clients on grounds that they did not receive adequate representation.

Hangers-on face somewhat different problems. Often they are among the most marginal members of the legal profession. Their legal training and skills are meager. Many would find it impossible to make a living on their own, and depend upon receiving a sufficient number of appointments. Consequently, they are highly dependent on the goodwill and cooperation of the court, and avoid doing anything to jeopardize it. Understandably, they are quite reluctant to burden the hard-pressed judge who appointed them with the necessity of hearing a time-consuming jury trial.

The problems of privately retained criminal specialists also include the practical considerations of making a living. Although they can control their work loads by refusing to take cases, they must have enough paying clients to maintain their incomes. Obviously, they cannot very often devote more time to cases than the client's financial resources justify. Their task, then, is to handle enough clients fast enough to make the fees obtained worthwhile. But they must do it in a way that encourages the clients to pay. Collecting fees from criminal defendants presents a peculiar challenge. Convicted defendants understandably lose their enthusiasm for paying. Enforcing collection (particularly if the client is in jail) is difficult, nasty, and time-consuming. Usually, therefore, trials must be avoided and clients must be motivated to pay *before* the case is concluded.[16]

One interesting problem faced by all defense attorneys is that of *client control*.[17] The challenges which privately retained lawyers face in justifying and collecting fees are part of it. But they, along with court-appointed attorneys and public defenders, have to convince their clients that (1) they have done a good job on their behalf, and (2) if a bargain has been struck with the prosecutor in return for a guilty plea, it ought to be accepted and formally entered in a courtroom ritual. Because the client has no choice but to accept the public defender or appointed attorney as his counsel, this control is more difficult for them.

The Strategic Situation of the Judge

The power of judges to pass sentence on convicted defendants most attracts our attention.[18] But judges also make a number of other decisions affecting the fates of defendants. They formally set bail levels. They may accept or reject

---

[16] Blumberg has summarized his thoughts about the role of retained counsel in the felony court he studied in a short article that will appeal particularly to readers with a cynical streak. Abraham Blumberg, "The Practice of Law as a Confidence Game," *Law and Society Review* 1 (1967), pp. 15-39. He observes "The criminal lawyer ... must solve three problems. First, he must arrange for his fee; second, he must prepare and then, if necessary, 'cool out' his client in case of defeat (a highly likely contingency); third, he must satisfy the court organization that he has performed adequately in the process of negotiating the plea, so as to preclude the possibility of any sort of embarrassing incident which may serve to invite 'outside' scrutiny" (p. 27).

[17] The term is used by Skolnick, "Social Control," p. 65. Skolnick points out a retained lawyer can withdraw from the case or increase his fee substantially if the client refuses his advice and insists on going to trial. The public defender is stuck with his client (and vice versa) (p. 66).

[18] It has also attracted the attention of scholars. Aside from studies of background characteristics and recruitment, sentencing is one of the few aspects of trial judges' behavior that has been studied. See, for example,

prosecutors' motions to dismiss or reduce charges and defense motions for directed verdicts of acquittal. They rule on requests for postponements, on motions to suppress evidence, on objections to questions asked of witnesses. Their instructions to juries and comments on the evidence help to shape verdicts. Their control over conduct in their courtrooms gives them considerable leverage over both prosecutors and defense attorneys. Clearly, judges are formidable decision-makers.

Like prosecutors, their discretion is impressive but not limitless. They cannot normally ignore rules of procedure and standards of fairness entirely, for fear of drawing the censure of the local bar and press and frequent reversal and chastisement by appeals courts. Furthermore, persons charged with crimes must have their cases handled expeditiously. Several factors make a current docket desirable. Personal pride and a desire to avoid the criticism of judicial superiors and the local bar are partly responsible.[19] But long delays in the trying of cases create two serious problems. Defendants unable to make bail languish in pretrial detention even though they have been convicted of no crime. And the prosecution's case deteriorates as witnesses move, die, and forget. Finally,

---

Edward Green, "Sentencing Practices of Criminal Court Judges," *The American Journal of Correction*, (1960), pp. 32-35; Robert M. Carter and Leslie T. Wilkins, "Some Factors in Sentencing Policy," *The Journal of Criminal Law, Criminology, and Police Science* 58 (1965), pp. 503-514; Frederick J. Gaudet, "Individual Differences in the Sentencing Tendencies of Judges," *Archives of Psychology* 32 (1938), reprinted in Glendon Schubert, ed., *Judicial Behavior* (Chicago: Rand McNally, 1964); and Albert Somit, Joseph Tanenhaus, and Walter Wilke, "Aspects of Judicial Sentencing Behavior," *University of Pittsburgh Law Review* 21 (1960), pp. 613-621, also reprinted in Schubert, *Judicial Behavior*, pp. 389-394. Most other significant questions about these judges (including just how they make decisions) have not yet been explored. By far the best effort to date is John Hogarth's outstanding study of Canadian judges, *Sentencing As a Human Process* (Toronto: University of Toronto Press, 1971).

[19] Skolnick, "Social Control," p. 55.

judges cannot entirely ignore the repercussions of their decisions. Few feel secure enough to dismiss or to direct a verdict of acquittal in serious cases without substantial grounds. Elected judges, in particular, as noted in Chapter 2, may be sensitive to the reactions of party officials, the criminal bar, and the public to their decisions.[20] Counterpressures for severity in dealing with convicted defendants may come from the police, prosecutors, and the press.

Guilty Pleas, Bureaucratic Realities, and Mutual Dependence

The prevalence of guilty pleas in state felony courts is hardly the result of massive outbreaks of conscience or remorse by defendants. They are the product of bargains struck between their attorneys and the prosecutor, with the judge ratifying the agreement and sometimes participating actively in its negotiation.[21] The process is usually referred to as *plea bargaining.*

Plea bargaining is vitally important to the criminal process. The whole system of criminal justice as presently constituted would break down without a speedy way to dispose of cases. Jury trials are slow and cumbersome. Because their length is unpredictable, the problems associated with scheduling other court business (particularly minimizing the time wasted by witnesses waiting for their cases to be called) are considerably complicated. Furthermore, considerable preparation for both prosecution and defense is required.

---

[20] In some jurisdictions, the political connections of defense attorneys can be used to obtain favorable treatment from judges. Blumberg, in *Criminal Justice,* p. 120, observed of the judges in the court he studied that "their ascendency to the bench was preceded by many years of clubhouse activity.... These contributions continue, because strong clubhouse ties are needed for re-election or promotion. The situation generates commitments and obligations to 'politically visible' lawyers in Metropolitan Court.... If they cannot receive payment in cash, they will accept payment 'in kind'—judicial favors dispensed at critical junctures in the criminal lawyer's practice."

[21] Often a separate set of negotiations between the lawyer and his client is necessary to convince the client he should accept the bargain. Sometimes, experienced criminals will bargain directly with the prosecutor, never relying on an attorney of his own at all.

If every case went to a jury, then, the system would soon be overwhelmed. Jails, already overcrowded in many places, would have to house even more defendants unable to make bail who were awaiting trial. Prosecutors, public defenders, and judges would be inundated. "Our office keeps eight courtrooms extremely busy trying 5 percent of the cases," observed a Manhattan prosecutor. "If even 10 percent of the cases ended in a trial, the system would break down."[22] Meanwhile, the lag between arrest and trial would rapidly increase. The number of convictions, even if the prosecutor won every trial, would fall dramatically. Private attorneys would encounter financial disaster as they were forced to accept meager fees inadequate to compensate them for the time spent preparing and actually trying cases.

If the adversary ideal of a jury trial in all or most cases is unattainable, what then? Some other acceptable way to handle cases generated by police arrests is essential. It must meet three requirements: (1) it must be efficient enough to dispose of all cases given existing manpower; (2) it must give at least the appearance of meeting the tenets of due process; and (3) it must permit both prosecution and defense to satisfy the demands placed upon them. Several possible ways of disposing of cases fail to meet all three conditions. The prosecutor cannot dismiss 90 percent of the cases brought to him, even though it would violate no provisions of due process and could be accomplished with available manpower. The number of convictions would fall dramatically, and adversely affect ongoing law-enforcement programs. Substantial increases in the number of prosecutors and judges to handle additional trials are unlikely. Local and state governments have neither the money nor the desire to increase appropriations for them substantially. Defense attorneys could solve the problem by automatically pleading clients guilty to whatever the prosecu-

---

[22] Quoted by Albert Alschuler, "The Prosecutor's Role in Plea Bargaining," *University of Chicago Law Review* 36 (1968), p. 55. The same situation apparently is found in Canada. Grosman, in *The Prosecutor* on p. 132, quotes a Canadian prosecutor: "If we fought out every case on our list, we'd be twenty thousand cases behind."

tor charged, thereby eliminating the need to bargain. But this would raise difficult problems in the area of client control. Nor can prosecutors so drastically undercharge every defendant that few hesitate to plead.

Under the circumstances, then, plea bargaining is inevitable. From the standpoint of judges, prosecutors, and defense attorneys, it is a welcome necessity. The judge's docket can be kept more or less current while formal requirements for due process are satisfied. The prosecutor is guaranteed a large number of sure convictions at relatively little cost instead of a series of time-consuming trials of somewhat doubtful outcome. Although defendants are convicted on fewer counts and receive lighter sentences than might be obtained after trials, the savings in time and effort and the certainty of obtaining conviction statistics more than compensates for this. Since they have the responsibility for representing every poor defendant, public defenders welcome the quick resolution of cases. Privately retained attorneys find it an attractive way to complete cases quickly enough for their clients to afford their fees. Appointed hangers-on correctly see it as the only course to follow if they want to receive appointments in the future. Finally, all defense attorneys can use the concessions won through plea bargaining to help in client control. They can point out that the client's jeopardy (i.e., the maximum sentence he could receive if convicted as originally charged) has been reduced by the dismissal of some counts or the lowering of others or both. If part of the agreement is probation or a light prison sentence, so much the better.

In a number of respects, then, everyone loses when a case goes to trial; everyone stands to benefit from the efficient disposal of cases through negotiated pleas. [23]

The manner in which people who have both conflicting and shared interests arrive at compromises is fascinating in itself. [24] The plea bargaining process is particularly interesting

---

[23] Whether the hapless defendant really benefits or not is discussed later in this chapter.

[24] For a fascinating analysis of bargaining strategy, see Thomas Schelling, "An Essay on Bargaining," *The American Economic Review* 66 (1956), pp. 281-306.

because it also demonstrates the complexities of mutual dependence among judges, prosecutors, and defense attorneys.

Paradoxically, it is because trials are possible in each case that they are not very probable. The major resource of both attorneys in plea bargaining is the threat to force a jury trial. Each recognizes that in most cases nobody really wants one. Yet, each side tries to convince the other that a trial will indeed take place unless an acceptable agreement is reached.[25] Each wants to extract maximum concessions by threatening to go to trial without actually having to carry out the threat.

Behavior throughout the life-history of a criminal case is shaped by the desire to negotiate a plea. This is evident at the outset when police and prosecutors are deciding what charges to bring. Sometimes defendants are charged with more serious crimes than the evidence (and the suspect's actions) justifies. It is common to bring a major charge and a number of "lesser included offenses," or to charge on as many individual counts of the same crime as possible. Blumberg reports that indictments for armed robbery typically include charges on the following: robbery first degree; assault second degree; assault third degree; grand larceny first degree; carrying a dangerous weapon; petit larceny.[26] A bad-check artist may be charged with 35 counts, one for each check the prosecutor knows about. In either case, he brings lengthy indictments in order to have concessions to offer and to provide an incentive to bargain. In the end, the armed robber may be allowed to plead to assault third degree with the other counts dropped; the check-forger pleads to one count in return for dismissal of the other 34.

In response, defense attorneys routinely tell clients to plead not guilty at their arraignments. This opens the possibility of bargaining. Ideally, of course, the goal is to convince the prosecutor to dismiss the case completely. What actually

[25] This is not true, of course, for those defense attorneys (both hangers-on and those in private practice) who have a reputation for never going to trial and who sacrifice clients' interest to obtain pleas.

[26] Blumberg, *Criminal Justice*, p. 57.

happens is that the parties agree on a plea to something between dismissal and the original charges, with an indication in many jurisdictions of what sentence will be recommended.[27] For retained attorneys, the negotiation period provides an opportunity to demonstrate the value of their services and effect collection of their fees.

Agreement on a negotiated plea can come at a number of points, including during the trial. Whenever it occurs, the final step in the process is the formal plea in open court. The ritual of these proceedings usually includes affirmations on the part of the defendant that his plea is made voluntarily and that he has neither been promised nor threatened with anything.[28]

The prosecutor must steer a delicate course between being too lenient in offering concessions and being so tough that he fails to induce a plea. His reputation is a very important factor in affecting the outcome of negotiations. If it is known that most defendants accept his offers and plead guilty, and that those who do not are usually convicted subsequently, he does not find it difficult to convince defense lawyers to plead their clients guilty. Defense attorneys in fact may accept settlements less attractive than they might wish, making it easier for the prosecutor to keep penalties in a reasonable relationship to the crimes committed. If, however, he begins to lose too many cases, it can begin a self-reinforcing spiral of defeat. Defense attorneys will be more likely to doubt the strength of his evidence or his ability to prove his case on the counts charged. As more defense lawyers take the gamble of

---

[27] A number of factors determine the final settlement: the reputation and skill of the attorneys; the seriousness of the offense and jury's probable reaction to it; the circumstances surrounding the crime; the personal characteristics of the defendant (and the victim).

[28] One task the defense attorney performs is to coach his client so that he gives the right answers when questioned by the judge as to whether he is really guilty, is entering his plea voluntarily, and has had any promises or threats made to him. For an example of a botched plea ceremony, see Blumberg, *Criminal Justice*, pp. 131-136. Newman, in *Conviction*, p. 7, provides an example of one flawlessly executed.

going to trial, the additional work generated by extra trials may indeed impair the ability of the prosecutor's office to prepare adequately for other cases going to trial. Furthermore, the prosecutor can no longer bluff the defense into believing weak cases are actually strong. His conviction rate begins to fall, further lowering his reputation and his ability to negotiate pleas in the future. It is not difficult to see why losing cases is regarded as a serious matter by prosecutors.[29]

As we have already mentioned, judges are in a position to help shape jury verdicts through their rulings, comments, and instructions. Because of this, their active support of the prosecutor can be an important factor in maintaining a winning reputation. Lacking active support, the judge's neutrality is essential. If he is so annoyed with the prosecutor that he exerts his influence to tip close trials against him, the danger of a downward spiral in reputation with all its consequences becomes distressingly real.

Judges can help prosecutors in several other ways. By far the most effective one is to create the impression that defendants who insist on trials receive harsher sentences than those who plead guilty. The incentive to plead is strengthened if the defendant's cellmate or attorney warns him the judge will "throw the book" at him if he's convicted after a trial. Another way is to accept the prosecutor's recommendation on sentence in most cases. By essentially delegating this right to determine the sentence to the prosecutor, the judge considerably strengthens the prosecutor's hand in negotiations with the defense.

The judge has a clear interest in helping prosecutors. If they are unable to obtain negotiated pleas, he faces the problem of coping with the resulting flood of jury trials. In addition, the prosecutor plays a key part in keeping the business of the court moving, for it is up to him to see that

---

[29] Skolnick, in "Social Control," p. 58, suggests the importance of winning as follows: "Credibility leads to victory, victory to the quasi-magisterial status, and quasi-magisterial status to enhanced credibility, all of which eases the task of the prosecutor."

some cases are always kept in reserve to fill unexpected gaps in the calendar.

Since defense attorneys have problems convincing clients to accept negotiated deals, judges cannot favor the prosecution too much. The number of jury trials, after all, also depends on the actions of local criminal specialists and public defenders. If the prosecutor is so stingy in offering concessions that the defense decides nothing is lost by taking a few more cases to trial, the judge's docket is just as cluttered as when the prosecutor begins losing too many cases. Thus, he may intervene to wring acceptable concessions from the prosecution as well as the defense during plea bargaining.

When a judge does decide to participate actively in plea bargaining, he is in a formidable position to be effective. If he chooses to exercise the full powers of his office, he can make the case difficult for either side. He can turn down requests for postponements, rule against a side on close questions, criticize and embarrass an attorney in open court before witnesses, clients, and the jury, and hand down sentences too light for the prosecutor or too harsh for the defense. More than anything else, it is their power to set sentence that makes judges so influential.

Defense attorneys depend upon judges for other things besides courteous treatment in court and acceptable settlements. They can be instrumental in helping a privately retained lawyer justify and collect his fee by permitting him to make some impassioned statements and granting motions that have little impact on the outcome of the case. In some jurisdictions, judges will grant postponements where the sole purpose is to further delay final action until the client has paid the latest installment on his fee.[30] Although public defenders have no fees to worry about, they are concerned about possible charges of incompetence or selling out. Furthermore, it is not always easy to convince a client to cop a plea (i.e., to plead guilty), especially when a prison sentence is

---

[30] Blumberg, "The Practice of Law as a Confidence Game," p. 30.

part of the deal. A strategic word or gesture from the judge can help the defender convince his client to accept a bargain enthusiastically.

Prosecutors cooperate with defense attorneys in many of the same ways—agreeing to postponements, helping to demonstrate the value of their services, and offering attractive concessions in return for a plea. Sometimes the concessions will be real, reflecting a weakness in the prosecutor's evidence, respect for the skill of defense counsel, or a defendant who arouses sympathy. But dismissal of multiple counts on the same charge, since conviction on all of them usually does not increase the severity of the sentence, is less meaningful even if an inexperienced defendant thinks otherwise. The same applies to reductions when the prosecutor has brought more serious charges than he intends to pursue for the express purpose of providing illusory concessions.

The considerations just mentioned help account for the final bargain reached in many cases. Other factors shape the outcome as well, including the client's attitude, the defense attorney's opinion on the probable guilt of his client, the attitude of the judge toward the particular crime, and the amount of publicity surrounding the case. Frequently, however, no special circumstances exist. In these cases, the standard terms found in unstated "recipes" for normal crimes determine the final agreement.[31]

Obviously, some cases do go to trial. A few involve serious crimes and notorious defendants in which both sides prefer a trial.[32] More often, defendants resist efforts to convince them to plead guilty and insist on a trial. Sometimes, defense attorneys convinced of a client's innocence will pass up

---

[31] Sudnow, "Normal Crimes," p. 317.

[32] Not all such cases, however, result in a trial. The prime example, of course, is the decision of Martin Luther King's assassin to plead in return for a 99-year sentence rather than risk the death penalty after conviction by a jury.

attractive settlements in an effort to obtain an acquittal.[33] Some defense lawyers will go to trial (if their work loads and the client's pocketbook permits) when they sense weakness in the prosecutor's evidence despite the obvious guilt of their client. But trials also result from simple impasses in negotiations where both prosecutor and defense feel they cannot accept the other's terms without damaging their reputations (and hence their effectiveness in the future). Going to trial occasionally makes subsequent threats to do so more credible and effective.

It is significant that so far we have barely mentioned the defendant, the individual presumably at the center of the criminal process. This is not an oversight but rather a reflection on the nature of the criminal process and the defendant's role in it.

It is tempting to conclude that the defendant is systematically victimized by the plea bargaining process. In many cases, however, he comes out ahead. In return for forfeiting his right to a trial, the guilty defendant pleads to less serious offenses than his actions justify, and often receives a lighter penalty as well. Unfortunately, the unknown proportion of innocent men caught up in the criminal process do suffer from the plea bargaining process. This would be less of a problem if pleas were truly voluntary and uncoerced. But in fact subtle and sometimes not so subtle pressures are brought to bear. These include intimations that if convicted after a trial, the defendant will receive a stiff sentence. Defendants unable to make bail are pressured when repeated delays prolong their stays in the uninviting pretrial detention jails.

---

[33] A defense attorney must sometimes advise clients to plead guilty even if he believes they are innocent. Defendants with serious criminal records, or those who commit certain crimes that prompt juries to convict no matter what the evidence is (narcotics cases are good examples) may be better off pleading if the settlement offer is attractive and the original charge carries a heavy sentence. A defendant enticed into selling dope to an undercover agent may risk going to trial by basing his defense on entrapment, but if he loses he may face a lengthy mandatory prison sentence. Pleading guilty to the less serious charge of possession may be the best strategy.

Ironically, the defendants most hurt by the system are those who do not play the game. If they either refuse to bargain and are convicted as charged, or if they merely plead guilty without negotiating any reduction of the charges, they may (1) be pleading to offenses they didn't commit but were charged with, (2) be convicted on more counts than others who engaged in the same actions, (3) receive harsher sentences than those who do bargain. Because of this, some defense attorneys feel they have an obligation to bargain to ensure their clients receive equal treatment.[34]

Summary

Throughout the examination of state felony courts, many characteristics typical of bureaucratic institutions have been described. In summarizing the politics of these courts, we shall make explicit five propositions about their bureaucratic qualities.

1. Although we may wish to use legal categories in *evaluating* the performance of state felony courts (Is due process honored? How about justice and fairness?), a bureaucratic perspective is more useful in *describing* how they function. Basically, their task is to process large numbers of individual cases or items much as a Social Security office or motor vehicle license bureau does.

2. Individual participants face problems familiar to bureaucratic organizations more than they encounter strictly legal problems. The "working judge" in these courts must be "politician, administrator, bureaucrat, and lawyer in order to cope with a crushing calendar of cases."[35] The prosecutor is burdened with an endless oversupply of cases that constantly threaten to overwhelm him, and which he must either get rid of (i.e., dismiss) or win. Retained defense attorneys are not in private practice in the traditional sense, but are participants in and manipulators of an ongoing bureaucracy. As Blumberg

---

[34] This argument is made by Polstein, "How to 'Settle' a Criminal Case," *Practical Lawyer* 8 (1962), p. 36.

[35] Blumberg, *Criminal Justice*, p. 123.

notes, "because they are so intricately enmeshed in the court organization, they cease being true professionals and instead function as 'fixers' for a fee." [36]

3. Secrecy and hostility toward outsiders are typical of the operation of state felony courts. Much of the actual work occurs in private. The public rituals, particularly the "plea copping" ceremony, provide little indication of how decisions are actually reached. Like the police and bureaucratic personnel generally, participants in felony courts resist outside scrutiny. In a sense, the hostility toward outsiders extends to defendants, who are considered to be transitory figures, potential sources of trouble, something to be processed.

4. A common attribute of bureaucracies—the displacement of the goals and values they ostensibly seek in favor of actions that insure the continued smooth functioning of the organization—is found in state felony courts as well. [37] It is not surprising, then, that *institutionalized evasions* of due process are found, or that defense attorneys are more concerned about the future of their relationships with other court regulars than their clients. Clients are too often merely means to bureaucratic ends. [38]

5. Mutual dependence and an understandable desire to have pleasant relationships with those encountered every day further mute overt conflict. As Jerome Skolnick points out,

---

[36] *Ibid.*, p. 104.

[37] Blumberg, in "The Practice of Law," p. 19, makes this point by observing: "Organizational goals and discipline impose a set of demands and conditions of practice on the respective professions in the criminal court, to which they respond by abandoning their ideological and professional commitments to the accused client, in the service of these higher claims of the organization." Grosman found the same to be true of Canadian prosecutors: "... often it is the administrative demands made upon him and the informal social relationships which develop within his operational environment that control his decision-making processes" (*The Prosecutor*, p. 3).

[38] This description is drawn from Blumberg, "The Practice of Law," p. 21.

the problem is not how to keep conflict between the prosecutor and defense within acceptable bounds, but how to maintain at least a minimum degree of adversariness.[39]

LOWER CRIMINAL COURTS

State felony courts are important because they have jurisdiction over most cases involving serious crimes. Lower criminal courts, which hear less serious offenses, derive their importance from the fact that, statistically speaking, they *are* the criminal system. It has been estimated that 90 percent of all criminal cases are heard in these courts.[40] If we want to learn about the experiences of our citizens who find themselves in criminal courts, this is the place to look.

In addition, nearly everyone charged with a felony is initially brought into a lower criminal court shortly after arrest for his arraignment. Here he is supposed to be informed of the charges against him, asked if he wants a preliminary hearing, informed of his right to counsel (and to have one appointed if he lacks sufficient funds), and have his bail set. With the exception of bail-setting, we shall ignore these functions to focus on the primary task of these courts.

The chief function of lower criminal courts is to try (and, if convicted, to sentence) those charged with petty offenses. Generally, these crimes carry rather modest maximum penalties.[41] Examples are drunkenness, disorderly conduct, va-

---

[39] Skolnick, "Social Control," p. 23. Blumberg, in "The Practice of Law," p. 24, makes a similar point: "The principals, lawyer and assistant district attorney, rely upon one another's cooperation for their continued professional existence, and so the bargaining between them usually tends to be 'reasonable' rather than 'fierce'."

[40] Robert W. Winslow, ed., *Crime in a Free Society: Selections from the President's Commission on Law Enforcement and Administration of Justice* (Belmont, Calif.: Dickenson, 1968), p. 313.

[41] In Detroit, for instance, the misdemeanor (early sessions) division of recorder's court tries all cases with a maximum of 90 days in jail or a $100 fine. In Maryland, these courts have jurisdiction of a specific set of offenses, some of which carry more severe penalties.

grancy, prostitution, petty theft, littering, simple assault, disturbing the peace, and traffic offenses. In urban areas they are known variously as magistrates court (St. Louis), municipal court (Baltimore), general sessions (District of Columbia), and by a host of other names. Their rural counterparts are frequently called justice of the peace courts. Because research has concentrated on the urban variety, the following description does too. Aside from a lower volume of cases and less hurried atmosphere, it is unlikely that the quality of justice dispensed by justices of the peace differs much from that of their urban counterparts.

Until the spring of 1972, the politics of these courts was less complex than in felony courts in many jurisdictions, primarily because the judge was the only major decision-maker present. Neither prosecutors nor defense attorneys appeared regularly. The prosecutorial function was performed by the police, and there was no requirement that defendants charged with misdemeanors had to be provided with legal representation. Defendants were even less active participants than in felony proceedings.

In other jurisdictions, however, the differences in the participants present were less pronounced. By 1970, nineteen states required the appointment of an attorney for indigents in most misdemeanor cases, and another twelve called for appointed counsel in the more serious misdemeanor cases. [42]

The differences among states are likely to diminish as the Supreme Court's decision in the *Argersinger* case is implemented. [43] The Court held, "Under the rule we announce today, every judge will know when the trial of a misdemeanor starts that no imprisonment may be imposed, even though local law permits it, unless the accused is represented by counsel." [44] Of course, the decision does not mean defense attorneys will always be present. Some misdemeanors do not provide for imprisonment upon conviction. Defend-

---

[42] Comment, "Right to Counsel; The Impact of Gideon v. Wainwright in the Fifty States," *Creighton Law Review* 3 (1970), pp. 119-133.

[43] Argersinger v. Hamlin 92 S.Ct. 2006 (1972).

[44] *Ibid.*, p. 2014.

ants can still be tried without an attorney on misdemeanors that do carry a possible jail sentence so long as judges do not actually impose a jail sentence. And it is entirely possible that the Supreme Court's ruling will be ignored in some jurisdictions.

Nevertheless, defense attorneys will undoubtedly appear in lower criminal courts more frequently. As a result, prosecutors will also appear more often. The most glaring abuses of the adversary ideal found in the description of lower criminal courts that follows will moderate somewhat. However, given the nature of the personnel who staff these courts, the types of offenses and defendants dealt with, and the extraordinarily heavy caseload, dramatic changes are unlikely. Thus, even though the studies upon which the following description of lower criminal courts is based were conducted before *Argersinger*, the basic characteristics of their operation as presented remain valid.

Bad as felony courts are in adhering to our ideals of what criminal justice should be like, they appear to be doing a marvelous job compared to lower criminal courts. The President's Commission on Law Enforcement and the Administration of Justice, which found many problems with the entire criminal justice system, concluded that "No findings of this Commission are more disquieting than those relating to the condition of the lower criminal courts." [45]

What was there about these courts that caused the commission so much concern? The answer is, practically everything. [46] Perhaps their only redeeming feature was their speed. In many jurisdictions, few defendants spent more than a day or two in jail awaiting trial. But there were considerable

---

[45] Winslow, *Crime in a Free Society*, p. 312.

[46] The description presented here is based primarily on two task force field reports on these courts in Baltimore and Detroit found in The President's Commission on Law Enforcement and Administration of Justice, *Task Force Report: The Courts*, pp. 121-138. See also Jerome Carlin, Jan Howard, and Sheldon Messinger, *Civil Justice and the Poor* (New York: Russell Sage, 1967), pp. 21-28; and Maureen Mileski, "Courtroom Encounters: An Observation Study of a Lower Criminal Court," *Law and Society Review* 5 (1971), pp. 473-538.

costs to be paid for this promptness. Because so little time was available for hearing cases, efficient routines for their disposal were developed. Prisoners were sometimes brought into court in groups of 25. Each stepped forward when his name was called. A majority pleaded guilty. If one of them decided not to, the rest waited while the "trial" commenced. Typically, the judge made no effort to explain the proceedings to those who asked for trials. They were not informed of their right to remain silent, to demand a jury trial, or to cross-examine witnesses. At the time the commission wrote its report, attorneys were not required for most misdemeanor cases, and few jurisdictions provided them for indigents.[47] People charged with vagrancy, disorderly conduct, drunkenness, simple assault, and the like rarely had their own attorneys. There is even some question as to whether they would have had an opportunity to retain one even if they had funds. Cases were prosecuted by a police officer, who may or may not have been the same officer who made the arrest. After the evidence was presented, the judge normally turned to the defendant and asked, "Well, what do you have to say for yourself?"[48] or something to that effect. Not surprisingly, the whole proceeding did not take more than a few minutes, and a conviction usually resulted.[49] The number of cases handled per hour in Detroit was estimated to be 13, including four trials.

The conviction rate was generally quite high, although

---

[47] The task force study in Baltimore found that even in cases where the penalty was great enough (6 months or a $500 fine) to entitle defendants to free counsel, the defendant still was not informed of his right to counsel. *Task Force Report: The Courts*, p. 124.

[48] *Ibid.*, p. 134. See also Caleb Foote, "Vagrancy-Type Law and Its Administration," *University of Pennsylvania Law Review* 104 (1956), pp. 603-650. Reprinted in William J. Chambliss, ed. *Crime and the Legal Process* (New York: McGraw-Hill, 1969), p. 320. Citations to Foote will be to pages in the Chambliss volume.

[49] In Detroit, for instance, 80 percent of these trials led to conviction (*Task Force Report: The Courts*, p. 133).

dismissals were not unheard of.[50] Sentences were not invariably harsh, either. About 50 percent of those convicted in Baltimore were imprisoned, and most of these (80 percent) were jailed because they could not pay their fines and had to "work it off."[51] In Detroit, 21 percent of those convicted were imprisoned, 31 percent fined, and the rest placed on probation or handed suspended sentences.[52]

Statistical descriptions fail to convey fully the nature of lower criminal courts. Those who have observed them invariably strive to depict their lack of decorum. The courtrooms are crowded, bubbling with noise, making it difficult to hear the proceedings. Defendants are herded about, dispensed with hurriedly and in an offhanded, disrespectful, and disinterested fashion. Most semblances of due process and fair hearing are absent. Defendants often are not informed of their rights, and don't understand what is going on. They either are not represented by counsel, or receive only perfunctory representation after a hurried conference lasting a few moments. In many jurisdictions, no record of the proceedings is kept. Finally, for all practical purposes, these are courts of last resort. Appeals are practically never taken.[53] What happens in them determines what happens to the accused.

---

[50] If cases bound over to the grand jury are excluded, about 71 percent of the dispositions during the last two months of 1965 in Baltimore's Municipal Court were convictions (*Task Force Report: The Courts*, p. 124). In that same year, about 88 percent of misdemeanors disposed of in the Detroit Early Sessions Court were convictions (p. 134, Table 5). However, a study in Chicago found that only 53 percent of cases decided on clear merit (and 37 percent of all cases) led to conviction (see Dallin H. Oaks and Warren Lehman, *A Criminal Justice System and the Indigent* (Chicago: University of Chicago Press, 1968), p. 138).

[51] *Task Force Report: The Courts*, p. 124.

[52] *Ibid.*, p. 134.

[53] In Baltimore, only 926 of over 39,000 convictions were appealed in 1964, less than 3 percent. Of these, 41 percent were convicted again on appeal (*Ibid.*, p. 125). Foote, in "Vagrancy-Type Law," p. 326, reports that one magistrate could recall only two appeals in 6 years. He cites other studies reporting appeal rates from lower courts of less than 1 percent.

Although we do not have studies of lower criminal courts from every urban area, there is little reason to doubt that the descriptions of Baltimore and Detroit are atypical. There is even some evidence that things might be worse in other jurisdictions. Caleb Foote did an extensive study of vagrancy and drunkenness law enforcement in Philadelphia in the early 1950s.[54] Defendants were rarely informed of the charges against them until *after* their trials were completed. With few exceptions, they were never asked to plead guilty or not guilty: "The proof in most cases consisted of the mere exhibition of a 'bum'... there was no evidence of habitualness in any habitual drunkenness prosecution observed...."[55]

Foote reports that during a drive on vagrants and drunks in Philadelphia, 55 defendants were disposed of in 15 minutes! Of these, forty were discharged, 15 found guilty:

Four of these committed defendants were tried, found guilty and sentenced in the elapsed time of seventeen seconds from the time the first man's name was called by the magistrate through the pronouncing of sentence on the fourth defendant. In each of these cases, the magistrate merely read off the name of the defendant, took one look at him and said, 'Three months in the House of Correction.'[56]

The following day, a defendant was found guilty and sentenced when the judge said to him, "You look like one, three months."[57] Dismissals were just as arbitrary. "Near the end of the line the magistrate called a name, and after taking a quick look said, 'You're too clean to be here. You're discharged.'"[58] In another instance, the defendant persisted in

---

[54] Foote, "Vagrancy-Type Law."
[55] *Ibid.*, p. 325.
[56] *Ibid.*, pp. 296–297.
[57] *Ibid.*
[58] *Ibid.*

claiming he had a job. "The magistrate asked him under whom he worked, what the first name of his boss was, and finally discharged him." [59] A final observation is noteworthy:

> Frequently defendants were not permitted to make any rebuttal, being cut off with some such remark as 'nothing you say will help,' or if rebuttal was permitted, the magistrate indicated he had already prejudged the case, making remarks such as these: 'You're a bum,' 'Well, what have you got to say for yourself?' 'What do you do for a living? Steal a little here and there?' [60]

It is not difficult to imagine how these courts go about setting bail for accused felons at arraignment. Generally, the amounts are standard and depend upon the offense. No attempt is made to ascertain whether the defendant could afford bail or how likely he would be to appear for his trial if bail were set at a reduced amount. Generally, the only time the brief routine is upset is when the prosecutor (who sometimes appears on more important cases) or the defense attorney (when one is present) attempts to get the amount changed. One study, not unexpectedly, found that while defense attorneys sometimes managed to have bail lowered, prosecutors were more successful in having it increased. [61]

Several miscellaneous observations about lower criminal courts are worth making. There are significant differences between magistrates. Foote reports that one magistrate in Philadelphia refused to hear routine drunkenness cases, causing the police to release the drunks they picked up when he

---

[59] *Ibid.*

[60] *Ibid.*, p. 323.

[61] Frederic Suffet, "Bail Setting: A Study of Courtroom Interaction," reprinted from *Crime and Delinquency* 12 (1966), pp. 318-331 in Richard Quinney, ed., *Crime and Justice in Society* (Boston: Little, Brown, 1969), p. 300. We shall examine the functioning of the bail system again in some detail in Chapter 10.

was sitting.[62] A study of Washington D.C.'s criminal courts discovered that there was a great deal of variation as to the number of cases judges could dispose of and in the extent of their leniency. These differences played an important part in deciding who was to be assigned to hear such cases.[63]

Judges are not immune to the pressures and the desire to cooperate that we found in felony courts. Foote reports that when the police, with the vigorous support of the newspapers, waged a campaign against "undesirables," there was a significant change in the way vagrancy cases were handled. He also found that drunks were sentenced to the house of correction when the arresting officer indicated he wanted them removed from the streets.[64]

One final question remains: Why do lower-level criminal court judges appear to place such low priority on adhering to traditional legal notions of dignity, due process, fairness, and the like? In brief, they act as they do because (1) they have not internalized standards of "proper judicial conduct"; (2) they have few incentives to adhere to notions of due process; and (3) they are confronted with situations which would make it difficult to do so anyway.

Judges in these courts are not among the most talented of lawyers. In fact, many of them are not lawyers at all. They do not keep up with current developments in case law. They are not interested in hearing strictly legal arguments and citations to appellate decisions. Although the evidence is little more than impressionistic and haphazard, it is not

---

[62] Foote, "Vagrancy-Type Law," p. 298. The *Task Force Report: The Courts*, p. 132, reports that a previous study in Detroit also found police shaping arrest to fit the predilections of whatever magistrate happened to be sitting.

[63] Harry I. Subin, *Criminal Justice in a Metropolitan Court* (Washington, D.C.: Office of Criminal Justice, U.S. Department of Justice, 1966), p. 69.

[64] Foote, "Vagrancy-Type Law," p. 316.

unreasonable to conclude that many of them simply are not very intelligent men.[65]

Nor are they likely to be held to high standards of conduct in their work. The defendants they encounter tend to be apathetic and defeated. They are rarely represented by counsel. Appeals are so infrequent that higher courts have almost no opportunity to try to enforce greater adherence to legal norms. Their decisions are routinely ignored by the press. The only other major outside actor in the courtroom, the policeman, is likely to approve of current practices. If external incentives are absent, so are internal ones. The work is not very satisfying. Courtrooms are crowded, noisy, and often rundown. The defendants are inarticulate, hostile, frequently filthy, sometimes still intoxicated. The judges are held in little esteem by the legal profession and they know it. Unless they are on their way up to a higher post, many feel that they have not quite made it. Resignation and defeat are probably common among them.

Finally, they are faced with the awesome task of somehow disposing of the large numbers of cases brought to them. If there are 125 drunks waiting in a basement holding pen for their cases to be heard, they must find a way to do it. Shortcuts are a necessity. In a sense, these judges are victims of circumstance. Given the work load, time constraints, and resources made available to them, there may be little else they could do no matter how noble their intentions.

CIVIL COMMITMENT OF THE MENTALLY ILL

Disparities between legal ideals and operating realities created by the strategic environment are not found exclusively in the

---

[65] For a lively, though unsystematic description of lower courts which supports this picture of such judges, see Howard James, *Crisis in the Courts* (New York: McKay, 1967), especially Chapters I and III. He estimates that 10 thousand of 15 thousand lower court judges in the United States are not attorneys, that half are not fit to serve, and that only one in 10 is really competent (see p. 4).

criminal process. Though no one is sentenced to prison in civil proceedings, striking similarities to the criminal process exist. This is particularly true of procedures used to commit those alleged to be mentally ill to mental hospitals. Technically, these are strictly civil cases. In the overwhelming majority of these cases, there is no prosecutor representing the state; no crimes are alleged to have been committed;[66] no statutes violated. The end result, however, is that people are placed against their will in institutions which resemble prisons in many respects.

Many readers of this book are probably only dimly aware that it is possible to commit individuals to mental institutions without their consent. Certainly, it is not something that receives much public attention or thought. Yet people are committed daily in every state. As we shall see in Chapter 11, the process is significant both in terms of the number of people involved and the impact it has on their lives. And, like the criminal process generally, there is an official myth about how the process ought to work opposed by a far less appealing reality.

Official Views of Commitment Proceedings

There is less consensus on the proper procedures for civil commitment than in the criminal area. In some states, the statutes embody essentially the same general principles found for the criminal process: presumption of sanity until it has been established otherwise; notification of the "charges" to the accused; the right to a hearing at which the "accused" is present; the right to counsel and a trial by jury; and individual consideration of each case on its merits. In other states, some of these provisions have been modified, presumably because of the medical considerations involved. For instance, sometimes hearings without the presence of the "accused" are permitted if it is felt the experience would be psychologically traumatic. For the same reason, jury trials may be prohibited or only granted at the discretion of the judge. The

---

[66] Psychopathic delinquency proceedings provide a rare exception to this statement.

right to counsel is not always absolute, but one common provision requires the state to appoint an attorney (called the attorney *ad litem*) charged with protecting the rights of the allegedly mentally ill.[67]

Despite this variation, some common elements are found in the procedures of most states. Proceedings are initiated either by a petition to the appropriate court alleging mental illness, or by the police as an emergency measure to deal with individuals exhibiting bizarre behavior. In some states, petitions must be signed by a relative or physician or both; elsewhere, a broader category of petitioners exists. The allegedly ill individual is also examined by physicians, usually psychiatrists. Then a judicial hearing of some sort is held where the result of the medical examination (and perhaps other evidence) is presented, and a final determination is made on whether to commit the individual.

Underlying all of these statutory provisions are two basic notions: Those who are the subject of commitment proceedings are to be presumed sane until a judicial official determines, on the basis of adequate evidence, that the presumption has been refuted; and the individual characteristics of each case are to be carefully considered.

The Reality of Commitment Proceedings

In practice, commitment works quite differently than the statutes say it should. The description below is a composite, drawn from a variety of sources.[68] The studies, done in

---

[67] For a comprehensive summary of the provisions of the various states regarding civil commitment, see Lindman and McIntyre, eds., *The Mentally Disabled and the Law* (Chicago: University of Chicago Press, 1961).

[68] Fred Cohen, "The Function of the Attorney and the Commitment of the Mentally Ill," *Texas Law Review* 44 (1966), pp. 424-469; Luis Kutner, "The Illusion of Due Process in Commitment Proceedings," *Northwestern University Law Review* 57 (1962), pp. 383-399; Dorothy Miller and Michael Schwartz, "County Lunacy Commission Hearings: Some Observations of Commitments to a State Mental Hospital," *Social Problems* 14 (1966), pp. 26-35; Thomas Scheff, Chapter 5, "Two Studies of the Societal Reaction" in *Being Mentally Ill* (Chicago: Aldine, 1966); and Thomas Scheff, "Social Conditions for Rationality: How Urban and Rural Courts Deal with the Mentally Ill," *American Behavioral Scientist* 7 (1964), pp. 21-27.

widely separate geographical areas using a variety of research techniques, have come to strikingly similar conclusions.

Perhaps most important, the presumption of sanity is a myth. Study after study shows that, to the contrary, there is a very strong presumption of insanity: Once a petition is filed alleging someone to be mentally ill, the entire process operates to confirm his illness. This comes out most clearly in the psychiatric interviews. One study found that the diagnostic psychiatric interviews lasted an average of only 10 minutes. [69] They consisted in part of a series of rapid-fire, general-knowledge questions ("What is 11 times 11?" "Who is president?" "What does 'a rolling stone gathers no moss' mean?" "What year was it 17 years ago?"). The examiners appeared to be looking for incorrect answers, ignoring the total number correct. Some psychiatrists appeared to have prejudged the cases before the interviews; some felt it was best to commit even if the evidence of mental illness was weak. [70]

The presumption of mental illness carried over to the judicial hearing as well. [71] One study found that 58 hearings averaged 4.4 minutes. [72] Another found a court disposing of them on an average of one every 1.6 minutes! [73] Furthermore, the judges frequently seemed to defer to the judgments of medical men in an unquestioning manner. Although a few perfunctory questions were asked, judges at such hearings seemed quite clearly to be performing a formality.

Even if he tried to adhere to the presumption of sanity, a judge might feel some pressure to err on the side of commitment. [74] He may well find he is not hurt if some people are

---

[69] Scheff, *Being Mentally Ill*, p. 144.

[70] This discussion is based on Scheff, *ibid.*, pp. 144–150. Also see Kutner, "The Illusion of Due Process," p. 38.

[71] See especially Scheff, *Being Mentally Ill*, pp. 132–133 and passim.

[72] Miller and Schwartz, "County Lunacy Commission Hearings," p. 28.

[73] Scheff, *Being Mentally Ill*, p. 134.

[74] *Ibid.*, p. 153.

committed who should not be. But there may be severe repercussions if he fails to commit someone who then goes on to perpetrate some serious crime.

A second significant conclusion obtained from the studies is that the safeguards embodied in formal procedures are often mere gestures.[75] The "accused" frequently is present at the hearing but is not told what the proceedings are about or what his rights are.[76] All he knows is that something having to do with what will happen to him is being discussed. Those who have observed these hearings also note that often the "accused" is not told of his right to have a lawyer represent him or to have a jury decide whether he should be committed. Sometimes the allegedly mentally ill person comes to the hearing under such heavy medication that he is unable to comprehend anything at all.

Nor does the attorney *ad litem* normally see that the safeguards are meaningful.[77] Although he is entitled (and perhaps obligated) to confer with his client before the hearing, he practically never does so. Even when an individual attempts to resist confinement, the attorney *ad litem* usually fails to inform him of his rights to counsel and a trial. Nor does he question the adequacy of the psychiatric examination nor insure that the required number of independent examinations have been conducted. In fact, he usually just sees that a few legal requirements are met, such as making sure the "accused" is served with a notice of the hearing. The attorney *ad litem* serves more as a cover to make sure that no legal errors are made that might create problems later.

The studies also show the very routinized and bureaucratized nature of the civil commitment procedure. Large num-

---

[75] Kutner, "The Illusion of Due Process," p. 325.

[76] Miller and Schwartz, "County Lunacy Hearings," p. 27; Scheff, *Being Mentally Ill*, p. 137.

[77] See especially Cohen, "The Function of the Attorney." He studied attorneys *ad litem* in Texas and Colorado. Undergraduates in the author's classes at the University of Michigan have found the same problems in Ann Arbor, Michigan.

bers of individuals are processed in an efficient manner, and regulars develop strong ties and mutual understandings among themselves. There is a marked similarity to the procedure already described in lower criminal courts. And like lower criminal courts, the decisions are practically invisible to the public at large.[78]

Although pressures for a high commitment rate do not seem to exist, there is a need to process cases rapidly. People in temporary confinement pending a final decision on their status must be accommodated.

It is not difficult to see why attorneys *ad litem* and psychiatrists behave as they do. The attorney *ad litem* is normally paid by the case. The more cases he handles, therefore, the more fees he receives. The quicker he disposes of cases, the more he gets, and the more time is alloted for his other legal business. Furthermore, if he begins questioning the proceedings, encouraging his clients to demand jury trials, and otherwise upsetting the efficient routine of commitment, he is unlikely to find himself appointed attorney *ad litem* again. Psychiatrists, too, are sometimes paid by the case. At $10 or $20 a case, they cannot afford to devote the time needed to do a decent psychiatric interview.

Furthermore, close working relationships develop among the judges, psychiatrists, and attorneys. As with criminal defendants, the allegedly ill individual is an intruder to be processed. Mutual deference is shown between judges and doctors. One study found that the judge invariably committed individuals who resisted confinement by attacking the psychiatrist's testimony. The only effective technique was to question the motives of those who had initiated the petition.[79]

---

[78] Other similarities to criminal proceedings exist. Kutner, in "The Illusion of Due Process," pp. 392-393, points out the use of warrants, police officers, judges, jurors, and incarceration in jails if hospitals are full. Also, many statutes use terminology borrowed from criminal procedure.

[79] Miller and Schwartz, "County Lunacy Hearings," p. 29.

Obviously, not everyone named in a petition for a sanity hearing is committed. Considerable variation in the proportion committed exists from one jurisdiction to another.[80] The extent to which reality veers from the statutory ideal also varies. But the general picture is fairly clear. Once proceedings are instituted, commitment is practically automatic. As one author put it, "The hearing serves only to validate decisions made in the unrevealed discretion of the physician according to the internal administrative procedure of the hospital where the accused is temporarily held."[81] And frequently, the psychiatrists are merely ratifying a decision made by private individuals. Hence, the legal process is used to bring the formal coercive power of the state to bear in order to carry out decisions made by private individuals (relatives, family doctors, and so on)—decisions which can deny a person his liberty for the rest of his life.

COMPENSATION OF ACCIDENT VICTIMS

A significant portion of the civil dockets of state courts consists of suits that seek compensation for injuries sustained in traffic accidents. Our brief survey of this topic will show how formal legal proceedings structure informal processes that determine the law-in-action. Our focus, then, is on the entire compensation process, not just those aspects of it that surface in litigation.[82]

If we look at who participates, the two most important positions turn out to be accident victims (claimants) and insurance adjustors. Although accurate nationwide statistics are not available, apparently a majority of claims are settled

---

[80] Scheff, in "Social Conditions," finds that in rural areas, more careful treatment of each case is given. Also, more people successfully avoid commitment than in the urban areas he studied.

[81] Cohen, "The Function of the Attorney," p. 436.

[82] Much of the following discussion is based on H. Lawrence Ross, *Settled Out of Court* (Chicago: Aldine, 1970), an excellent survey of the whole area.

without the participation of attorneys.[83] Neither claimants nor adjustors are formally part of the legal process. But outcomes of their informal interactions are significantly shaped by the existence of the possibility that the claimant will retain an attorney, opening the possibility of a trial.

There are a variety of reasons why adjustors like to settle claims without having to deal with an attorney. For one thing, it is much quicker.[84] This is important to adjustors because there is substantial pressure on them from the company to settle cases quickly,[85] since it is cheaper for the company to do so. Legal costs to one insurance company were $221 when the plaintiff was represented but did not go to trial, and $740 when trials were held,[86] but only $3 for unrepresented clients. Furthermore, settlements were both more frequent and larger when clients were represented.[87]

An attorney can hardly net his client less than he would have received had he accepted the adjustor's last offer before retaining him. This provides the attorney with a strong incentive to obtain at least the adjustor's figure plus enough to cover his fee. Furthermore, the attorney is likely to be a far stronger and more skillful negotiator than the average claimant.

Thus, the existence of formal litigation procedures opens the possibility of the participation of attorneys, and this, in

[83] *Ibid.*, p. 166. Several factors affect the likelihood of representation. Attorneys are more often retained by claiments who (1) live in metropolitan areas, (2) come from particular ethnic groups, and (3) sustain more serious injuries (pp. 196-198).

[84] *Ibid.*, p. 229. Here Ross found that the mean time lapse in days to settlement was 242 for unrepresented claimants and over 600 for those represented. Though due in part to the greater seriousness of claims where counsel is retained, this does not fully account for the substantial difference found.

[85] *Ibid.*, p. 19, observes "Unclosed files form visible accumulations and generate complaints to managers and supervisors, whereas closed files trouble no one." Interestingly, there is more incentive for adjustors to settle cases quickly than to settle them cheaply.

[86] *Ibid.*, p. 139. These figures are for 1962.

[87] *Ibid.*, p. 194, Table 5.5.

turn, encourages adjustors to engage in behavior that minimizes the likelihood that an attorney will be retained. For instance, they do not normally wait for potential claimants to contact them. A delay increases the chances that an attorney will be retained. Instead, the adjustor contacts the accident victim and frequently comes to a quick settlement. Particularly if the claim is small, the adjustor will offer a settlement even if the question of liability is not clear.

For a variety of reasons, adjustors are frequently unsuccessful in settling a claim before an attorney enters the picture. At this point, the claimant ceases to play an important role, if only because his attorney instructs him to refuse any contact with the insurance company. The adjustor and the claimant's attorney become the principal participants. However, the adjustor's incentive to avoid a trial by reaching a negotiated settlement is typically not diminished.

The claimant's attorney, too, has an interest in reaching a negotiated settlement, opening the door to serious negotiation. In this regard, it is important to understand the relationship of the attorney to the claimant.

These cases are usually handled on a contingent-fee basis. There is no initial cost to the victim. His lawyer is paid a percentage (usually between 30 and 40 percent) of the final award, creating a strong mutuality of interest between lawyer and client. But this mutuality of interest is not complete. Poorer accident victims may be anxious for an immediate award, even if it is considerably less than what could be obtained by holding out. Some lawyers find they must lend poor clients money so they will resist the temptation to accept an immediate but modest settlement from the insurance company in return for an unconditional release (which absolves the insurance company from any further claim).[88] On the other hand, the client may refuse a settlement, hoping

---

[88] Jerome Carlin, *Lawyers on Their Own* (New Brunswick, N.J.: Rutgers University Press, 1962), pp. 79-80. For an excellent description of accident litigation in Chicago from the plaintiff's attorney's viewpoint, see pp. 71-91.

that his award from a jury would be much larger, thus forcing his attorney to incur the extra expense and trouble of a trial. The lawyer, meanwhile, usually much prefers to take a sure 30 to 40 percent of a smaller, effortless, and relatively costless out-of-court settlement.

The lawyer may have other strategic considerations that are of no concern to his clients. Some accident litigation specialists have reputations for never going to trial.[89] Their livelihood depends upon the cooperation of insurance adjustors, insurance lawyers, and judges. As a result, they may be given minimal awards (under $300) in worthless cases. Other specialists, however, depend upon reputations for hard bargaining, competence, and a willingness to go to trial. They, too, are concerned with the impact of each case on the future. Thus, they may wish to go to trial on good cases even when the clients are willing to accept the proposed settlements, simply to bolster their reputations for future negotiations.[90] Of course, not all attorneys handling these cases are specialists. These men generally are worried less about how their performance might affect their effectiveness in future dealings with the same adjustor.

The formal bargaining situation between the claimant's attorney and the adjustor has several interesting attributes, particularly when compared to other bargaining situations (labor disputes, international relations). According to Ross, these characteristics can be summarized as follows:

The number of parties and issues is minimal, and there is relatively little interrelationship between one negotiated agreement and another. The

---

[89] *Ibid.*, p. 75. Carlin reports that half of the specialists in accident litigation do not normally try cases.

[90] These considerations are also found to some extent in relationships between insurance companies and the lawyers who represent them. Disputes over whether compromise offers should be accepted or not occur frequently. If the defense attorney has been hired on a case-by-case basis (rather than on salary), he bills his client for the work done on each case. Consequently he is not always interested in disposing of cases as quickly and expeditiously as possible.

balance of power is often one-sided, and agreements are retrospective rather than prospective in orientation. The bargaining is entirely distributive. Finally, the consequences of failure, although not trivial, are not catastrophic, so the achievement of a bargain is unheroic.[91]

Because bargaining occurs repeatedly between sophisticated parties, it is not surprising that informal rules condition the outcome.[92] These include:

1. Yield from an initial demand. This leads claimants' attorneys to demand more and adjustors to offer less initially.
2. Balance concessions. A concession by one party must be followed by one from the other. A critical element is not the offering of a concession, but its magnitude.
3. Never retract a previously made offer.
4. Bargain in good faith.

Formal legal procedures leading to litigation can largely be understood as bargaining ploys. Filing suit, for instance, is a symbolic way of indicating that you mean business. It also may signify the plaintiff's attorney's conclusion that he is not getting anywhere with the insurance company adjustor, and that he may as well try his luck with their attorney by filing suit and bringing him into the negotiations. Once a suit is filed, the standard initial response of defense attorneys is to resist. Theoretically, of course, suits could be terminated if defendants agreed to pay whatever amount was sued for, but this usually occurs only when the insurance company did not believe the plaintiff would ever actually sue.

Several other things happen once a suit is instituted. Procedures for obtaining more information about the nature of and circumstances surrounding the injuries are made available. These pretrial discovery techniques—depositions, interrogatories, and pretrial conferences—help both sides learn

---

[91] Ross, *Settled Out of Court*, p. 144.
[92] *Ibid.*, pp. 149–150.

more about how much the other side's case is worth. While uncertainty is reduced in this sense, anxiety is increased by the possibility that the other side will go to trial as a result of the new information.

As the months pass, the delay becomes increasingly significant. Client pressure for some immediate compensation may encourage the plaintiff's attorney to propose or accept less than he had previously demanded. Meanwhile, the case of either side may be weakened if witnesses die or disappear as the delay continues.

Finally, the pretrial conference can function as a mechanism for arriving at a compromise. Frequently there is a settlement that both sides are willing to accept, but one which neither is willing to propose. An offer to settle for less money may be interpreted by the other side as a sign of weakness, prompting him to hold out for even further concessions. In a situation where both sides are sensitive about saving face and reputation, proposals from a third party (such as the judge) may be especially efficacious. Moreover, the judges who hear pretrial conferences are more than disinterested parties. They have as much desire to see cases settled as do judges handling criminal cases, and for many of the same reasons. If most accident cases went to juries, trial dockets would be overwhelmed. [93] Therefore, judges frequently push for settlements. And they have the resources to make compelling arguments for their acceptance by both parties. Either side may think twice before rejecting a compromise the judge strongly supports, not only because the judge (or a colleague) will hear the case when it is tried, but also because judges usually are regarded as knowledgeable about what the outcome of trial would be.

Hence, as in criminal cases, everyone has an interest in reaching a compromise. The attrition of cases through settle-

---

[93] Another incentive to see cases settled without trial is that trial verdicts expose a judge to the risk of reversal by a higher court following an appeal. By cutting down on the number of trials, he reduces the chances of being reversed.

ment at every step of the way to trial attests to how successful the parties are in reaching them. A study of accident claims in New York City estimated that 193,000 accident victims sought to recover damages in 1957. Of these, fully 116,000 or about 60 percent were able to settle without instituting suit.[94] This same study found that of the 77,000 suits filed, 29,000 were settled before both sides were ready for trial. Of the remaining 48,000 cases, settlements were reached before trial began in all but 7,000. Only 2,500 of these went to verdict, with the others being settled before the trial was completed.[95] Most defense and plaintiff's attorneys face real limitations, however, in the sort of settlements they can accept. Both are concerned about their reputations, particularly if they derive a major portion of their livelihoods from such cases. To give too much to the other will encourage aggressive demands in the future and make reasonable settlements more difficult. It also may require going more often to trial—an expensive and time-consuming process. In addition, both have the problem of securing an agreement that they can sell to their clients. It requires considerable skill on the part of the attorney to obtain a settlement acceptable to his client by threatening to go to trial without actually having to follow through and try the case.

Two other characteristics of accident compensation deserve comment. One is that those routinely involved in the process (adjustors, attorneys for both claimant and insurance company, judges), particularly in nonmetropolitan areas, come to know each other quite well. As with criminal cases, they develop their own community in which their ties to one another are closer than the ties of litigants to their own attorneys. This is beautifully illustrated by Claude Brown in *Manchild in the Promised Land*. As a young boy, Brown was hit by a bus, and went to court with his father:

---

[94] Marc Franklin, Robert Chanin, and Irving Mark, "Accidents, Money, and the Law: A Study of the Economics of Personal Injury Litigation," in *Dollars, Delay and the Automobile Victim* (New York: Bobbs-Merrill, 1968), p. 73.

[95] *Ibid.*, p. 38.

When we went into the courtroom, the lawyer went up to where the judge was sitting and started talking to him. They seemd to be friends or something. Almost everybody there seemed to be friends—the bus driver, the other lawyer, the people from the bus company. The only ones who didn't seem to be friends with anybody was me and Dad.[96]

The second is that the law-in-action differs considerably from what we would expect based on the content of formal law, just as it does in the criminal area. According to Ross, if the rule of contributory negligence [97] were rigidly adhered to by insurance companies, most claims would be denied.[98] In practice, tort law-in-action is considerably more liberal than the formal law.[99] The explanation for this resembles that offered for the discrepancy between the adversary ideal and bureaucratic reality of state felony courts. Organizational and bureaucratic factors make it impossible for adjustors or attorneys to give cases the full individualized treatment which formal theory says they deserve. Instead various shortcuts (such as determining liability by the type of accident—red light, rear-ender, uncontrolled intersection—and whether traffic laws were violated) and standard formulas for determining awards and settling claims are relied upon.

[96] Claude Brown, *Manchild in the Promised Land* (New York: Signet Books, 1965), p. 96. Ross, *Settled Out of Court*, p. 83, confirms this by observing that claimants' attorneys report getting along better with adjustors than with their own clients.

[97] This rule denies compensation to victims of torts when their own negligence contributed, even if only slightly, to the occurrence of the injury.

[98] Ross, *Settled Out of Court*, p. 234.

[99] *Ibid.*, p. 240.

CHAPTER 7
THE OPERATION OF FEDERAL DISTRICT COURTS

COEXISTING with the 50 state court systems is the federal court structure. At the lowest level—the trial court level—are 93 district courts scattered throughout the United States and its overseas possessions. These courts serve as focal points for the individuals and interactions that constitute the federal legal process.

In the criminal area, federal courts have jurisdiction whenever there is an infraction of a federal statute. Major categories of cases include selective service violations, motor vehicle theft across state lines, robbery of a bank where deposits are federally insured, embezzlement from such a bank, fraud against the government, immigration violations, income tax evasion, IRS liquor laws, narcotics, theft of government property, mail crimes, interference with federal justice, and espionage and sabotage.

On the civil side, district courts have jurisdiction over cases or controversies involving the Constitution, a federal law, or a treaty. Thus, major challenges on constitutional grounds to the policies and actions of local and state governments are frequently taken to federal court. The federal district courts also have jurisdiction when the United States is a party in a case, or when a state is a party (unless suit was brought against it by an individual or foreign country).[1] It is not surprising that a major portion of the cases eventually heard by courts of appeals and the Supreme Court originate here.

Much of a district court's civil docket is comprised of cases which are there because of its *diversity jurisdiction*. Any two citizens of different states can sue each other on a civil matter in federal district court provided the sum of money at issue exceeds $10,000. Since *citizen* is defined to include corporations, major corporations often find themselves in litigation in these courts.

In this chapter, we shall look at the federal legal process from the perspective of district courts by examining the politics of interaction among the major participants and the environmental and political factors that condition it.

A NATIONAL SYSTEM OF COURTS

The Judiciary Act of 1789, which created the lower federal courts, sought to establish a national system of courts. In a number of respects the attempt has been successful.[2]

Federal district courts all have the same basic jurisdiction. This means that, in broad terms, the same types of cases will be heard, and the same categories of actors and interests will be involved. The same list of significant participants in the work of these courts is found in each district. It includes judges, U.S. magistrates, U.S. marshals and their deputies, clerks, bailiffs, probation officers, the U.S. attorney and his

---

[1] Cases involving representatives of foreign governments (such as ambassadors) and citizens of the same state disputing land originally granted by more than one state may also be heard. See Henry J. Abraham, *The Judicial Process* (New York: Oxford University Press, 1968, 2nd ed.), p. 157. As a practical matter, such cases do not account for a significant portion of the docket.

[2] The struggle between *nationalists* and *antifederalists* over the organization and jurisdiction of the federal judiciary was a protracted one. For an interesting history of the struggle, see Richard J. Richardson and Kenneth N. Vines, *The Politics of the Federal Courts* (Boston: Little, Brown, 1970), Chapter 2.

assistants, personnel from federal investigative agencies, and a subset of local lawyers who appear regularly in federal court. Moreover, their functions, duties, and responsibilities, in general terms, are identical throughout the country. In the criminal area, for instance, investigators initiate the criminal process and gather the evidence, prosecutors handle the in-court litigation, judges supervise the courtroom procedure and decide questions of law, and defense attorneys represent defendants. To the extent that patterns of interaction between them are determined by their formal duties, the patterns will be much the same wherever the district court is located.

In many ways the major participants and the basic patterns of interaction between them resemble what we have found in state courts. The distinctive jurisdiction of federal courts, however, brings about the involvement of a unique set of interests, attorneys, and defendants which differentiate them from state courts. The frequent appearance here of governments and various political and economic groups is especially important. We have seen that federal courts are the usual forum for challenges to state and local governmental action by interested groups on constitutional grounds. Groups that are regulated or affected by federal statutes also utilize the federal courts. Those involved in both types of litigation tend to be well-organized, well-financed, and nationally based. As noted previously, much of the litigation of large corporations takes place here as well.

The private citizens involved in civil litigation with the government tend to be drawn from the higher economic levels of society. These include property holders whose land is needed for federal highways or construction projects, and defaulters on government-subsidized loans and government-insured mortgages. Criminal defendants too are more likely to come from a middle-class background, because of the nature of many of the crimes over which the district courts have jurisdiction—embezzlement, forgery, counterfeiting, mail fraud, and income tax evasion.

Representing these higher-status litigants are higher-status attorneys. Although it is a simple procedure for any local attorney to be admitted to the federal bar, the attorneys who appear with some regularity are distinguishable from those whose practice leads them to state courts.[3] Many are former assistant U.S. attorneys. In general, their legal training and skills are above average. Because a number of attorneys are intimidated by the prospect of appearing in U.S. district court, a certain degree of prestige attaches to those that do.

Another element contributing to the national character of the system of district courts is their common position in the judicial hierarchy. All are coequal as courts of original jurisdiction for cases arising within their districts. The decisions rendered are subject to review by a court of appeals and ultimately the U.S. Supreme Court. General supervision is provided by the Judicial Conference of the United States, and the judicial conferences of the 11 circuits. The Administrative Office of United States Courts also provides some general, uniform administrative supervision and record-keeping.

Furthermore, similar factors condition the behavior of all district judges. The federal rules of civil and criminal procedure provide a common guide. The perception of legitimacy attending the decisions and orders of courts of appeals and the Supreme Court, and the anticipation of possible reversal from above, shape the behavior of all. Within the same circuit, of course, the behavior of district judges is even more similar. Since they all look to the same appellate body, the judges within a circuit look to and cite the same body of decisions and rulings.

The effectiveness of courts of appeals in guiding the behavior of judges in the circuit is enhanced by communication among them. A study of such communication concluded that

---

[3] This discussion is based on evidence obtained by the author in the course of his research on U.S. attorneys. For a description of the research, see James Eisenstein, *Counsel for the United States: An Empirical Analysis of the Office of United States Attorney* (Ph.D. diss., Yale University, 1968).

differences in the judicial behavior of U.S. trial judges from circuit to circuit persist because for these judges the circuit is a semi-closed system, a nearly self-contained organizational unit within which there is considerable interaction among its members and almost no interaction between the members of one unit (circuit) and another.[4]

The presence of communication and the patterns of interaction which result do much to shape the character of the district courts.

Since many of the participants with whom district judges interact are organized on a nationwide basis, they contribute a parallel unifying tendency. The FBI and other federal investigative agencies are centrally based, and nationwide policies are established in Washington. Policy for the federal prison system is made by the Bureau of Prisons.

A more significant unifying element, however, is provided by the official legal representatives of the federal government in district court—the U.S. attorneys. All matters handled by U.S. attorneys' offices are formally within the jurisdiction and control of the Department of Justice. Standard procedures and policies are spelled out in a *United States Attorney's Manual*. From time to time, the department seeks to achieve uniformity in the way specific criminal statutes are enforced by announcing policies in the *U.S. Attorney's Bulletin* which is sent to each office on a regular basis. The department also sets forth standard policies for the handling of certain civil cases. To enforce its policies the department periodically inspects the office procedures, operations, and record-keeping of the U.S. attorneys' offices. There are also review attorneys in Washington who oversee the handling of specific cases. Of course, the obstacles to enforcing their uniform standards and policies are formidable and the department's success in doing so is far from complete. Later in this chapter, we shall describe the difficulties the department

---

[4] Robert A. Carp, "The Scope and Function of Intra-Circuit Judicial Communication: A Case Study of the Eighth Circuit," *Law and Society Review* 6 (Feb., 1972), p. 407.

encounters in attempting to do this. Nevertheless, the supervision and coordination the department provides U.S. attorneys contributes substantially to uniformity in the federal court system.

Another unifying tendency is that the participants who interact in federal court each have their own common procedures for recruitment. The appointment process for judges and U.S. attorneys has already been described. Assistant U.S. attorneys are chosen formally by the attorney general. As a practical matter, the local U.S. attorney (sometimes in consultation with local political organizations) makes the choice. The chief probation officer is chosen by the judges, and each judge personally interviews and selects his own clerk, bailiff, and other members of his staff. Agents of the FBI and other federal investigative agencies are recruited and trained by the central organization in Washington and dispatched to the various regional offices.

Why would similarities in the formal methods of recruitment for these positions tend to unify the federal court system? First, the methods by which participants are recruited help to determine what their resources are when they interact with others, who has access to them, and who they choose to consult for advice and guidance. Second, the method of recruitment affects the type of people chosen. As noted in Chapter 4, judges and U.S. attorneys are typically higher-status, politically active lawyers. Assistant U.S. attorneys are generally recent law school graduates, often with ties to local political organizations. Clerks, bailiffs, and probation officers generally do not have legal training and come from modest but solidly middle-class backgrounds. Agents of the FBI and Secret Service are less likely to reflect the social composition of the district because they are recruited and assigned centrally. To the extent that these common attributes lead to uniform behavior, the recruitment process contributes to similarities in patterns of interaction throughout the country.

LOCAL INFLUENCES ON DISTRICT COURTS

In their book on federal courts, Richardson and Vines observe that "Although the representative functions of courts have rarely been recognized in legal theory, the linkage between political officials and the territory they serve is not just a legislative function."[5] The point is well taken. Most of the participants in the federal court system are influenced to a significant extent by the social and economic conditions, values, and structures of political power within their local districts. Differences in the nature of the locally generated influence are translated into differences in behavior. Thus, while the unifying factors described in the previous section lead to similarities among federal district courts, significant differences can also be found.

Federal judicial districts[6] have been superimposed on the basic constituent components of the federal system—the states. There is at least one judicial district for each state and no district crosses a state boundary. This fact has profound consequences.

Most significantly, it permits the intrusion of state and local politics into the recruitment process. Frequently, when the territory of a government agency's jurisdiction coincides with the boundaries of a political subdivision, those who wield power within that subdivision seek to influence the personnel and policies of the agency.[7] In the case of federal

---

[5] Richardson and Vines, *The Politics of the Federal Courts*, p. 36.

[6] This discussion applies only to those districts apportioned among the 50 states and the District of Columbia. It excludes the districts of Guam, the Canal Zone, the Virgin Islands, and Puerto Rico.

[7] An interesting illustration of this phenomenon is described by Mike Royko in his journalistic political biography of Mayor Daley, *Boss* (New York: Dutton, 1971). Royko observes that Chicago ward bosses were extremely unhappy when police command districts were reorganized so they no longer coincided with ward boundaries. When they corresponded, the ward bosses were able to select the police commanders in their districts.

judges and U.S. attorneys, this tendency is reinforced by the provision for Senate confirmation. Because district lines do not cross state lines, senators (and other local and state politicians working through their senators) are able to exert considerable influence.[8] The result is that appointees are not merely residents of the district as the statute requires. Typically, they are politically prominent residents, successful participants in the local political culture, sharers of its values, and susceptible to its continued influence.

We do not yet have systematic studies of precisely how key participants in federal district courts perceive and react to pressures generated by the political and social values of their districts. Because of the importance of the question, however, it is worth speculating on the mechanisms which translate district pressures into decisions. Logically, we would expect the relationship to be most evident when decisions must be made on issues that evoke strong feelings within the community. In the recent past, decisions involving race (particularly school desegregation) in the South are the most notable examples. Fortunately, this is one area where some research findings do exist.

The only way to comprehend fully the pressures brought to bear on southern federal judges and U.S. attorneys who were perceived in their communities as taking a prointegration stand is to actually experience them. Those who have are understandably reluctant to relive the details. The private mental anguish, the late night phone calls, the subtle insults and social snubs from long-time friends and acquaintances, the shrinking or disappearance of the circle of friendly social contacts undoubtedly contributed to these pressures, though detailed autobiographical accounts of them are not available. However, outside observers who have written about school desegration provide a few examples of the public insults and pressures that were brought to bear. Judge J. Skelly Wright of New Orleans, who played the central role in the desegregation of that city's schools in the fall of 1960 was subject to

---

[8] For a brief description of senatorial courtesy, see Chapter 3, p. 37.

harsh public abuse.[9] Referring to Judge Wright and two colleagues, a Louisiana legislator publically denounced a federal court ruling as "claptrap." "We are only saved from the hands of these demagogues by the hand of the Lord when he takes them."[10] Indeed, Wright became the primary target of abusive legislators.[11] They called for his imprisonment; they cheered when a group of segregationists carried a coffin with his blackened effigy.[12] Federal legislators joined in the criticism. Congressman Otto Passman termed the decisions rendered "outrageous." Senator Russell Long denounced Wright in a speech to the state legislature.

The U.S. attorney in the same district, who came to play a major role in the later stages of the crisis, also came in for his share of criticism. Senator Ellender, who had voted to confirm the U.S. attorney's appointment several years before explained, "He came highly recommended. I didn't know he was going to turn coattail."[13]

Such pressures are strong enough to affect the careers of these men. One southern U.S. attorney involved in local desegregation controversy told the author local resentment and hostility were so strong that he was able to earn only $3,000 in his law practice the year after he left office. Judge Wright was promoted to the appeals court, but to the Washington D.C. Circuit, not the Fifth Circuit (which is located in New Orleans).[14] Judge J. Waites Waring came under such

[9] For an account of Judge Wright's role in the crisis, see Jack W. Peltason, *Fifty-eight Lonely Men* (New York: Harcourt, Brace, and World, 1961), Chapter 8. See also Robert L. Crain, *The Politics of School Desegregation* (Garden City, N.Y.: Doubleday, 1969), Chapter 15.

[10] Quoted by Peltason, *Fifty-eight Lonely Men*, p. 235.

[11] *Ibid.*, p. 236.

[12] *Ibid.*, p. 240. Richardson and Vines, in *The Politics of the Federal Courts*, p. 99, report that judges like Wright and Frank Johnson of Alabama have experienced the desecration of relatives' graves and cross-burnings on their lawns.

[13] Quoted by Peltason, *Fifty-eight Lonely Men*, p. 229.

[14] Wright was initially destined for the Fifth Circuit, but his appointment was blocked by Louisiana's senators (Richardson and Vines, *The Politics of the Federal Courts*, p. 99).

intense social pressure for his early dissents on the constitutionality of segregation that he retired from the bench in Charleston, South Carolina, and left the state.[15]

The strategic situation of federal judges in the South has been summarized best by Peltason.

> The district judge is very much a part of the life of the South. He must eventually leave his chambers and when he does he attends a Rotary lunch or stops off at the club to drink with men outraged by what they consider "judicial tyranny." A judge who makes rulings adverse to segregation is not so likely to be honored by testimonial dinners, or to read flattering editorials in the local press, or to partake of the fellowship at the club. He will no longer be invited to certain homes; former friends will avoid him when they meet him on the street.[16]

The number of federal judges is small enough and their communications with one another frequent enough that instances of pressure and abuse become widely known. These incidents are significant for their effect on the behavior of other judges as well as for the impact they may have on any specific case.

In this regard, it is significant that the recruitment process typically selects men who are predisposed to be susceptible to such pressures. It is not only that district judges are long-time residents of their districts and consequently are intimately tied to the social and political life there. They also share local attitudes toward blacks and segregation. Men who deviate sharply from local values are not normally appointed.[17] Personal interviews with southern U.S. attorneys,

[15] Peltason, *Fifty-eight Lonely Men*, p. 10.

[16] *Ibid.*, p. 9.

[17] Decisions even seem to reflect differences in attitudes toward the racial question found within the southern elite. Traditionally, southern Democrats have been the champions of segregationist values while Republicans have been more moderate in their attitudes. A comparison of the decisions of Republican and Democratic judges in the South found Republicans more likely to rule in favor of blacks than their Democratic brethren. Kenneth Vines, "Federal District Judges and Race Relations Cases in the South," *Journal of Politics* 26 (May, 1964), reprinted in Theodore Becker, ed., *The Impact of Supreme Court Decisions* (New York: Oxford University Press, 1969), p. 84. (Page numbers refer to the Becker volume.)

assistants, probation officers, and court clerks which the author conducted revealed how closely these men adhere to local values and attitudes on race.[18] A published opinion by the segregationist Judge Davidson of Dallas demonstrated the same point. "The Dallas Plan would lead, in the opinion and the light of history and unquestionable sources to an amalgamation of the races. . . . In no clime and in no nation have the races ever amalgamated that it has not been to the disadvantage of both. . . . "[19] And another Mississippi federal judge, Harold Cox, ruling in a voting rights case, observed: "I think that the Court could take judicial notice of the illiteracy that is prevalent among the colored people, and I do know that of my own knowledge, and the intelligence of the colored people don't [sic] compare ratio-wise to white people. . . ."[20]

The anticipations of the distinctly unpleasant consequences that would flow from antisegregation rulings served to reinforce the segregationist inclinations of many southern federal judges when deciding civil rights cases. Indeed, some rationalized their decisions by claiming they were obligated to reflect faithfully the views of their districts. A Mississippi federal judge, Sidney Mize, included the following in a dissent from a three-judge panel opinion. "It is the universal conviction of the people of the South also that the judges who function in the circuit should render justice in individual cases against a background of, and as interpreters of, the ethos of the people whose servants they are."[21]

A study of the decisions rendered by district court judges

---

[18] Eisenstein, *Counsel for the United States*. One former U.S. attorney in the Deep South proceeded to give the author a straight segregationist line, complete with assertions of innate inferiority and laziness among blacks.

[19] Quoted in Peltason, *Fifty-eight Lonely Men*, p. 121.

[20] Quoted by Charles V. Hamilton, "Southern Judges and Negro Voting Rights: The Judicial Approach to the Solution of Controversial Social Problems," *Wisconsin Law Review* 1965 (1965), pp. 1–31. Reprinted in Rita James Simon, ed., *The Sociology of Law* (San Francisco: Chandler, 1968), p. 520. (Page numbers refer to Simon volume.)

[21] Quoted in Richardson and Vines, *The Politics of the Federal Courts*, p. 106.

between May 1954 and October 1962 in 11 southern states provides systematic evidence for the relationship between district attitudes and judicial behavior. [22] Studies of southern political behavior have established that the higher the proportion of blacks found in a political jurisdiction, the less favorably they have been treated. Precisely the same pattern is found in these courts. The higher the proportion of blacks in the district, the less likely the court was to rule favorably in their cases. [23]

Other participants in the federal legal process are fully aware of these processes and adjust their behavior accordingly. Courts of appeals' criticism and reversal of district judges' decisions have at times been explicit and blunt. [24] During the Kennedy and Johnson years, the Department of Justice centralized the prosecution of all civil rights cases in its Civil Rights Division. Despite the obstacles that attorneys dispatched from Washington encountered in southern courtrooms, the department did not feel it could entrust these cases to the locally based U.S. attorneys' offices. [25]

Other evidence of the influence of southern values on the operation of federal courts exists. For years, blacks were excluded from federal juries throughout the South. [26] The only positions they held in these courts were custodial jobs.

---

[22] Kenneth Vines, "Federal District Judges."

[23] *Ibid.*, p. 82. The Pearson product-moment correlation between proportion of blacks and favorable rulings is −0.48.

[24] Richard Harris, *Decision* (New York: Dutton, 1971), p. 28, reports the Fifth Circuit unanimously overruled a decision of G. Harrold Carswell's in a theater desegregation case, declaring it "clearly in error." See also Peltason, *Fifty-eight Lonely Men*, pp. 116–122.

[25] The Nixon administration, whose commitment to civil rights is generally felt to be somewhat weaker than either Johnson's or Kennedy's, reversed this policy and permitted southern U.S. attorneys to exercise primary responsibility for the prosecution of civil rights violations.

[26] Sheldon Goldman and Thomas Jahnige, *The Federal Courts as a Political System* (New York: Harper & Row, 1971), p. 91.

They were even required to sit in sections of federal courtrooms designated for "colored." [27]

It is important to recognize, however, that the history of the school-desegregation controversy in the South provides a number of examples of courageous judges who withstood local pressures and moved vigorously to strike down segregation and other forms of racial discrimination. [28] As one student of voting rights decisions in the South concluded: "While it may be true that community pressures buttress some judges' segregationist attitudes, it is not true that community pressures will control the result of the litigation.... The fact is that community pressure has not proved to be an insurmountable obstacle. [29]

Although the relationship between local values and attitudes is clearest in cases involving racial questions in the South, other examples can be found. [30] In some small midwestern and large urban districts there is substantial antipathy towards the federal government. Attempts by the Justice Department to direct the activities of U.S. attorneys' offices are resented. Department attorneys dispatched from Washington to handle cases sometimes meet with frosty receptions from judges who regard them as intruders who are "taking cases away from the local U.S. attorney." Cooperative judges sometimes "order" the U.S. attorney to do what he has been pleading with the department to let him do. There are even instances where judges have called press conferences to publicly defend and praise U.S. attorneys in open conflict with the department.

Local characteristics and values serve to localize the federal

---

[27] Richardson and Vines, *The Politics of the Federal Courts*, p. 45.

[28] For examples, see Peltason, *Fifty-eight Lonely Men;* Crain, *The Politics of School Desegregation*; and Hamilton, "Southern Judges and Negro Voting Rights."

[29] Hamilton, "Southern Judges and Negro Voting Rights," p. 532.

[30] The examples presented here are drawn from the author's research cited previously.

court system by affecting the types of cases heard. The incidence of certain offenses is concentrated. Districts in major port cities and along the Mexican border have large numbers of immigration cases. The bulk of "moonshine" cases are brought in the southeastern part of the United States. Serious drug offenses and major corporate income tax cases are concentrated in larger urban districts.

Interesting disparities in the handling of these cases result. In some districts, a tolerant view is taken of moonshining to the point where the judges refuse to impose jail sentences upon conviction. Former officials of the Tax Division in the Department of Justice have reported that local hostility to the federal income tax laws in several districts has produced a like refusal to impose harsh sentences for tax evasion. Consequently, such cases were rarely brought in these districts. In urban districts, violations of federal marijuana statutes are ignored in favor of hard drug cases. But many smaller rural jurisdictions rarely see a heroin case. Marijuana violations that are ignored in large districts are pursued vigorously here. This reflects both community attitudes toward such offenses and their relative significance in the absence of more serious violations. Similar patterns are found with respect to prosecutions for sending obscene material through the mails. Prosecutions are typically brought in small midwestern or southern districts in which the material is received, rather than in the more tolerant districts (such as southern California) where the material is produced and mailed.

Of course, not all differences found in the way cases are handled can be attributed to local attitudes and values. Individual predelictions of federal prosecutors and judges that are independent of local influences also make themselves felt. Identical offenses are treated differently by different judges within a single district. The prosecutive policies of a U.S. attorney's office have changed significantly when a new U.S. attorney is appointed.

PATTERNS OF INTERACTION: U.S. ATTORNEYS, JUDGES, AND THE DEPARTMENT OF JUSTICE

As we describe the politics of interaction among the major participants in the work of federal district courts, we shall focus on the relationships between the U.S. attorneys' offices and judges on the one hand, and U.S. attorneys and the Department of Justice on the other. To keep the discussion manageable, only the criminal process will be examined. As Figure 1 suggests, this represents only a fraction of the significant interactions. But it also suggests the value of selecting

Figure 1. Interactions in federal district courts. Solid line indicates significant direct interaction while the dashed line indicates indirect and/or minor interaction.

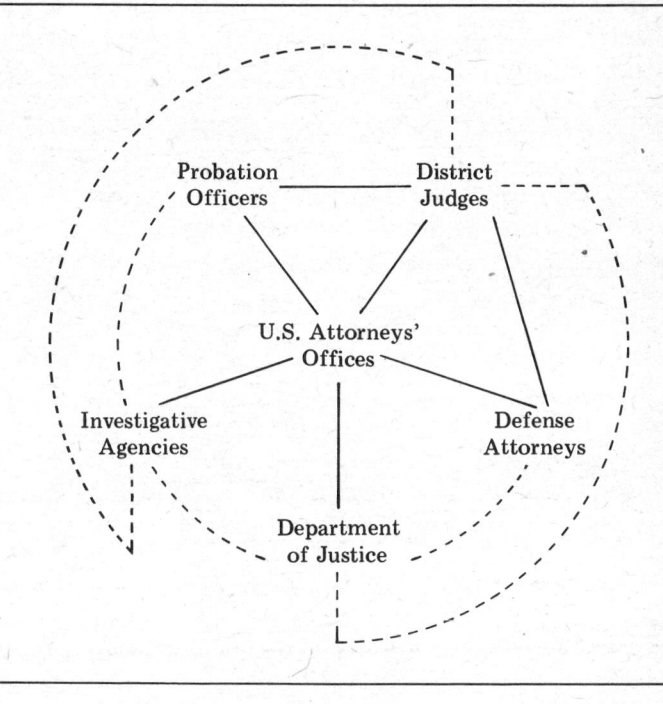

these two sets of relationships. U.S. attorneys are at the hub of the federal criminal process at the district court level.

Two quotations summarize the relationship between U.S. attorneys and judges. A former U.S. attorney recalled, "I got along fine with judges. Whenever they said 'frog,' I leaped. I really tried to anticipate their every need." A federal judge boasted, "I'm in the good position. The U.S. attorney wants plenty from me, and I don't want anything from him."

Indeed, the judge controls many things a U.S. attorney or assistant U.S. attorney wants. Judges control the scheduling of cases. They can grant or deny postponements. They control behavior in their courtrooms. Judges participate in trials by asking helpful or embarrassing questions and, on occasion, by making insulting comments about the attorney's case or his performance. They rule on motions, admissibility of evidence, objections, and the content of the charge to the jury; these decisions can be crucial to the outcome of a case. They have the power to sentence convicted defendants. Whether courtroom appearances are pleasant, tolerable, or horrid experiences is very much under the control of the judge. And the success of an attorney in the courtroom can affect his future career prospects as well as his self-esteem.

The former U.S. attorney's comment that he tried to "anticipate their every need" is not an idle one. Substantial evidence was found that the behavior of U.S. attorneys and their assistants is shaped in a number of ways by the stated and merely anticipated wishes of the judges. The types of cases authorized and declined, the number of counts charged, the forms used for pleadings, courtroom demeanor, the types of arguments used, even the way the office is administered are all affected by anticipations of what judges want.

The judge quoted above was exaggerating a bit, however, when he claimed there was nothing he would want from the U.S. attorney. Though the U.S. attorneys' resources are limited, they are not insignificant. The government is the single largest source of cases. To a considerable extent, how current a judge's docket is depends upon the number of cases brought by the U.S. attorney's office and the way in which they are handled. An unprepared, inept, or ornery U.S. attorney can significantly impede the progress of such cases. U.S. attorneys are also in a good position to assist the judges in other ways: They can help them avoid error and reduce their anxiety and uncertainty by demonstrating integrity, skill, and trustworthiness. Yet, while judges' resources rest on legally defined rights which permit them to make binding decisions on matters of vital importance to U.S. attorneys, the U.S. attorneys' resources consist primarily of opportunities to comply with judges' wishes, thus winning their gratitude and respect.

The attitudes and behavior of U.S. attorneys and judges toward one another each vary along a single dimension. When they are combined, they determine the overall quality of the relationship between them. These dimensions are illustrated in Figure 2. Some U.S. attorneys are more willing than others to accommodate judges' preferences and requests. For their part, judges differ in the extent to which they seek to influence how the U.S. attorney conducts himself. Five basic patterns result. The four in each corner are fairly clear-cut. As one moves toward the middle of the continuum the

Figure 2. Patterns of U.S. attorney-judge interaction.

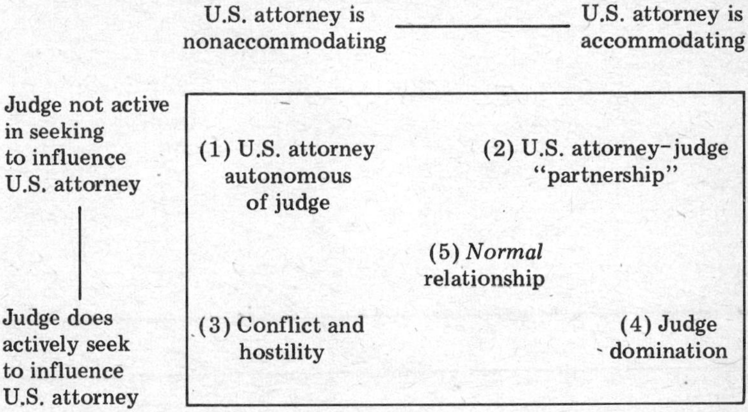

	U.S. attorney is nonaccommodating		U.S. attorney is accommodating
Judge not active in seeking to influence U.S. attorney	(1) U.S. attorney autonomous of judge		(2) U.S. attorney-judge "partnership"
		(5) *Normal* relationship	
Judge does actively seek to influence U.S. attorney	(3) Conflict and hostility		(4) Judge domination

picture becomes clouded. In the *normal* districts at the center of the diagram, elements of each of the other four patterns are found in rich and complex conglomerations.

If anything, the relationships between U.S. attorneys' offices and the Department of Justice are even more complex. The department has formal authority to oversee the entire operation of U.S. attorneys' offices. As indicated, it has established standard operating procedures and policies in many areas. It has access to much of the same information as the man in the field. It has review attorneys who follow the progress of cases and who may request progress reports and even issue directives on what should be done. As a last resort, the department can take over a case completely by dispatching one of its attorneys to the district.

The department has other resources as well. There is considerable expertise in Washington that hard-pressed U.S. attorneys' offices can call upon. It also has a limited supply of trial attorneys who can be assigned to help out an office with an unusually pressing case load. Finally, it can be a "heat shield," taking the blame for decisions that are unpopular with judges and other significant people in the district.

We can only summarize the attitude of many people in the department toward most U.S. attorneys' offices. Basically, there is considerable resentment when they perceive that U.S. attorneys do not recognize the necessity of establishing nationwide policies, and when field personnel are unwilling to rely on the department's knowledge and expertise. There is also conflict over whether important cases should be tried by field personnel or department attorneys. The result is a widespread and persistent desire to increase Washington's control over U.S. attorneys' offices.

U.S. attorneys' offices, not surprisingly, usually resist such control. If anything, their resentment toward the department prompts them to protect and expand their autonomy. Resentment of the department has several sources: the usurpation of prosecutive decisions; the feeling that it is a reflection on their competence when the department takes over a case or issues directives; the annoyance with repeated requests for time-consuming reports; delays in receiving replys to requests for information or authorizations for settlements; and the difficulties requests and demands can create in the district.

The behavior of U.S. attorneys toward the department and the department toward each district can each be located along a single dimension. Some U.S. attorneys are eager to do whatever the department requests. Others would rather be caught with their pants down than comply. For its part, the department largely ignores many districts, and delegates considerable discretion to the U.S. attorney's office. Other districts become the objects of formidable efforts to exert control. Not surprisingly, the position of each participant in the relationship frequently falls somewhere in between these extremes. (See Fig. 3.)

The interaction of U.S. attorneys' offices and the department along these two dimensions produces the five patterns depicted in Figure 3. Two basic characteristics of the rela-

Figure 3. Patterns of U.S. attorney-department interaction.

	U.S. attorney's office strongly resists department control efforts	U.S. attorney's office willingly accepts department control efforts
Intensive department efforts to control U.S. attorneys	(1) Protracted, intense conflict; circumscribed autonomy	(2) Office *controlled* by department
	(5) *Normal* relationship	
Minimal efforts by department to control U.S. attorneys	(3) Conscious autonomy from department	(4) Voluntary compliance of office

tionship are summarized by it: the level of conflict; and the locus of effective decision-making.

Relationships are smoothest in the fourth pattern. U.S. attorneys in such districts voluntarily seek to comply with department policies and directives. The department finds little reason to attempt actively to supervise the U.S. attorney's office because it thinks the U.S. attorney's office adheres to its general policies. Where the department has less confidence in the willingness or ability of an office to follow policy guidelines it may engage in active supervision despite the fact that the U.S. attorney really is willing to follow national policies (pattern 2). Although relationships are smooth on the surface, an undercurrent of tension and resentment exists. It is difficult for members of the U.S. attorney's office to avoid feeling somewhat offended. Tension also underlies the outwardly smooth relationships with districts we identify as displaying *conscious autonomy*. The department grants autonomy to the field office because it feels the U.S. attorney has been following its policies. But the U.S. attorney believes that his decisions result from his own interpretations of what should be done. Overt conflict is relatively infrequent because the U.S. attorney freely chooses to do what the department wants him to do. Underlying tension is generated by the omnipresent "What if?" question. What if the U.S. attorney wanted to do something the department opposed (or vice versa)?

Both seek to avoid confrontation. As a result, there is typically give-and-take negotiation and persuasion when disagreements arise. In fact, the avoidance of genuine conflict by negotiation is predominant in all but the first pattern. Even there the level of conflict is circumscribed: Violent disagreements may be raging in some policy areas, but the normal pattern of negotiation and persuasion will be found simultaneously in others.

Three factors operate to limit the frequency and extent of overt conflict: the common desire most humans have to avoid unpleasant confrontations and promote friendly relationships with those they often deal with; the recognition that they depend upon one another to achieve common goals; and the personal friendships that frequently develop between individuals in Washington and in the field.

The second characteristic of department-U.S. attorney relationships depicted in Figure 3—the locus of effective decision-making power—is best conveyed by describing the balance between central control and field autonomy found in the *normal* relationship (pattern 5).[31] The basic elements of this relationship can be summarized as follows:[32]

1) The department nearly always prevails on matters it considers to be important. General policy decisions made in Washington, especially those prohibiting particular actions, are implemented in the field.
2) The department can prevail on less important matters *when it so desires*.
3) U.S. attorneys very often prevail in disputes if (a) the dispute does not involve disagreement over a major departmental policy; and (b) the U.S. attorney vigorously battles for his position.
4) Many routine decisions (whether to prosecute a particular case, who to hire for the office staff, etc.) are left to the U.S. attorney's discretion.

Generalizations about the overall balance between field autonomy and central control in the operation of U.S. attorneys' offices are risky, particularly when there is such variation between districts. Nevertheless, the impression one receives from studying their operation is that there is rather less control from Washington than in most federal bureaucracies.

In part, this results from significant limitations on the department's ability to exert control. With few exceptions, the department can succeed in securing compliance with any

---

[31] The other four patterns differ from the normal in obvious ways.

[32] This discussion is drawn from Eisenstein, *Counsel for the United States*, Chapter IV, pp. 79-83.

given policy or decision. But it lacks the manpower to prevail in very many of them. It must pick and choose. U.S. attorneys can make it costly to the department to enforce its will—costly in terms of manpower, time, money, and psychic energy. That is why the department must delegate many decisions to the field. It also helps to explain why a U.S. attorney, if he is inclined to fight hard, is able to prevail in disputes that do not fall into the limited group the department assigns top priority. Of course, the U.S. attorney faces similar limitations; there are only so many battles he can wage with the department.

The department's ability to control decisions made in the field is also hampered by its lack of information. Although it has some information about cases (it receives copies of the investigative reports which the FBI submits to the U.S. attorneys, for example), the men actually handling cases in the field have superior information. In criminal cases they often know the investigator personally, have interviewed the witnesses, and are generally able to gain a better feel for the case than the department review attorney. U.S. attorneys and assistants also know the characteristics of other major participants—judges, opposing attorneys, defense witnesses. They also may have a reliable notion of how a local jury would react to the case. With this information, they are in a strong position to claim a better basis for deciding what course of action is most appropriate. When the field attorney has special expertise in the particular area of law involved, his position is further strengthened.

Finally, U.S. attorneys are in a stronger strategic position than most federal bureaucrats who head field offices. As noted, it is difficult to fire them. Having to resign under pressure or being dismissed loses some of its sanctioning power, moreover, because U.S. attorneys are usually able to reenter private practice with ease. The knowledge that U.S. attorneys are men of political substance also strengthens their positions. They have political contacts and support. Otherwise they would never have become U.S. attorneys. The possibility that they could mobilize this support in a dispute with the department structures the behavior of both U.S. attorneys and the department. Also, U.S. attorneys often are able to rely upon the support of others, such as judges, who play crucial roles in the federal legal process. If a U.S. attorney can anticipate cooperation and support from them in disputes with the department, it gives him a tremendous advantage.

THE SIGNIFICANCE OF DISTRICT SIZE

The foregoing description of the relationship between U.S. attorneys and judges on the one hand, and U.S. attorneys and the Department of Justice on the other provides the necessary background for understanding the significance of district size.

The inclusion of at least one district in each state guarantees substantial differences in the size of the population contained in each district. This results in what Richardson and Vines call "judicial malapportionment." [33] The number of districts within a state varies between one (25 states) and four (California, New York, and Texas). The population per district also varies. The 1960 population of the Southern District of Alabama, for example, was under 650,000 while the Eastern District of Michigan had over 5.5 million people. [34] The number of judges and assistant U.S. attorneys shows a corresponding variation. As of 1968, for instance, the District of Vermont was authorized only one assistant and handled a total of 85 cases. The Southern District of New York had nearly 70 assistants and handled some 1,800 cases. [35] The case load per judge also varies, though the differences are less extreme.

---

[33] Richardson and Vines, *The Politics of the Federal Courts*, pp. 43-45.
[34] *Ibid.*, p. 40.
[35] U.S. Department of Justice, *Annual Report of the Attorney General*: 1968 (Washington, D.C.: U.S. Government Printing Office, 1968), Table V, pp. 93-94.

If we would place each district in its appropriate location in Figures 2 and 3 above, and compare its relative position on each figure, a rough, though by no means perfect, correspondence would emerge. Districts dominated by the judge would exhibit either the voluntary compliance or controlled pattern in their relationships with the department. Where there is conflict and hostility between U.S. attorney and judge, we would also tend to find the *conscious autonomy* or *conflict* pattern in their relationship with the department.

To the extent that there is systematic correspondence, it is primarily a function of district size. The smallest districts tend to locate in the lower right-hand corners of Figures 2 and 3 (pattern 4). As district size increases, they tend to move upward, and to the left. The largest districts are concentrated in the upper left, exhibiting both autonomy from judges and protracted conflict with circumscribed autonomy from the department (pattern 1).[36]

What is there about district size that accounts for this? Basically, there are four mechanisms through which size of district is translated into differences in behavior patterns.

First, the strategic situation of the U.S. attorney varies with size. Regardless of how large the office is, there is only one U.S. attorney. When important cases arise in a district, the department generally deals directly with him. The more cases handled in a district, the more frequent are the occasions of contact over important cases. Moreover, the larger districts, primarily because they are situated in urban centers, account for more than their share of significant cases. U.S. attorneys in large districts come to be regarded as more

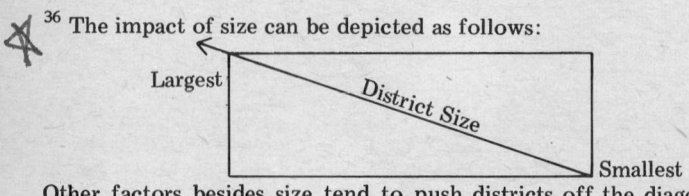

---

[36] The impact of size can be depicted as follows:

Largest ◁——————————
        | *District Size* |
        ————————————▷ Smallest

Other factors besides size tend to push districts off the diagonal into patterns two and three.

important in the eyes of the department, and they come to regard themselves in the same light.

The additional time U.S. attorneys in large districts spend dealing with the department is symptomatic of a variety of other transformations in the nature of the job. In the smaller districts, the U.S. attorney is no more than a first among equals. He has to pull his share of the routine case load. Hence, he is subjected to the same pressures from judges, investigators, and department review attorneys that his assistants are.

As district size increases, the U.S. attorney is forced to become more of an administrator. He is less vulnerable to the pressures generated on trial attorneys by private attorneys, judges, and department supervisory personnel. And, as the content and quality of his work experiences shifts from those of the trial attorney to those of the administrator, there is an inevitable effect on his perspectives and behavior. Because he thinks primarily about administrative problems, he is likely to be more conscious of his office's prerogatives and its influence in relationships with others. He becomes less concerned with particular cases and more interested in how the office can handle recurring problems in its relationships with judges and the department.

This produces two effects: His desire for independence and autonomy increases because he sees them as means to achieve the increased flexibility needed to cope with administrative problems; his skills in dealing with others so that he is capable of enlarging his autonomy will improve as he is forced to confront a series of crises.[37]

Finally, the position of the U.S. attorney relative to the

---

[37] A less important but nonetheless intriguing mechanism pushing U.S. attorneys in large districts toward a more militant defense of office autonomy is the existence of a tradition of independence found in some of them. It is reinforced by the active concern of former members of the office. These alumni constitute a standing body of influential members of the federal bar who, through both informal processes of socialization and advice-giving, renew and strengthen the incumbent's resolve to resist encroachments upon the office's autonomy.

judges is strengthened in larger districts. There is still only one U.S. attorney in the largest districts, but there are over a score of judges. Where there are but one or two judges, the U.S. attorney is little more than another federal trial attorney to the judges, albeit one with a presidential appointment. But the status of each judge vis-à-vis the U.S. attorney in a 20-judge district is not as likely to impress either judge or U.S. attorney. This diminished stature of the judges in larger districts is reinforced by the reduced importance of any single judge to the successful functioning of the U.S. attorney's office. For clearly, if the lone judge in a district is unhappy with the performance of the U.S. attorney's office, life can be difficult indeed. But in a 10-judge district, the consequences of strained relations with one of them are less grim. In addition, as the number of judges increases, the probability of their assuming a cohesive and consistent stance in dealing with the office drops sharply.

The second mechanism which translates size of district into autonomous behavior patterns can be found in the relative value of the resources which U.S. attorneys have for dealing with other participants.

The additional manpower available in larger districts reduces the dependence of the U.S. attorney on others. He has greater flexibility in scheduling the work of his office. A long trial in a small district can exhaust the available supply of good trial attorneys and force the U.S. attorney to seek the cooperation of judges to postpone other difficult trials in the interim. Similarly, the U.S. attorney in a larger district will have fewer occasions when he must rely upon the department for an emergency loan of a trial attorney to bail him out when the trial calendar gets too heavy.

The greater number of specialized cases in larger districts and the availability of assistants to try them facilitates the development of expertise within the office. This reduces the need to seek advice and trial assistance from the department or judges when unusual cases arise. The largest districts are able to have specialists in torts, mail fraud, and appellate brief writing. Small offices find it difficult to develop expertise in any such specialized area. In fact, they sometimes must call upon the department for assistance in writing briefs for the district court.

Another resource stems from the complexity of internal organization in larger offices. From the perspective of outsiders, the lines of authority and responsibility for decisions are blurred. It is easier, for example, to delay and put off the department by referring its requests and orders up and down the organization.

The significant and more interesting cases in larger districts serve as a resource in another way as well. They provide assistant U.S. attorneys with attractive incentives to join the office and to help defend its autonomy (and hence its control of such cases) from Washington. The reason most men seek to become assistant U.S. attorneys, after all, is for the experience. The trial of important cases provides the experience assistants seek most. Thus the quality of those seeking assistantships is higher, and the morale of those who succeed is higher. Because the pool of available legal talent is both larger and of higher quality in large metropolitan areas, assistants in large offices are generally more competent. It is easier to resist the department's attempts to take over the best cases when there are top-notch assistants available to try them.

Finally, the influence of a U.S. attorney's political sponsors is greater in larger districts. Politically influential men in large urban areas are likely to swing more weight with a national administration than are their country counterparts. The backing of the mayor of Philadelphia or Chicago (if he is of the president's party) counts for more than that of the mayor of Asheville or Billings. The significance of this factor is diminished, however, by the fact that U.S. attorneys from smaller districts (particularly in the South) frequently have the backing of senators who have attained considerable influence.

The third mechanism in the relationship between size and behavior patterns consists of the greater desire for autonomy evinced by U.S. attorneys who head large offices. The reasons for this have already been suggested: the uniqueness of their position vis-à-vis others; their greater resources; local traditions of independence.

Finally, U.S. attorneys in large districts enjoy greater autonomy because other participants who might resist them encounter obstacles they would not face in smaller districts. Judges have relatively less prestige and control over the cases tried by a large office. They are less likely to deal with an accommodating U.S. attorney. The department, too, finds itself dealing with more independent-minded men who are less susceptible to influence, and who need rely less on it for expertise, temporary manpower, and advice.

The relationship between the size of the organization and its behavior is not confined to the operation of federal district courts. Although rural state courts have not been studied extensively, there is some evidence that the differences between them and urban state courts are a function of size.[38] Beyond this, the processes and relationships illustrated here may well represent more general phenomena found throughout the political process. A study of the rate of innovation in local health departments found that the most powerful predictor of innovation was size.[39] At least a partial explanation for this seems to be that with increasing size, the motivation to innovate, the resources available to carry out innovation, and the lack of obstacles to hinder it all favored greater innovation.[40]

A COMPARISON WITH STATE COURT SYSTEMS

State and federal courts both deal with the same general categories of problems. Both are subject to pressures from the local community. Frequently, they both have jurisdiction over the same case. Most civil cases meeting the jurisdictional

---

[38] Thomas Scheff, "How Urban and Rural Courts Deal With the Mentally Ill," *American Behavioral Scientist* 7 (1964), pp. 21-24.

[39] Lawrence Mohr, "Determinants of Innovation in Organizations," *American Political Science Review* 63 (1969), p. 126.

[40] *Ibid.*

requirements of the federal courts can be brought in state courts as well. Moreover, in whichever forum a diversity case [41] is heard, the same law is applied, since in these cases federal courts must apply the law of the state in which they are located.[42] Many infractions of federal criminal law violate state statutes as well.

Trials in civil and criminal cases are generally as uncommon in federal courts as in the state courts. For fiscal year 1967, for instance, only 11.5 percent of the federal civil cases terminated went to trial. Just over 14 percent of the criminal cases concluded that year involved trials; over 70 percent consisted of guilty pleas.[43] In addition, the jury-selection process in both jurisdictions has failed to recruit a representative cross section of the adult population.[44]

The development of close working relationships among major participants is a recurrent pattern in the operation of state courts, as Chapter 6 has demonstrated. The same phenomenon appears in federal district courts. Mutual support, dependence, and friendship among the regulars develops and tends to weaken the vigor of the adversary ideal. But the extent and consequences of interdependence are significantly diminished in federal courts, and this leads to important differences in their patterns of operation.

What accounts for the diminished intensity of mutual supportive relationships and the closer adherence to formal legal norms in federal district courts? For one thing, as noted at the outset of this chapter, the status of major participants (prosecutors, judges, defendants and plaintiffs, attorneys) is

---

[41] As noted, a *diversity* case is one in which the federal court has jurisdiction because a citizen of one state is suing a citizen of another state.

[42] It was not always so. Prior to the Supreme Court's decision in Erie Railroad v. Tompkins (1938), federal judges applied the principles of an evolving federal common law.

[43] Goldman and Jahnige, *The Federal Courts as a Political System*, p. 105.

[44] *Ibid.*, p. 91.

generally higher than that found in state courts. Associated with the higher status of these participants is a greater acceptance of the ideals of the adversary process—equal justice and due process. These values tend to be inculcated more systematically in higher-status law schools. They are congruent with other attitudes held about government and politics among these strata of society. In addition, higher-status lawyers have been found to experience less pressure from clients to engage in unethical practices.[45] All the major participants—private large-firm attorneys, government lawyers, and judges—tend to share values and ideals and reinforce each others' affirmations of them.[46]

The activities of federal courts are also more visible than those of most state trial courts. The judicial conference of each circuit keeps watch over administration and case loads in the district courts. The more prominent members of the bar practice there, and are able to use their contacts in legal, governmental, and political circles to call attention to practices they find objectionable. In most districts, a local newspaper reporter covers federal court. Decisions made there are more visible to hierarchical superiors. Because many litigants are wealthy and highly motivated to win their cases, a larger proportion of cases are appealed.[47] Unlike local prosecutors, the U.S. attorney has a supervisory body that has access to information about his decisions and is able to exert authority and influence over their content. Because visibility is higher, deviations from accepted practices relating to due process, equal justice, and the adversary ideal are more likely to be detected and criticized.

The pressure created by the heavy case load found in state

---

[45] See Jerome Carlin, *Lawyers' Ethics* (New York: Russell Sage, 1966), especially Chapter 4.

[46] *Ibid.* Carlin found that higher-status attorneys reported general support for the canons of ethics among their associates. See his Chapter 6.

[47] Goldman and Jahnige, in *The Federal Courts as a Political System*, estimate that approximately five of every eight civil cases and about half of the cases of convicted defendants are appealed. See p. 104.

courts is generally less intense at the federal level. True, there has been a steady rise in the number of cases. Between fiscal years 1960 and 1970 the number of civil cases commenced increased by approximately 75 percent, and the number of criminal cases by about 35 percent.[48] But the district courts have not been overwhelmed by this increase. For one thing, the number of judges increased nearly 40 percent during this same period.[49] In addition, the procedures used to handle cases also helped. Extensive use of pretrial discovery and pretrial conferences has proved effective for reducing civil trials.[50] On the criminal side, federal prosecutors have more control over case load than do their state counterparts. Normally, no federal investigative agency can make an arrest unless it has obtained prior authorization from a U.S. attorney's office. This results in fewer premature arrests that are difficult to dismiss. The superior quality of the investigative work results in stronger cases which result in guilty pleas.

Several significant consequences result from this diminished interdependence among major participants in federal district courts. Adherence to official norms of due process and the adversary ideal is much higher than in state courts. This does not mean that bargaining is not conducted to arrive at negotiated pleas of guilty. But the bargaining is less intense and generally involves somewhat less coercion. Since fewer cases are brought where the evidence is weak, there are fewer temptations to offer substantial reductions in charges. In addition, federal prosecutors have less flexibility in reducing charges, since federal law provides for fewer "lesser included offenses." Bargaining more often involves the *number* of

---

[48] U.S. Bureau of the Census, *Statistical Abstract of the United States* (Washington, D.C.: U.S. Government Printing Office, 1971), p. 152.

[49] *United States Government Organization Manual: 1960–1961* and *1971-72* (Washington, D.C.: U.S. Government Printing Office). There were 241 district judges apportioned among the 50 states and the District of Columbia in 1960–1961 and 331 in 1971–1972.

[50] Richardson and Vines, in *The Politics of the Federal Courts*, p. 86, found that approximately 40 percent of some 15,000 pretrial conferences held in 1960 resulted in a settlement.

counts charged than their seriousness. Finally, federal prosecutors are seldom able to bargain on sentence. In many state courts, judges routinely accept the prosecutor's recommendations on sentence. Although some exceptions are found, most federal judges refuse to bargain over the sentence and even feel it is improper to ask the government if it has anything to say regarding the sentence.

Other differences are evident in the treatment of criminal defendants. Proceedings are conducted at a slower pace and with considerably more decorum, formality, and dignity. Many federal judges make genuine efforts to ascertain if defendants understand the nature of the proceedings and the significance of any voluntary actions or waivers. Hesitation at the time of the plea prompts many federal judges to insist on a plea of not guilty and a trial.

Attorneys who have practiced in both state and federal courts often describe the difference between them as being "like night and day." Unlike state courts, the requirements of the adversary ideal are taken seriously. Efforts to adhere to them are genuine rather than perfunctory. Although it would be an exaggeration to claim that the adversary ideal is realized, it is approximated.

Our brief consideration of the politics of federal district courts will conclude with a final significant comparison of them to state courts. Although local values, attitudes, and political processes are reflected in the behavior and decisions of federal district courts, the relationship is considerably weaker than at the state level. State courts are usually intimately intertwined in the local political culture. Federal prosecutors, judges, and supporting personnel are part of two worlds—the federal as well as the local. They look for approval and support beyond the district as well as within it, not exclusively within it as their local counterparts must.[51]

---

[51] Richardson and Vines, in *The Politics of the Federal Courts*, reach similar conclusions. ". . . It would seem the southern federal judges are less affected by political pressures than are many other political officials in the South" (p. 98). The reasons they cite include security of tenure, the absence of the need to run for reelection, and pressures from federal appellate courts.

Once again, the handling of litigation involving racial questions in the South provides the best evidence for this assertion. When civil rights advocates have had a choice between state and federal courts to press their claims, they have consistently opted for the federal forum. The performance of federal judges in the years immediately following the Supreme Court's 1954 desegregation decision has aptly been summarized by Jack Peltason: "Judges may not have required much action; still they are the only ones to require any action. . . . Whatever desegregation there has been has come about because a judge has insisted on it."[52]

[52] Peltason, *Fifty-eight Lonely Men*, p. 134.

CHAPTER 8
THE STRATEGIC ENVIRONMENT OF APPELLATE JUDGES

THE U.S. SUPREME COURT

NO other component of the legal process has captured as much interest and attention as the U.S. Supreme Court. Thus far, this book has deliberately refrained from discussing it in any great detail. If the lack of emphasis helps readers avoid the common misconception that the Supreme Court is *all* there is to the legal process, it has served a useful purpose. Nevertheless, no one can deny the Court's significance or the necessity of examining the politics of its functioning.

Unlike the other aspects of the legal process described herein, the Supreme Court is a unique institution. It consists of a single group of nine men and a small supporting staff located in Washington, D.C. We encountered problems in generalizing about state courts and lower federal courts because of the wide variation in their environmental contexts and operating characteristics. Such problems do not arise here. Furthermore, there is less variety and complexity in the immediate operating environment of the Court. Police, prosecutors, and lower-court judges deal with a number of other people on a variety of matters in an official capacity. The justices interact primarily with each other and their law clerks. Formal public interaction with outside participants is largely confined to attorneys presenting oral arguments, and only a small proportion of their total time is consumed by oral argument.

What is it like to be a justice of the U.S. Supreme Court? Understandably, we cannot describe the personal and psychological reactions of those chosen to serve. But they all are exposed to the distinctive institutional environment of the Court, and must respond to it. We can say something about that.

The Work of the Court

How do cases come to the Court? Very few fall within the Court's original jurisdiction as spelled out in the Constitution. As a practical matter, nearly all are brought to the Court by litigants who lost their cases in a federal court of appeals or state supreme court. With a few exceptions, this means that all of its cases originated in a federal district court or a lower state court.[1] The trial record, which along with briefs and oral arguments provides the information upon which the Court's formal opinions are based, is made in these lower courts. The quality of the factual material and information about the case contained in the record depends in part upon the performance of these lower courts. Furthermore, the nature of the issues raised is partially determined by intermediate appellate courts.[2]

About 10 percent of the cases decided by the Court come to it on a writ of appeal. Although appellants have a right to

---

[1] One major exception is the provision for initial consideration by a panel of three federal judges of requests for injunctions of governmental actions challenged on constitutional grounds. For a brief description, see Henry Abraham, *The Judicial Process* (New York: Oxford University Press, 1968), p. 163.

[2] Richardson and Vines' study of civil liberties cases in courts of appeals led them to observe that "one of the important political functions of the appellate process in the federal courts is the metamorphosis of cases, the transformation of cases that were routine trial types into cases with greater political significance as civil liberties issues." (See "Review, Dissent, and the Appellate Process: A Political Interpretation," in Herbert Jacob, ed., *Law, Politics, and the Federal Courts* (Boston: Little, Brown, 1967), p. 112.)

appeal certain categories of cases to the Supreme Court, it can and often does refuse to hear these cases. It claims they do not present "substantial federal questions" or that it lacks jurisdiction for other reasons. In either event, appellants who believe the Court erred in refusing to hear their cases are out of luck. There is no one else to appeal to.

The remaining 90 percent of the cases decided by the Court come by way of losing litigants' petitions for *writs of certiorari*.[3] There are no restrictions on who may petition for certiorari. As a result, the Court is confronted with an immense and growing number of them.

The procedures for reviewing and deciding whether to grant a writ of certiorari are significant because they are primarily responsible for determining the Court's agenda. Petitions *in forma pauperis* prepared by indigent defendants are placed on the *miscellaneous docket*.[4] The normally stringent rules for certiorari petitions are relaxed.[5] The chief justice's law clerks prepare memoranda summarizing each *in forma pauperis* petition, and they are circulated among the other justices. Petitions not filed *in forma pauperis* are placed on the appellate docket and a copy is distributed to each justice. The decisions as to whether petitions on the miscellaneous and appellate dockets will be granted or denied are made at a conference of all the judges. To speed the process, the chief justice prepares a *special list* consisting of petitions he considers to be without merit. Unless another justice objects to the inclusion of a petition on the list, it is rejected without discussion or a vote. In order for a petition to be

---

[3] If granted, the writ of certiorari orders certified records of the case to be sent to the Supreme Court. In other words, the Court formally agrees to hear the case.

[4] The description of the certiorari process is drawn from Sheldon Goldman and Thomas Jahnige, *The Federal Courts as a Political System* (New York: Harper & Row, 1971), pp. 128-129; and Anthony Lewis, *Gideon's Trumpet* (New York: Random House, 1964), Chapters 1-3.

[5] There must be 40 printed copies, for example, and they must be on 6 1/8" X 9 1/4"-paper.

granted, four affirmative votes are necessary (the so-called *rule of four*).

This process of reviewing petitions for certiorari consumes a good deal of the Court's time. Thus, a major activity of the Court is deciding what to decide.

Since it takes substantially more time to dispose of the cases that are accepted for formal decision, the justices have no choice but to deny most petitions for certiorari if they are to escape being inundated by an impossible number of cases. Thus, about 9 out of every 10 petitions for certiorari are unceremoniously denied.

Cases receiving the full treatment of a formal written opinion take a good deal of time to decide. There are oral arguments to be heard, lengthy briefs to be read, a secret conference where the case is discussed and a preliminary vote taken, and the drafting of a formal written opinion (including, often, one or more dissents). It is not surprising that the Court is able to render only between 100 and 150 full opinions a year.[6]

The power of the Court to pick and choose the cases it will hear (no matter how many cases are appealed to it) is essential. Such a procedure not only permits it to regulate the number of cases it decides, but also *which* cases. It can avoid deciding politically sensitive cases if it wishes, or it can postpone them until a more auspicious time.

The Court's discretion over its work load is limited by significant formal restrictions and rules that guide it in deciding what cases it will hear. For instance, cases must involve real disputes with real parties. Advisory opinions on real or hypothetical questions are not rendered. Furthermore, the Court cannot seek out controversial and important questions to rule on. It must wait for cases embodying these questions to reach it in the normal course of litigation. The Court also

---

[6] The statistics on the Court's work load for the 1965–1966 term are typical. It disposed of 2,683 cases, but only 342 were actually decided on the merits. Of these, only 107 were full written opinions. (Abraham, *The Judicial Process*, p. 181).

refuses to decide cases that it believes involve political questions that are the responsibility of the other branches of government.[7]

As a practical matter, however, these are not significant restrictions. Most important conflicts in our domestic political life manage to find their way to the Court. And since the Court itself enforces its own restrictions, it can change its mind on whether it has jurisdiction, whether a *substantial federal question* exists, or on what the definition of a *political question* is. Many scholars, including Justice Jackson, believed the apportionment of state legislatures clearly involved a political question so that the Court could not and would not rule on the issue.[8] Yet the Court embarked on a series of historic reapportionment decisions starting with *Baker* v. *Carr*[9] less than a decade after Justice Jackson's observation.

Two other features of the day-to-day activities of the Court are particularly noteworthy. First, the justices work very hard. The pressure of work is relentless. Small wonder that one observer of the Court claimed the justices lived a life of "unremitting toil" or that Justice Murphy remarked that often he was "rushed beyond belief."[10] Henry Hart summed

---

[7] The limits on the Court's jurisdiction are discussed by Justice Robert Jackson in *The Supreme Court in the American System of Government* (Cambridge, Mass.: Harvard University Press, 1955), pp. 2-27. No one has succeeded in defining what a *political question* is. One observer, Jack W. Peltason, regards them as "Those which judges choose not to decide, and a question becomes political by the judges' refusal to decide it." See *Federal Courts in the Political Process* (Garden City, N.Y.: Doubleday, 1955), p. 10. The Court's formal justification for not hearing them is that they raise issues that properly are the concern of the legislative or executive branches, not the judicial. See also Abraham's discussion of political questions in *The Judicial Process*, pp. 364-369.

[8] Robert Jackson, "The Supreme Court as a Political Institution," in Alan Westin, ed., *The Supreme Court: Views from the Inside* (New York: Norton, 1961), p. 154.

[9] 369 U.S. 186 (1962).

[10] Quoted by J. Woodford Howard, Jr., "On the Fluidity of Judicial Choice," *American Political Science Review* 62 (1968), p. 50.

up the situation well: "... the Court has more work to do than it is able to do in the way in which the work ought to be done."[11] Second, for all its prominence, the Court really consists of a rather small number of people. Not counting clerical personnel, there are but 20 law clerks in addition to the nine justices.

The Dynamics of Decision-making

We might begin by first placing this whole discussion in perspective. How the Supreme Court's decisions are really reached and what accounts for the justices' votes and opinions has generated a formidable amount of thinking, research, and writing among legal scholars and political scientists. One unfortunate and unintended by-product of this intensive scholarly attention, however, is an exaggeration of the significance of these questions. Ultimately, the most important contributions of the Court to American politics stem from the impact its decisions have on society.[12] In Chapter 12, this will be examined in some detail.

This does not mean that we should not be interested in how the Court arrives at its decisions. In deciding which cases to hear and which to reject, it determines what issues will be placed on the agenda for possible implementation.[13] The content of decisions on the cases it does accept determines in

---

[11] Henry Hart, Jr., "The Time Chart of the Justices," *Harvard Law Review* 73 (1959), pp. 84-101, reprinted in Robert Scigliano, ed., *The Courts* (Boston: Little, Brown, 1962), p. 276.

[12] Most of the major studies of the impact of Supreme Court decisions are discussed and analyzed by Stephen Wasby, *The Impact of the United States Supreme Court: Some Perspectives* (Homewood, Illinois: Dorsey, 1970). See also Theodore Becker, ed., *The Impact of Supreme Court Decisions* (New York: Oxford University Press, 1969).

[13] Although debate rages over whether the Court intends denials of certiorari to serve as implicit affirmations of the lower courts' decisions, there is no question that the refusal does have a practical impact. For a discussion of what important cases were refused during one term, see Fowler V. Harper and Alan S. Rosenthal, "What the Supreme Court Did Not Do in the 1949 Term," *University of Pennsylvania Law Review* 99 (1950), pp. 293-325, reprinted in Robert Scigliano, ed., *The Courts* (Boston: Little, Brown, 1962), pp. 312-320.

part what the reactions of lower courts, governmental officials, and private citizens will be as efforts to implement them are made. Their decisions can have far-reaching effects on the very nature of our society.

The specific questions that students of the Supreme Court have sought to answer differ. Sometimes the focus is on how and why the Court reached a specific decision or group of related decisions. Alternatively, scholars have sought to describe and explain the behavior of a single justice as he coped with the totality of issues before the Court. Finally, attempts are made to isolate general variables that account for the behavior of the justices as a group on all cases.

At the risk of considerable oversimplification, two general approaches taken by those seeking to answer these questions can be identified. The first, or *eclectic* approach relies primarily on analyses of written opinions, although studies of individual justices make use of a variety of other sources of information (biographical data, letters, the justices' personal papers). Their explanations emphasize the impact of precedent and law, the judicial philosophies of the various justices, their social and political values, and the development of trends in the Court's reasoning.[14]

The second approach seeks to be more rigorous and systematic, relying heavily on quantifiable empirical data and sophisticated mathematical techniques used by behavioral scientists to analyze it. The language of opinions and biographical information on the justices are hardly utilized at all. Rather, the chief source of data consists of the votes of the justices on nonunanimous cases. Several techniques are used to analyze this data, including bloc analysis, Guttman scaling, and correlational analysis. There would be little value in describing these techniques here, but we can briefly summarize the major findings that have resulted from their use.

[14] For two excellent examples of this approach, see J. Woodford Howard, Jr., *Mr. Justice Murphy* (Princeton, N.J.: Princeton University Press, 1968); and Alpheus T. Mason, *Harlan Fiske Stone: Pillar of the Law* (New York: Viking, 1956).

For some time, observers of the Court had noticed that certain justices tended to vote together frequently. Systematic analysis of patterns of agreement and disagreement among the justices (the substance of bloc analysis) not only confirmed this, but provided precise descriptions of the make-up and cohesiveness of these blocs.[15] The blocs showed remarkable persistence across time, and can be characterized according to the ideological position (conservative or liberal) taken by their members on the cases.

The use of Guttman scaling and correlational analysis carries bloc analysis forward by looking at voting patterns in cases dealing with the same general issues. Guttman scaling is one technique used to determine if there is an underlying dimension that accounts for responses (in this instance, votes on cases). The major finding of Guttman-scaling research is that the ability repeatedly to scale cases dealing with two broad topics—civil liberties (the C scale) and economic liberalism (the E scale)—suggests the existence of underlying attitudes toward these two questions among the justices that shape their behavior.[16]

Those who have adopted this more systematic approach for

---

[15] The pioneering work in bloc analysis was conducted by C. Herman Pritchett. See especially *The Roosevelt Court: A Study in Judicial Politics and Values 1937-1947* (New York: Macmillan, 1948). Brief summaries of other applications of bloc analysis to judicial behavior can be found in Glendon Schubert, "Behavioral Research in Public Law," *American Political Science Review* 57 (1963), pp. 236-238; and Goldman and Jahnige, *The Federal Courts as a Political System*, pp. 155-159.

[16] It is obviously impossible to summarize the extensive literature that has been produced on judicial behavior. The most important work is perhaps Glendon Schubert's *The Judicial Mind* (Evanston, Ill.: Northwestern University Press, 1965). Other important books and articles include: Pritchett, *The Roosevelt Court*; Pritchett, *Civil Liberties and the Vinson Court* (Chicago: University of Chicago Press, 1954); Schubert, *Quantitative Analysis of Judicial Behavior* (Glencoe, Ill.: Free Press, 1959); S. Sidney Ulmer, "Toward a Theory of Sub-Group Formation in the United States Supreme Court," *Journal of Politics* 27 (1965), pp. 133-152; Ulmer, "The Dimensionality of Judicial Voting

the most part reject traditional explanations of judicial behavior relying on judicial philosophy, adherence to precedent, or the neutrality that may be adopted with the assumption of the judicial role. Instead, as already suggested, they look to the social and political attitudes of the justices. This position has been succinctly summarized by the best known and most prolific scholar among them, Glendon Schubert, who wrote that "differences in the attitudes of the Justices towards the basic issues raised by the cases that the court decides account for differences in the voting behavior of judges. In short, Supreme Court Justices vote as they do because of their attitudes towards the public policy issues that they decide." [17]

The arguments over the validity and soundness of these two approaches have consumed considerable amounts of time, energy, paper, and ink. Serious questions have been raised about the methodology and conclusions of both approaches. [18] This is hardly the place to enter into the fray. Instead, we shall discuss, in summary fashion, several out-

---

Behavior," *Midwest Journal of Political Science* 13 (1969), pp. 471-483; Fred Kort, "Simultaneous Equations and Boolean Algebra in the Analysis of Judicial Decisions," in Thomas Jahnige and Sheldon Goldman, eds., *The Federal Judicial System* (New York: Holt, Rinehart and Winston, 1968), pp. 166-180; Harold J. Spaeth, "Judicial Power as a Variable Motivating Supreme Court Behavior," *Midwest Journal of Political Science* 6 (1962), pp. 54-82; Spaeth, "Warren Court Attitudes Towards Business: The 'B' Scale," in Glendon Schubert, ed., *Judicial Decision-Making* (New York: Free Press, 1963), pp. 79-108.

[17] Glendon Schubert, "Judicial Attitudes and Voting Behavior," *Law and Contemporary Problems* 28 (1963), pp. 100-142, reprinted in Jahnige and Goldman, eds., *The Federal Judicial System*, p. 277.

[18] Theodore Becker, *Political Behavioralism and Modern Jurisprudence* (Chicago: Rand McNally, 1964) surveys and critiques a variety of approaches to the study of the Supreme Court. See also Douglas Rosenthal, "Schubert, The Judicial Mind"—Book Review, *Yale Law Journal* 77 (1968), pp. 1432-1446; Howard, *Mr. Justice Murphy*; Wallace Mendelson, "The Neo-Behavioral Approach to the Judicial Process: A Critique," *American Political Science Review* 57 (1963) pp. 593-603; and Glendon Schubert, "Ideology and Attitudes: Academic and Judical," *Journal of Politics* 29 (1967), pp. 3-40.

standing characteristics of the decision-making process.

We might begin by presenting the idealized official textbook version that often accompanies traditional views of the nature of law. According to official myth, Supreme Court justices are isolated from the normal flow of politics and events in society. Cloistered in their chambers in the Supreme Court building, they are depicted as arriving at considered and independent judgments on each of the cases presented based on their reading of the Constitution, statutes, and precedent. Decisions are rendered almost automatically—a mechanical tallying of the individual independent judgments arrived at by each justice.

The reality of Supreme Court decision-making is quite different. If we examine the nature of the task facing the justices, the unreality of such idealized notions of how the justices make their decisions is evident. They deal with questions of considerable importance that normally involve a conflict between two or more valued principles. The competing positions are well argued by competent attorneys on each side. The justices are as a rule extremely intelligent and proud men. They are forced to interact with eight other men and to come up with some sort of decision.

Under such circumstances, we would expect to find that the process of arriving at decisions is extremely complex and difficult to reconstruct. Furthermore, the justices often have a hard time making up their minds. The questions are not only difficult; they also are decided in conjunction with the other judges. Shifts in opinion, bargaining, fierce arguments, personal friendships and animosities, and patterns of specialization in which certain judges look to colleagues whom they feel have particular expertise in certain types of cases are likely to be found.

In recent years, a number of scholars have been able to penetrate the veil of secrecy that has surrounded the Supreme Court's decision-making.[19] Their primary source of

---

[19] See especially Walter Murphy, *Elements of Judicial Strategy* (Chicago: University of Chicago Press, 1964); Howard, "On the Fluidity of Judicial Choice"; and Mason, *Harlan Fiske Stone.*

data has been the private papers of a number of former justices. They include records of how the justices voted on each case after it was initially discussed in conference, the marginal comments made on draft opinions, notes written to and received from other justices, and memos to law clerks.

The conclusions of this research have confirmed what logic based on the nature of the Court's task suggests. For one thing, the justices are not isolated either from society or its politics. One of the striking patterns that emerges in Alpheus Thomas Mason's fascinating biography of Chief Justice Stone is the extent and content of his correspondence with friends and acquaintances in the legal profession. A constant stream of letters reached him commenting on the latest decisions of the Court, and included both praise and criticism of his own decisions. [20] He could not possibly have had the feeling that nobody was reading or criticizing his opinions or the decisions of the Court.

Justices have also taken active roles in the selection of new members of the Court. The intense activity of Chief Justice Taft in the selection of both lower federal court judges and members of the Court has been well documented. [21] Political activities have extended to other spheres as well. Louis Brandeis, who was a close confidant of Woodrow Wilson, continued to advise him on a variety of matters after his

---

[20] Mason, in *Harlan Fiske Stone*, observes that "By 1930 Frankfurter's communiques appeared with such regularity that if no word had come from Cambridge on a Wednesday following the delivery of opinions on Monday, the Justice was apt to ask his law clerk for an explanation" (p. 305). In one such letter, Frankfurter observed, "I have just finished the reading of the January 6th batch of opinions . . . and I find I am deeply in your debt—all of us are, who really care about our constitutional system and your Court. . ." (quoted on p. 296). This communication went both ways. At one point, Stone suggested Frankfurter write an article on a topic of concern to Stone, which Frankfurter proceeded to do (see p. 303).

[21] See Murphy, *Elements of Judicial Strategy*, pp. 74-76; David J. Danelski, *A Supreme Court Justice is Appointed* (New York: Random House, 1964), passim; Murphy, "In His Own Image," 1961 *Supreme Court Review*, p. 159; Murphy, "Chief Justice Taft and the Lower Court Bureaucracy," *Journal of Politics* 24 (1962), p. 453.

elevation to the bench, including key appointments and major questions of foreign policy.[22] During the Roosevelt administration, Brandeis was able to secure the appointment of men he recommended to important posts, and apparently was not reluctant to communicate his views on current policy to them.[23] More recently, Justice Fortas continued to serve as an advisor to President Johnson, and Chief Justice Berger worked actively among members of the Senate for the confirmation of President Nixon's nominees to the Court.

The intensity and frequency of interpersonal interaction among the nine justices themselves is even more pronounced. Personal friendships and animosities indeed develop.[24] Normally these relationships do not determine absolutely votes or the content of written opinions. On occasion, friends find themselves in disagreement and enemies who are barely on speaking terms are in agreement. But opportunities to communicate on points of disagreement or to bargain on the working of an opinion are probably opened or closed depending on the quality of personal relations among the justices. When there is sharp disagreement on the Court, patterns of friendship serve to sustain the minority dissenting bloc.[25]

The notion that the justices arrive at independent conclu-

---

[22] Murphy, *Elements of Judicial Strategy*, pp. 148-149.

[23] *Ibid.*, pp. 150-151. Murphy observes that both Taft and Stone also played a role in shaping executive branch policy through their contact with the incumbent president. For a description of Stone's relationship with President Hoover, see Mason, Chapter 17, "Friend of President Hoover," in *Harlan Fiske Stone*. Murphy also reports that Stone worked through Frankfurter to get the Roosevelt administration to retain J. Edgar Hoover as FBI director (see p. 155).

[24] This discussion is drawn from Murphy's description of interpersonal relations on the Court. *Ibid.*, pp. 49-56.

[25] Mason, in *Harlan Fiske Stone*, refers to the dissenting bloc of Holmes, Brandeis, and Stone as "The Three Musketeers." At one point in his career, Stone wrote, "It is a great comfort that when one starts out to 'proclaim the truth' he can usually count on such staunch supporters as Justice Holmes and Justice Brandeis" (quoted on p. 254). Mason goes on to observe that Holmes and Stone "instantly 'hit it off'."

sions on each case is equally erroneous. There is not only substantial interaction among them during the period in which decisions are reached, there is also a good deal of true persuasion. Arguments appealing to logic, precedent, the well-being of the Court as an institution or even of society as a whole play an important role in the give and take of discussion during formal conferences and private meetings between individual justices. The same is true of the frequent written communications passed between them.[26] There is substantial evidence that persuasive techniques are often effective. Justices have admitted to changing their minds on the basis of the arguments of others.[27]

But other processes besides persuasion are to work in the communications network. Bargaining is one. This is most evident at the opinion-writing stage of the decisional process. In order to forge a majority, maintain its cohesion in the face of a large minority, or even to hold a dissenting bloc together, a good deal of give and take on the lines of argument and on specific wording occurs.[28] Even subtle threats to change one's vote on a case or to write a dissenting opinion unless certain changes are made, while gently conveyed, do not appear to be uncommon.[29]

The foregoing discussion illustrates five techniques which justices can utilize to influence the outcome and content of decisions: persuasion on the merits of the case; persuasion based on personal regard and friendship; bargaining; threats; and influencing the selection of new members of the Court.[30]

The interaction among the justices in the decision process

---

[26] See Murphy, *Elements of Judicial Strategy*, pp. 43-49.

[27] *Ibid.* Murphy quotes Justice Jackson as saying, "I myself have changed my opinion after reading the opinions of other members of this Court" (p. 44).

[28] *Ibid.* For specific examples, see pp. 56-68.

[29] *Ibid.*, pp. 54-56.

[30] *Ibid.*, Chapter 3.

produces a situation where preliminary decisions are fluid and the final outcome in doubt. The justices' perceptions of what issues are raised by a case may change during this process, as may their views of the fact situation.[31] Tentative decisions reached after reading the briefs, hearing oral arguments, discussing the case in conference, and even reading draft opinions are not stable. Newcomers to the Court appear particularly likely to change their positions.[32] But as noted, veteran justices also change their minds on the merits. At times, they have been known to abandon strongly held views in the face of arguments appealing to their sense of loyalty to the Court as an institution or to notions of the public interest. This primarily takes the form of withholding a dissent and acquiescing in the majority opinion when it is felt a unanimous opinion is necessary.[33] Even the pressures of time—the necessity of arriving at *some* decision because other important cases require attention—affect outcome.[34]

Reading the formal opinions and dissents that emerge from the decision-making process, one could easily get the impression that there was never any doubt in the minds of the justices on the correctness of their conclusions. But the definite and self-assured tone of many opinions conceals the agonizing doubts that lie behind them. Some of the most famous dissents in the decade studied by Professor Woodford Howard were written by men who originally agreed with the

---

[31] For an excellent treatment of the fluid nature of decision-making on the Court, see Howard, "On the Fluidity of Judicial Choice," p. 50.

[32] *Ibid.*, p. 45.

[33] A notable example was Justice Murphy's reluctant decision to write a concurring opinion rather than issue an already written ringing dissent in Hirabayashi v. United States, a case dealing with the policy of internment of Japanese-Americans during World War II. See Murphy, *Elements of Judicial Strategy*, pp. 46–47.

[34] Howard, "On the Fluidity of Judicial Choice," p. 50. For an excellent discussion of the role the chief justice can play in the small-group interaction of the Court, see David J. Danelski, "The Influence of the Chief Justice in the Decisional Process," in Walter Murphy and C. Herman Pritchett, eds., *Courts, Judges, and Politics: An Introduction to the Judicial Process* (New York: Random House, 1961), pp. 497–508.

majority; sometimes minority opinions were transformed into majority opinions between the initial vote and the final decision. We can appropriately end this examination of the politics of the Supreme Court by repeating the words of Professor Howard. His study of the private papers of several justices serving during the 1940s tempts him to conclude that "hardly any major decision in this decade was free from significant alteration of vote and language before announcement to the public." [35]

U.S. COURTS OF APPEALS

U.S. Courts of Appeals comprise the middle level of the federal judicial system, between the federal district courts and the U.S. Supreme Court. There are 11 such courts, the District of Columbia Circuit plus 10 judicial circuits encompassing the 50 states. As with federal district courts we find that national uniformity is tempered by local conditions and individual proclivities.

The situational context in which judges of the courts of appeals find themselves is far less complex than that faced by trial-level judges, however. Most interaction occurs between the judges themselves (both face to face and through written communication), between judges and their law clerks, and between judges and the attorneys who argue cases before them. Evidently, there is even less personal interaction among the judges on some courts of appeals than on the Supreme Court. In his study of the Second Circuit Court of Appeals under Judge Learned Hand, Professor Marvin Schick reports that because a number of judges commuted daily, the court was far less close-knit in its interaction patterns than was the Supreme Court. [36] Several of the judges rarely communicated except by letter. However, this situation is probably quite different from many of the other circuits.

---

[35] Howard, "On the Fluidity of Judicial Choice," p. 44.

[36] Marvin Schick, *Learned Hand's Court* (Baltimore, Md.: Johns Hopkins Press, 1970), p. 74.

THE STRATEGIC ENVIRONMENT OF APPELLATE JUDGES

The activity and decisions of the courts of appeals are also characterized by a marked lack of visibility and drama. Press coverage is meager. The excitement of decision day in the Supreme Court, when opinions are read aloud, is absent. In the Second Circuit, at least, opinions are not read but merely handed to the clerk when they are ready to be issued.[37] Even when the Court of Appeals for the Second Circuit (one of the most important tribunals in the entire judicial system) is hearing oral arguments, the courtroom is nearly devoid of spectators.[38]

The Work of Courts of Appeals

There are two principal sources of cases: appeals from federal district courts and appeals from the decisions of various federal independent regulatory agencies and commissions. Practically all matters heard, then, have already been initially processed and a decision has been reached by another body. In addition to the absence of cases appealed from state supreme courts, there is another significant difference in the composition of these courts' dockets when compared to that of the Supreme Court. Courts of appeals cannot control the number or type of cases heard. Anyone losing in a district court or regulatory agency proceeding can appeal if he follows procedural rules and is willing to spend the money. Thus, courts of appeals are not faced with the task of deciding what to decide, but must render a decision on the merits for every case properly appealed to them.[39]

Only a small proportion of the decisions that could be appealed to them are, however. About 4 percent of district

---

[37] Schick, *Learned Hand's Court*, p. 113.

[38] *Ibid.*, p. 73.

[39] Richard J. Richardson and Kenneth N. Vines, *The Politics of Federal Courts* (Boston: Little, Brown, 1970), cite figures from 1963 that show 398 cases were disposed of by consolidation with other cases raising similar questions and another 1,441 disposed of without a hearing, frequently because the appeal was withdrawn by the appellant. This accounts for approximately 37 percent of the 5,011 cases disposed of that year (see Table 2, p. 120).

court decisions [40] and 1 or 2 percent of administrative agency decisions [41] are actually appealed. Nevertheless, the number is still substantial and apparently growing rapidly. [42] Of course, not all of these cases require full consideration. In a substantial minority (on the order of 20 to 25 percent) of cases in which briefs are filed and oral arguments heard, a very brief *per curium* opinion is issued. [43]

At first blush, the courts of appeals apparently perform only a screening and filtering function, winnowing out cases unworthy of Supreme Court consideration. This is only partially correct, however. As noted earlier in this chapter, broad issues not present at earlier stages are sometimes injected into cases at the courts of appeals level, essentially transforming the nature of the case. [44]

Although the case load per judge is not overwhelming, [45] courts of appeals judges evidently are under considerable time pressure. [46] It may be less oppressive than that experienced by Supreme Court justices, but nevertheless is probably sufficient enough to condition their behavior.

The Dynamics of Decision-making

In many respects, the general procedures used to decide cases follow those of the Supreme Court. Briefs are submitted and

---

[40] *Ibid.*, p. 117.

[41] Goldman and Jahnige, *The Federal Courts as a Political System*, p. 105, quoting Martin Shapiro.

[42] In 1960, 3,899 cases were filed; in 1963, it was 5,437, and in 1968, 9,116. Administrative Office of the United States Courts, *Annual Report of the Director, 1960, 1963, 1968* (Washington, D.C.: U.S. Government Printing Office).

[43] See Richardson and Vines, *The Politics of Federal Courts*, p. 121; and Schick, *Learned Hand's Court*, p. 94.

[44] See footnote 2 and accompanying text above.

[45] Richardson and Vines, *The Politics of Federal Courts*, p. 121, Table 3, found that the average number of cases terminated per judge in 1963 varied from 38 to 86, depending on the circuit.

[46] Schick, *Learned Hand's Court*, especially pp. 70–71.

read, oral arguments heard, a conference held in which cases are discussed, a vote taken, and assignment of the opinion made. There is one crucial difference, however. With very few exceptions, decisions are not rendered by the entire complement of judges on the court, but rather by panels composed of three of the judges. [47] There are several significant ramifications of this procedure. [48]

First, the method of assigning judges to cases assumes considerable importance. The composition of the panel can affect the outcome of the case. The chief judge [49] of the circuit normally makes the assignment, giving him considerable potential influence over the outcome of cases. [50] Second, the overall composition of a court of appeals does not permit prediction of the outcome on a specific case. A seven-judge court composed of two liberals and five conservatives may render liberal decisions when the two liberals are on the same panel. Similarly, it is not meaningful to speak of the Supreme Court reversing the court of appeals for a particular circuit unless a rare *en banc* decision is referred to. Third, this procedure can and evidently does sometimes lead to intracircuit conflict. Similar cases may be decided differently because of changes in the composition of the panels that decided them. Finally, the fact that only three judges sit on each case facilitates the process of arriving at unanimous

---

[47] In special circumstances, the entire compliment of judges may sit *en banc*. Only a minimal proportion (less than 2 percent) of cases are decided in this manner, however. For a discussion of the criteria used to determine when a case should be heard *en banc*, see Schick, *Learned Hand's Court*, pp. 118-122.

[48] The following discussion draws heavily on Richardson and Vines, *The Politics of Federal Courts*, pp. 122-123.

[49] The judge who has the longest service on the appeals bench automatically serves as chief judge until he reaches the age of 70.

[50] There is little evidence on the extent to which this potential is realized. In his description of the Second Circuit, Schick, in *Learned Hand's Court*, p. 76, says only that "the panels are composed in a manner that equalizes the work of the judges and provides as many combinations of judges as possible."

decisions. The frequency of nonunanimous decisions is considerably lower than on the U.S. Supreme Court. In recent years it was in the neighborhood of 10 percent of all cases.[51] Of course, the existence of three-judge panels is not the only reason for the high proportion of unanimous decisions. But it is a factor, if only, as Professor Sheldon Goldman has observed, because a judge who wishes to dissent must do so alone.[52]

The description of decision-making procedures is complicated somewhat by intercircuit differences. A notable example is found in the variation found in the rate of dissent. For instance, in a study of courts of appeals cases reviewed by the Supreme Court between 1957 and 1960, it was found that the Washington, D.C. Court of Appeals had been divided in 60 percent, whereas the figure for the Second and Fifth Circuits was about 30 percent, and for the Ninth, but 11 percent.[53] The D.C. Circuit also has the highest rate of nonunanimous decisions for all cases (over 15 percent) regardless of subsequent Supreme Court review. In contrast, the Sixth Circuit Court of Appeals renders nonunanimous decisions in less than 3 percent of its cases.[54] The rules of procedure followed may also differ, though these differences have been reduced by the adoption, in 1968, of standard rules of procedure.[55] Finally, differences are found in the internal decision-making mechanisms utilized. For instance, the Second

[51] Goldman and Jahnige, *The Federal Courts as a Political System*, p. 193; Schick, in *Learned Hand's Court*, p. 108, cites a figure of 15 percent for the Second Circuit. Approximately half of the Supreme Court's decisions are nonunanimous.

[52] Sheldon Goldman, "Conflict and Consensus in the United States Courts of Appeals," *Wisconsin Law Review* 1968 (1968), p. 481.

[53] Louis S. Loeb, "Judicial Blocs and Judicial Values in Civil Liberties Cases Decided by the Supreme Court and the United States Court of Appeals for the District of Columbia Circuit," *The American University Law Review* 14 (1965), p. 149.

[54] Goldman, "Conflict and Consensus," p. 464. These figures are for fiscal years 1962–1964.

[55] Schick, *Learned Hand's Court*, pp. 85–86.

Circuit follows the unusual and probably unique practice of requiring each judge on a panel to write a memorandum stating his views of the case and his vote before the conference is held. [56]

Evidently, many of the same characteristics of decision-making on the Supreme Court are found in the courts of appeals as well. For example, there is evidence that fairly stable blocs of justices form in 8 of the 11 circuits. [57] Furthermore, it appears possible to identify these blocs according to the decisional tendencies of their members along liberal-conservative lines. [58] One study was able to demonstrate a link between *left* and *right* blocs on the D.C. Court of Appeals on one hand, and analogous blocs on the Supreme Court on the other by examining voting patterns on cases appealed from the D.C. Circuit and heard by the Supreme Court. [59]

Further evidence of the influence of ideological and attitudinal factors in the decisions of appeals judges comes from the finding that judges whose votes are liberal in one type of case also tend to be liberal in other areas. Thus, judges who tended to favor the defendant in criminal cases also supported civil liberties claims and labor unions or employees in disputes with management. [60] There also is a relationship between partisan affiliation and votes. Sheldon Goldman found that "In general, the Democrats appear relatively more 'liberal' than Republicans in cases which involve what might be called 'economic liberalism.' However, Democrats and Republicans appear equally 'liberal' on the criminal and civil liberties categories." [61]

---

[56] *Ibid.*, p. 96.

[57] Goldman, "Conflict and Consensus," p. 473.

[58] Goldman, "Conflict and Consensus," Table 2, p. 467.

[59] Loeb, "Judicial Blocs," pp. 152-155.

[60] Sheldon Goldman, "Voting Behavior on the United States Courts of Appeals, 1961-1964," *American Political Science Review* 60 (1966), Table 4, p. 378.

[61] *Ibid.*, p. 381.

Interestingly, the judges themselves also attributed lack of unanimous decisions to attitudinal differences on specific issues; most, however, did not believe that general ideological stances (liberal versus conservative for example) explained differences on specific issues in any consistent fashion.[62]

Finally, courts of appeals judges are no more insulated from society and its politics than their brethren on the Supreme Court. Like other federal judges, many have been extremely active politically prior to appointment. And if Justice Stone had frequent contact with Felix Frankfurter at the Harvard Law School, Justices Jerome N. Frank and Charles Edward Clark of the Second Circuit had frequent and intense interaction with their friends and former colleagues at Yale.[63]

Despite the presence of a number of these and other factors that would seem to encourage disagreement and dissent, however, there are obviously forces operating in the dynamics of decision-making in these courts that tend to produce consensus. Professor Goldman has identified five "rules of the game" based on his interviews with courts of appeals judges that appear to perform this function:[64] (1) There is evidently a strong belief among these judges that they ought to follow precedents, particularly those of the Supreme Court, regardless of their personal views; (2) the judges seek *just* or *fair* decisions, and despite the ambiguity of the term and potential conflict with the norm of following precedent, this appears to contribute to unanimous decisions; (3) decisions must be justified in a reasonable fashion in written opinions; (4) the judges generally seek to maintain cordial relationships with their colleagues both on and off the bench; (5) finally, a good deal of give-and-take is accepted in the decisional process. Thus, as in the Supreme Court, the bargaining over the wording of opinions, and the changes in

---

[62] Goldman, "Conflict and Consensus," p. 475.
[63] Schick, *Learned Hand's Court*, p. 124.
[64] Goldman, "Conflict and Consensus," pp. 476-480.

the votes of individual judges and the decisions ultimately reached occur in the courts of appeals as well. In the words of one observer,

> It is very difficult to get unanimity on the Court but the judges on the circuit try to reach consensus. It is a bargaining, give-and-take process as each judge is a different being with different views. Often a judge would rather bargain with his peers and achieve a decision, although not as broad-sweeping as he would want but nevertheless in the right direction, than write a ringing dissent while having no influence on the outcome of the case.[65]

Our discussion of courts of appeals concludes with two observations about this bargaining process. First, because only three judges are involved, the negotiations need be considerably less complex to reach agreement than in a nine-member body. Second, despite the presence of many of the same factors that produce frequent dissents on the Supreme Court—particularly the necessity of deciding issues that raise fundamental questions upon which the justices have personal values and attitudes—the elements in the strategic environment of judges on the courts of appeals which discourage dissents appear to operate effectively in the overwhelming majority of cases. Unanimity characterizes their decisions to a degree much greater than at the Supreme Court level.

STATE APPELLATE COURTS

Twenty-two states have intermediate appellate courts between their major trial-level courts and the highest appellate tribunal.[66] Despite their probable significance, practically nothing is known about the dynamics of their functioning or

---

[65] *Ibid.*, p. 479.

[66] Council of State Governments, *State Court Systems: A Statistical Summary* (Chicago: Council of State Governments, 1970 revised edition), Table 4. The average term of judges on these courts is 7.8 years.

even of their structure and procedures.[67] However, limited information is available about state supreme courts, and the following discussion will deal with them.

It is impossible to make meaningful generalizations about the strategic environments of state supreme court judges. The information available by no means covers a representative sample of all such courts, and no comprehensive studies have been conducted. Even more significantly, substantial differences are found among these courts in a number of important respects.

Formal recruitment procedures are identical for judges in the federal court system. But as noted in Part II, practically every form of recruitment found in the legal process is used to select state supreme court justices. This immediately suggests that differences in behavior are likely. In Chapter 4, for instance, differences in the decisional tendencies of state appeals court justices according to their party affiliation were described, and the strength of this relationship was found to depend on the method of selection.[68] Additional evidence for this exists. Several studies of the Michigan Supreme Court have found that fairly cohesive blocs form, based on the party affiliation of the judges.[69] Furthermore, when they decide cases that deal with issues that sharply differentiate the positions of the two parties, their decisions are consistent with their party affiliation.[70] Democrats are con-

---

[67] One exception is Daryl R. Fair, "State Intermediate Appellate Courts: An Introduction," *Western Political Quarterly* 24 (1971), pp. 415-424. Fair describes the basic institutional and structural characteristics of the 19 intermediate appellate courts in existence in 1969.

[68] See Chapter 4, p. 63.

[69] Glendon Schubert, *Quantitative Analysis of Judicial Behavior* (Glencoe, Ill.: The Free Press, 1959), pp. 129-142; and Sidney Ulmer, "The Political Party Variable on the Michigan Supreme Court," *Journal of Public Law* 11 (1962), pp. 352-362.

[70] Schubert, in *Quantitative Analysis*, studied workmen's compensation in the 1954-1957 terms. Ulmer, in "The Political Party Variable," replicated and extended Schubert's study to cover workmen's compensation and unemployment compensation cases in the 1958-1960 terms.

siderably more inclined to side with the employee, Republicans with the employer on workmen's compensation cases. The close link between party affiliation and decisional tendencies apparently is forged at least in part through the recruitment process. Although candidates for the supreme court in Michigan run on a nonpartisan ballot, they are nominated by the parties at their state conventions and are clearly tied to their respective parties in the course of the campaign. The contrast with Wisconsin, a state with a similar political system and party structure, is instructive.[71] There, no consistent differences are found in the behavior of Republican and Democratic judges on workmen's compensation cases; indeed, voting blocs based on party do not appear to form at all on the Wisconsin Supreme Court.[72] Elections to the Wisconsin Supreme Court appear to be truly nonpartisan. Candidates are nominated in a nonpartisan primary. They generally draw bipartisan support for their candidacy. Party does not play a significant role in the rhetoric of the campaign. In addition, the election is held in the spring, and not in conjunction with November national elections as in Michigan.

The evidence on the links between recruitment and behavior suggest that, given the variety of techniques used to select state supreme court justices, generalizations covering all state supreme courts are not likely to be valid.[73]

State supreme courts also differ from one another in the procedures used to decide cases. Although there are some

---

[71] For an excellent discussion of this contrast, along with data from Wisconsin, see David W. Adamany, "The Party Variable in Judges' Voting: Conceptual Notes and a Case Study," *American Political Science Review* 63 (1969), pp. 57–73.

[72] *Ibid.*, p. 63.

[73] This is emphatically demonstrated in the case of the Pennsylvania Supreme Court. Although judges are elected on a strict partisan basis, and although there are a number of split decisions, cohesive blocs (including those that might be based on similar party affiliation) do not exist. See Henry R. Glick, *Supreme Courts in State Politics* (New York: Basic Books, 1971), pp. 107–108.

basic similarities (all generally require the submission of briefs and the presentation of oral arguments; all hand down formal written opinions), they do not exhibit the same degree of uniformity found in U.S. Courts of Appeals.[74] Some are able to control their dockets by refusing to hear cases. Others are required to render decisions on everything properly appealed to them. As noted, 22 are assisted in the task of reviewing decisions of trial courts by intermediate appeals courts. Techniques for assigning opinions and arriving at decisions also vary widely. All judges participate in all phases of decision-making on some courts, but in others a single justice is assigned primary responsibility for reading the briefs, hearing the oral arguments, and drafting the opinion.[75]

A third likely source of variation in the behavior of state supreme courts stems from the ways in which judges conceive of the nature of their job. Henry Glick's study of the role perceptions of judges on the supreme courts of New Jersey, Louisiana, Pennsylvania, and Massachusetts provides a fascinating (though admittedly not a representative) picture of these differences.[76] Pennsylvania judges see their task primarily as processing litigation smoothly; in New Jersey, there is considerable emphasis on the lawmaking functions of the court.[77] Similar patterns are found in the orientation of the judges toward the extent to which they should make law as opposed to merely interpreting it. New Jersey judges emphasize the lawmaking aspect; Pennsylvania and Louisiana judges see themselves as law-interpreters.[78] Differences are also

---

[74] For a general description of these differences, see Herbert Jacob, *Justice in America* (Boston: Little, Brown, 1965), pp. 173-174.

[75] In some courts, opinions are sometimes assigned to judges on the basis of their perceived expertise in a particular area. See Glick, *Supreme Courts in State Politics*, pp. 110-111. Glick also notes that sometimes the conclusions of the opinion-writer are accepted with little criticism or revision by the rest of the court.

[76] *Ibid.*

[77] *Ibid.*, Table 2-1, p. 34.

[78] *Ibid.*, Table 2-3, p. 41.

found in attitudes toward how decisions should be reached, the importance of precedent, and the proper techniques for resolving disagreements (persuasion; compromise; or voting). [79]

Yet, that supreme court justices perceive their roles differently in these four states is not conclusive evidence that differences in patterns of behavior exist. <u>Their behavior may or may not be consistent with these role perceptions.</u> However, evidence based on other data suggests that differences do indeed exist in patterns of behavior. We have already seen the link between recruitment and decisional patterns on the Michigan and Wisconsin courts. We can also seek clues to the amount of conflict on state supreme courts and the effectiveness of mechanisms to control it by referring to the frequency of nonunanimous decisions. The differences are substantial. The proportions of dissenting opinions in 1965–1966 were 40.2 percent in Pennsylvania, 31.8 percent in Louisiana, and only 7.1 and 1.6 percent in New Jersey and Massachusetts respectively. [80] A small sample of cases from all state supreme courts decided in 1964 shows similar variation. [81] The existence of relatively few dissenting opinions does not necessarily mean there is agreement, however. It means only that whether the judges agree or not, dissents are not written. Indeed, there is some evidence to suggest that unanimous opinions mask individual disagreements fairly often in some states. [82]

[79] *Ibid.*, Tables 4-1, p. 75; 4-2, p. 76; and 5-1, p. 90.

[80] *Ibid.*, p. 64.

[81] Robert J. Sickels, in "The Illusion of Judicial Consensus: Zoning Decisions in the Maryland Court of Appeals," *American Political Science Review* 59 (1965), Table 1, p. 100, looked at the 25 most recent cases decided by each. In 31 states, including Massachusetts and New Jersey, there were two or less dissents among the 25. Nine states had three, four, or five dissents, and the remaining ten (including Louisiana and Pennsylvania) had six or more.

[82] *Ibid.* Sickels notes that while unanimous opinions in zoning cases are the rule, substantial disagreement on how such cases should be decided is revealed by reading the opinions of the various judges. The outcome

The foregoing summary of some major differences found in the operations and procedures of state supreme courts suggests the existence of significant relationships between the political culture of the state, its method of recruiting the judges, and their patterns of behavior. The precise nature of these relationships and their frequencies will not be known until systematic and comprehensive studies are conducted.

There are enough similarities in the strategic position of these courts relative to inferior courts and in the nature of the tasks that they perform, however, to produce patterns that resemble those found in the higher federal courts. The influence of individual judges in the deliberations of their courts varies according to their intellectual competence, persuasive abilities, and personal characteristics.[83] Chief judges in particular are in a strategically advantageous position.[84] Regardless of whether dissenting opinions are issued or not, give-and-take bargaining is probably common.[85] Finally, the fluidity that characterizes U.S. Supreme Court decision-making is found at the state level as well, as the following observation of a state supreme court justice suggests:

In this last session... I had six dissenting opinions to file at the conference. In three cases I got one other judge to dissent with me and we may get others.... In three other cases, my dissents changed the

---

depends upon who is assigned the task of writing the opinion, and the other judges acquiesce in his decision. And Glick, in *Supreme Courts in State Politics*, p. 63, discovered the existence of a set of "informal rules of the game" in interpersonal relations that tend to produce agreement. More significantly, he found that in New Jersey in particular (which has few dissents), the judges felt compromise was the appropriate means to resolve differences (see Table 5-1, p. 90).

[83] See Glick, *Supreme Courts in State Politics*, Chapter 5, especially p. 112.

[84] *Ibid.*, pp. 115-117.

[85] *Ibid.*, pp. 72-75.

opinion of the whole court. The case was reassigned. The opinion you read in the book is not necessarily the first one arrived at by the court. Here, the dissent may become the majority as a result of the conference.[86]

[86] *Ibid.*, p. 98.

PART FOUR
THE IMPACT OF THE LEGAL PROCESS

"IT'S not relevant," cries the student. Predictably, *relevant* is often nothing more than a code word to legitimize demands that material which conforms to personal ideological outlooks be covered to the exclusion of everything else. But the demand for relevance implicitly raises what is perhaps the most significant question for students of politics: So what?

So what? What difference does it make that the recruitment and behavior of individuals in the legal process is political? In fact, what difference does the legal process make from any perspective?

The answer, of course, varies according to your interests and values. But if you think that what happens to people is important, that it makes a difference if someone is evicted from his apartment, jailed, or even executed; if it makes a difference that his property is seized to pay alleged debts, or that he is compensated for injuries resulting from someone else's negligence or aggressiveness, then the legal process is extremely relevant.

CHAPTER 9
AN OVERVIEW OF THE IMPACT OF THE LEGAL PROCESS

THE NUMBER OF PEOPLE AFFECTED

PRACTICALLY everyone is affected by the legal process all the time. Certain behavior is deterred by the possibility of arrest and punishment, while other behavior is encouraged. Sometimes we consciously change our behavior to avoid a direct impact of the legal process upon us. Thus, we slow down when we see someone else getting a speeding ticket. We put money in the parking meter. We resist the temptation to shoplift. On the civil side, tenants pay their rent to avoid eviction or a lawsuit; newspapers try not to slander private individuals.

But the legal process affects many persons much more directly. The ultimate penalty, execution, was carried out on over 3,800 people between 1930 and 1964.[1] Many more, of course, have been imprisoned. The President's Commission on Law Enforcement and

---

[1] U.S. Bureau of Prisons, *National Prison Statistics* (Washington, D.C.: U.S. Government Printing Office, 1966), Vol. 31, p. 1. No executions were carried out in the late 1960s and early 1970s pending the outcome of litigation challenging the constitutionality of the death penalty.

Administration of Justice estimated that some 426,000 were in correctional institutions on an average day in 1965.[2] In addition, there are at least 400,000 patients in mental institutions.[3] Of course, some of these people voluntarily enter these institutions. Others, only technically voluntary admissions, are those who agreed to sign themselves in when faced with the alternative of being committed. But a large proportion—estimates range as high as 90 percent for state mental institutions—are involuntarily committed through civil court proceedings.[4] Those who are involuntarily committed find themselves in surroundings that do not differ very much from those of most prisons.[5]

The number of people arrested and prosecuted, of course, is larger still. The FBI collects reasonably accurate statistics on the number of arrests made for the seven felonies that make up its crime index. In 1969, over 485,000 such arrests occurred.[6] Although figures on arrests for all offenses are not available, there are estimates. The FBI put the figure at 7 million arrests for all criminal offenses except traffic violations. This produces an arrest rate of 47 per 1,000 for people

[2] The President's Commission on Law Enforcement and Administration of Justice, *The Challenge of Crime in a Free Society* (Washington, D.C.: U.S. Government Printing Office, 1967), p. 171.

[3] U.S. Bureau of the Census, *Statistical Abstract of the United States* (Washington, D.C.: U.S. Government Printing Office, 1971), Table 107, p. 74. Several experts testifying before Congress place the number considerably higher—at 650,000 and even 800,000 (U.S. Senate, Committee on the Judiciary, *Constitutional Rights of the Mentally Ill, Hearings Before the Subcommittee on Constitutional Rights*, 87th Cong., 1st sess. 1961, pp. 11 and 41).

[4] Committee on the Judiciary, *Constitutional Rights of the Mentally Ill*, p. 43.

[5] For an excellent description of life in "total institutions" such as prisons and mental institutions, see Erving Goffman's fascinating book, *Asylums* (Chicago: Aldine, 1962).

[6] U.S. Bureau of the Census, *Statistical Abstract of the United States*, Table 229, p. 145.

over 10 years of age.[7] Of course, not all arrested are prosecuted, not all prosecuted are convicted, and not all convicted are imprisoned. But arrest alone is a rather significant event for an individual.

Estimates of arrests for moving traffic violations are even more difficult to obtain. A study of 508 cities with 1960 populations of over 25,000 found that 104 traffic arrests were made per 1,000 of population. However, tremendous differences exist among communities. Although Boston and Dallas are about the same size, Boston police issued 11,242 one year while their colleagues in Dallas handed out 273,626![8]

Finally, as any driver in urban or suburban America knows, there is the parking ticket. The number issued each year must be staggering. Ann Arbor, Michigan, a city of a little more than 100,000 had 17,064 moving violations and 217,679 parking tickets in one year, more than two for each resident.[9]

The number of people employed in the criminal justice system provides another measure of its scope. In October 1969, there were 730,000 full-time jobs at the federal, state, and local levels with a yearly payroll amounting to more than $7 billion.[10]

On the civil side, we have already mentioned involuntary commitment of the allegedly mentally ill. Divorce is another

---

[7] Federal Bureau of Investigation, *Uniform Crime Reports* (Washington, D.C.: U.S. Government Printing Office, 1968), pp. 32-33. Lee Silverstein estimates there were about 300,000 felonies and 4,470,000 misdemeanor arrests in 1962. *Defense of the Poor in Criminal Cases in American State Courts: A Field Study Report* (Chicago: American Bar Foundation, 1965).

[8] John A. Gardiner, *Traffic and the Police* (Cambridge, Mass.: Harvard University Press, 1969), pp. 7-8.

[9] Ann Arbor Municipal Court, *Annual Report,* July 1, 1967-June 30, 1968. More than $365,000 was collected on parking tickets.

[10] United States Law Enforcement Assistance Administration and United States Bureau of the Census, *Expenditures and Employment for Criminal Justice System, 1968-1969* (Washington, D.C.: U.S. Government Printing Office, 1970), Tables 1 and 2, p. 11.

important area. About 715,000 couples went through the process in 1969, and their 900,000 or so children were inevitably affected as well.[11]

Nearly 200,000 bankruptcies were filed in the year ending June 30, 1968.[12] Wage garnishments, court orders requiring employers to withhold a portion of an employee's wages so it may be transferred by the court to a creditor, are even more numerous. One very conservative estimate puts the number at over one million each year in the United States.[13]

The number of civil suits of all types, if one includes actions in small claims courts, suits for back rent, claims for injuries suffered in automobile accidents, and so forth is immense. One study found that in 1957, 77,000 lawsuits arising from automobile accidents were begun in New York City alone.[14] In suburban Nassau County, New York, with a population of about one million, around 3,500 civil cases were begun in 1963.[15] Even in the rarefied atmosphere of federal district courts (where the amount at issue must be at least $10,000), over 86,000 civil cases were begun in the year ending June 30, 1970.[16]

Although they are not parties to a lawsuit, men and women sitting on juries directly participate in the legal process. There

---

[11] U.S. Bureau of the Census, *Statistical Abstract of the United States*, Table 79, p. 60.

[12] Administrative Office of the United States Courts, *Tables of Bankruptcy Statistics, 1968* (Washington, D.C.: U.S. Government Printing Office, 1968).

[13] Herbert Jacob, *Debtors in Court* (Chicago: Rand McNally, 1969), p. 26.

[14] Marc Franklin, Robert Chanin, and Irving Mark, "Accidents, Money, and the Law: A Study of the Economics of Personal Injury Litigation," in *Dollars, Delay, and the Automobile Victim* (New York: Bobbs-Merrill, 1968), p. 38.

[15] Kenneth Dolbeare, *Trial Courts in Urban Politics* (New York: Wiley, 1967), p. 35.

[16] U.S. Bureau of the Census, *Statistical Abstract of the United States*, Table 245, p. 152.

are probably at least 100,000 jury trials begun each year.[17] This means it is very likely that close to a million people serve as jurors.

Additional examples illustrating the scope of the legal process can be dredged up to the point of oppressiveness for the reader. If the figures just presented are beginning to swirl, it may help to condense the message of the preceeding paragraphs: Substantial numbers of Americans are touched in rather direct ways each year by the legal process.[18]

WHAT VALUES ARE AFFECTED?

When we ask ourselves what politics involves, we usually think of how material values (such as wealth and physical well-being) are distributed by governmental decisions. But the allocation of symbolic or psychological values is equally important. The decisions of government have psychological as well as material impact on people. People are threatened, reassured, given status and prestige, or degraded by what government does.[19] Everything that men value, both symbolic and material, that is affected by the political process generally is affected also by the legal process.

Consider, for example, the impact of arrest and a stay in jail. For many, the psychological costs are extremely high. Jail is a degrading experience. The prospect of having an

---

[17] Harry Kalven and Hans Zeisel, *The American Jury* (Boston: Little, Brown, 1966) report that in 1955, 80,000 criminal jury trials were begun and 60,000 completed (p. 12).

[18] There is some evidence on frequency of type of contact. A survey study conducted in Wisconsin determined how many had participated in the past five years as a litigant, defendant, witness, or juror. The number was about 14 percent. See Herbert Jacob, *Justice in America* (Boston: Little, Brown, 1965), p. 120.

[19] The importance of the symbolic and psychological dimensions of politics has been described in penetrating fashion in the work of Harold Lasswell. See his *Politics: Who Gets What, When, How* (New York: World, 1958), Chapter 2; and Lasswell and Abraham Kaplan, *Power and Society* (New Haven: Yale University Press, 1950). For a more recent treatment of this question, see Murray Edelman, *The Symbolic Uses of Politics* (Urbana, Ill.: University of Illinois Press, 1967).

arrest record and being an ex-jailbird can produce a good deal of mental anguish. Psychological wounds are probably even more traumatic among those who are the victims of homosexual rapes. Prison rapes are not extraordinary occurrences, either. One study of the Philadelphia prison system estimated that during a one-year period in the late 1960s, over 2,000 violent homosexual assaults on nonconsenting jail inmates occurred.[20] The periodic suicides that occur in pretrial detention facilities provide additional testimony to the psychological burdens of imprisonment.[21]

The material consequences of imprisonment are also profound. The physical conditions in the jails that house defendants awaiting trial are typically poor and frequently horrible. These facilities are usually quite old, overcrowded, dirty, and without recreation facilities. Meanwhile, the structure of one's normal life on the outside deteriorates, sometimes irretrievably. Detainees frequently lose their jobs. Their families are often forced to move, sell possessions, and go on welfare. Installment debts become overdue. Their spouses often desert them. Whether arrested suspects in pretrial detention deserve these things is irrelevant to the fact that their imprisonment affects them in a most immediate and profound way.

Additional examples, while easy to produce, really aren't necessary. Whether it is eviction from your living quarters, the loss of custody of your children, or the imposition of a substantial fine, the impact of the legal process on the whole range of human values is both evident and substantial.

HOW MUCH ARE VALUES AFFECTED?

It is not always possible to measure in a meaningful way the magnitude of this impact on values. How can the cost of a

---

[20] Alan J. Davis, "Sexual Assaults in the Philadelphia Prison System and Sheriff's Vans," *Transaction* 6 (1968), pp. 8-15.

[21] In 1969, eight men committed suicide in New York City prisons. See "Detention Centers 60 percent over Capacity," *The New York Times*, January 22, 1970.

prison rape or false arrest be assessed? Sometimes the question itself is not even meaningful. To a man about to be executed, *everything* is at stake. But by two scales, the amount of money changing hands and the time spent in prison, we can attempt to understand how much people are affected.

Insurance companies paid out over $4.5 billion in 1969 to cover claims of bodily injury and property damage resulting from automobile accidents.[22] We cannot credit this entire sum to the operation of the legal process, of course. But as the description of accident litigation suggests, settlements reached in the vast majority of claims are shaped by the knowledge that a lawsuit and trial are possible. We do know that about $10 million changes hands as a result of court verdicts in these cases in New York City each year.[23]

Studies of accident litigation find tremendous variation in the amount of compensation that victims received. Research done on serious accidents revealed that nearly 48 of every 100 persons injured received nothing from the person who injured them or from his insurer.[24] About 10 percent of those who did recover damages were still out over $800 in lost wages and medical bills. Yet a third of the victims received awards more than double their dollar losses. In New York City, 36 percent of the victims of minor accidents received no compensation. The average award of those who did collect was just slightly above their average cash outlay.[25]

---

[22] U.S. Bureau of the Census, *Statistical Abstract of the United States*, Table 858, p. 538.

[23] Franklin, Chanin, and Mark, "Accidents," p. 38. The total amount involved was estimated at $220 million (verdicts plus settlements). Significantly, $77 million of it went to attorneys as fees.

[24] Clarence Morris and James Paul, "The Financial Impact of Automobile Accidents," in *Dollars, Delay, and the Automobile Victim* (New York: Bobbs-Merrill, 1968), p. 6.

[25] Accidents studied involved injuries described as "slight shock, contusion." The average award was $510, $90 above the expense incurred. Despite the minor nature of these accidents, victims recovered $22 million and their attorneys received somewhat less than $15 million (Roger B. Hunting and Gloria S. Neuwirth, *Who Sues in New York City* (New York: Columbia University Press, 1962), p. 39).

AN OVERVIEW OF THE IMPACT OF THE LEGAL PROCESS 213

Massive sums of money are transferred as the result of other types of cases as well. In fiscal 1969, U.S. attorneys throughout the country were responsible for imposing nearly $69 million in fines, forfeitures, penalties, and other civil judgments.[26] Over $36 million was actually collected that year.[27] In fiscal year 1968, the city of Ann Arbor, Michigan collected close to $440 thousand in parking and traffic fines.[28] Over $92 million was distributed to creditors from the assets of people who went bankrupt in fiscal year 1968.[29] Close to $1.75 million was distributed by the probate court of Cuyahoga County (Cleveland, Ohio) in a little less than a year from the estates of intestate decedents (people who died without wills).[30]

These figures provide at best only a sketchy notion of the amount of money that changes hands as a direct result of the legal process. The total would surely be something over $10 billion, perhaps much more. Clearly, whatever the precise figure, the legal process is a major factor in the transfer of wealth through governmental action.

The other major value affected by the legal process that can be measured is time spent in prison. Here again, figures are incomplete and difficult to obtain. The length of the sentence imposed is not identical to time actually spent in prison. The vast majority of prisoners are released considerably before their sentences are completely served. In fiscal year 1968, for instance, first-time offenders released from

---

[26] United States Department of Justice, *Annual Report of the Attorney General* (Washington, D.C.: U.S. Government Printing Office, 1969), p. 110.

[27] *Ibid.*, p. 102.

[28] Ann Arbor Municipal Court, *Annual Report*, July 1, 1967–June 30, 1968.

[29] Administrative Office of the United States Courts, *Tables of Bankruptcy Statistics.*

[30] Based on a sample of every twentieth estate closed or released from administration between November 9, 1964 and August 8, 1965. The author is indebted to Professor Richard Wellman of the University of Michigan Law School for this data.

federal prisons served only 54.5 percent of their average sentence; the average time they spent in prison was slightly over 19 months.[31]

RATE OF DISTRIBUTION OF VALUES

The time it takes the legal process to allocate values is also important. One of the major results of civil litigation, in fact, is to affect *when* values are allocated.

Forcing someone to file suit will delay the final settlement. As noted, insurance companies usually profit from delay because many plaintiffs may be unwilling or unable to wait for settlement, and consequently accept a smaller compromise offer.

Although the mass media occasionally describes the delays encountered in civil courts (focusing on the penniless widow who must wait five years to win her suit for the wrongful death of her husband), hard data on this is difficult to find. We do have some information, however, on civil cases filed in the major civil court in Manhattan in the mid-1950s.[32]

The average delay for all cases not receiving priority was just under 15 months.[33] In other words, the average litigant had to wait about that long after his suit was filed before it was actually heard. If we examine those cases which have received the most attention in discussions of delay—personal injury suits involving jury trials—the average delay is about two and a half years.[34] A large proportion of these cases (41 percent) are given preferential treatment, however, particularly when the plaintiff is elderly or destitute. Then the delay is just under 16 months.[35] Of course, as was shown in Chapter

---

[31] U.S. Bureau of the Census, *Statistical Abstract of the United States*, 1970, Table 238, p. 157.

[32] See Hans Zeisel, Harry Kalven, Jr., and Bernard Buckholz, *Delay in the Courts* (Boston: Little, Brown, 1959).

[33] *Ibid.*, p. 21.

[34] *Ibid.*, p. 46.

[35] *Ibid.*

6, most personal injury cases are settled out of court. Thus we must look beyond figures for cases that go to trial. An analysis of personal injury cases in which a jury was requested shows that the average time lapse between filing and settlement is 21 months.[36] Another study found similar results; in a majority of more serious accidents in which there was an award, it took more than a year.[37]

The importance of delay in criminal cases is even more profound. If the defendant is out on bail he usually is happy to postpone his trial for as long as possible. This delays the start of a possible prison term. Until his trial, he at least is free to go about his normal activities. But perhaps more important, the longer the delay the more the prosecution's case decays. Witnesses die, forget, and move. New evidence is increasingly hard to obtain as the crime recedes in time.

If the defendant is unable to make bail, however, delays work a real hardship. He suffers all of the material and psychological hardships of pretrial detention. He is unable to help in the preparation of his case. The longer he waits for trial, the stronger is the temptation to plead guilty, especially if by doing so the time already spent in prison is applied against his sentence.

How long is the delay in criminal cases? In Washington, D.C. in 1962, the average was 51 days; in Philadephia in 1954 it was 33; in Los Angeles in 1963, 78 days; in 1962 in New York City, 30 days; and in the federal courts in fiscal year 1960, over 25 days.[38] Since these figures are averages, some defendants spend much longer periods awaiting trial. A month or two in jail where conditions are likely to range from bad to nearly intolerable is a long time, especially in light of the fact that these men have not been convicted of a crime and are presumed innocent.

---

[36] *Ibid.*, p. 56.
[37] Morris and Paul, "The Financial Impact," p. 14.
[38] Daniel Freed and Patricia M. Wald, *Bail in the United States* (Washington, D.C.: U.S. Government Printing Office, 1964), pp. 9–18.

CHAPTER 10
THE IMPACT OF THE CRIMINAL PROCESS

IN the preceding chapter, we sketched the impact of the operation of the legal process. Here, we shall examine the dynamics of this impact in the criminal process at the trial court level and below.

THE IMPACT OF THE POLICE

Sgt. Paul E. Fabian, 1970's "Policeman of the Year," described how he came to use his award-winning technique for gathering information from juvenile narcotics users: ". . . I thought about how the state gives immunity once a year to persons who turn in unregistered guns. I also thought about how grand juries and investigation commissions are able to offer immunity to helpful witnesses. And I asked myself, 'Why can't I do it?' And I did."[1] The fact that the technique was illegal (as Sgt. Fabian, his chief, and his county district attorney freely admitted) seemed to pose no serious handicaps.

This illustration of how police can shape the impact of the legal process through the exercise of their discre-

---

[1] "Policeman Fights Drugs by Blocking Prosecution," *The New York Times*, October 7, 1970.

tion is typical in all respects but one: Because the story appeared on the first page of *The New York Times'* second section, it was uncharacteristically visible to the public.

Discretion is the key to understanding how the police influence what the impact of the legal process is. By discretion, I mean the ability to choose between several significant alternatives without incurring severe sanctions for picking one over the other. The absence of severe sanction is critical to the notion of discretion. Theoretically, I can cross a bridge or jump off it. But unless I happen to be suicidal, the costs of jumping are too high to say I really have a meaningful choice.

Two components of the working environment of the police account for much of their discretion. The first is the ambiguity of many statutes and policies they enforce. The second is the low visibility of their decisions. Even if sanctions are theoretically possible, they cannot be applied if police command officers don't know how their men are acting.

A result of this discretion is that the critical question of who will police the police is best answered by "no one." In a number of important areas, either the police must police themselves or nobody will. The President's Commission on Law Enforcement and Administration of Justice summarized what these areas are: "The Police must make important judgments about what conduct is in fact criminal, about the allocation of scarce resources, and about the gravity of each individual incident and the proper steps that should be taken." [2]

Discretion in Order Maintenance

Studies of police behavior without exception agree on one fundamental fact. Police use their discretion. In part, they do so because it is unavoidable. But they also actively desire to use their discretion. The choices they make shape what law-in-action is.

---

[2] The President's Commission on Law Enforcement and Administration of Justice, *Task Force Report: The Police* (Washington, D.C.: U.S. Government Printing Office, 1967), p. 14.

One of the most significant patterns to emerge from the exercise of discretion is that police underenforce the law.[3] Numerous situations and actions that could lead to a legitimate arrest are either ignored entirely or handled by some means short of an arrest—a lecture, a warning, a sympathetic expression of concern, temporary detention in the field and release, or even a cuff or two. This is particularly true in high crime areas. Descriptions of police on patrol consistently point out that minor traffic violations, drunkenness, petty gambling, minor scuffles, and so forth are frequently overlooked. Underenforcement arises from necessity, not laziness. There are too many violations, too few police, and not enough hours in a day to even approach full enforcement.

The fact of underenforcement gives added significance to decisions to actually make an arrest. When everyone who could legitimately be arrested cannot be, what determines who will? From the standpoint of someone who is arrested, the decision is crucial. For him, the police determine what the law-in-force is. For all *practical* purposes, behavior the police ignore is "legal." He is not sanctioned by government for engaging in it. Acts that attract an arrest or some other police sanction are, for that person at that particular time, "illegal."

Just as clear violations of statutes may be legal for practical purposes when they are ignored, so, too, can "objectively legal" acts which do not violate statutes become illegal as a practical matter if they result in an arrest. In all likelihood,

---

[3] A number of studies of police have reached this conclusion. See, for example, James Q. Wilson, *Varieties of Police Behavior* (Cambridge, Mass.: Harvard University Press, 1968), p. 49; Michael Banton, *The Policeman and the Community* (London: Tavistock, 1964); Wayne La Fave, *Arrest: The Decision to Take a Suspect into Custody* (Boston: Little, Brown, 1965); Egon Bittner, "The Police on Skid-Row: A Study of Peace Keeping," *American Sociological Review* 32 (Oct., 1967), pp. 699-719. For a theoretical and legalistic discussion of underenforcement, see Joseph Goldstein, "Police Discretion Not to Invoke the Criminal Process: Low Visibility Decisions in the Administration of Justice," *Yale Law Journal* 69 (1960), pp. 543-594.

this is what happened to a group of 15 students in California. None of the 15 had received moving traffic violations in the preceding year. All promised to continue driving safely and to avoid attracting attention to themselves. Their cars were inspected for defective equipment and repaired where necessary. The only thing they did was place Black Panther bumper stickers on their fenders. At the end of 17 days, the students had received 33 traffic citations, and thorough searches were conducted of the cars of five.[4]

It is not always easy to determine when behavior is "objectively illegal," that is, clearly violates some statute. In a number of situations encountered in order maintenance, citizens' behavior is of ambiguous legality. At what point can someone who has been drinking be classified as drunk? When does exuberance become a public nuisance or disturbing the peace? When does a poor loafer become a vagrant and loiterer? Similarly, it may be difficult to determine who is to blame in a fight or whether a somewhat willing female has been raped.[5] The exercise of discretion in these situations of ambiguous legality is unavoidable.

The conditions under which a patrolman makes discretionary order-maintenance decisions in the field affect how they are made. To maintain control, establish his dominance, reduce his fear of being attacked, and obtain respect and deference, he must act quickly. He has no time to obtain the facts, to find out whether the scruffy black man is a nuclear physicist on his way to help a friend move, a dope peddler, or what. His cynicism and suspiciousness make it unlikely that he will believe what he is told anyway. He necessarily relies upon external cues—age, race, dress, speech, and general de-

---

[4] F.K. Heussenstamm, "Bumper Stickers and the Cops," *Trans-Action* 8 (Feb., 1971), pp. 32-33.

[5] One study found that the police decided one in five reported rapes were unfounded and no criminal violation had occurred. "Police Discretion and the Judgment That a Crime Has Been Committed: Rape in Philadelphia," *University of Pennsylvania Law Review* 117 (1968), p. 281.

meanor—when making decisions. In other words, he looks for characteristics associated with trouble and criminality in previous encounters (being black, poor, or young; using particular speech mannerisms; slouching or acting insolent).

Characteristic patterns in the way police approach encounters with citizens in the field shape the nature of law-in-force. This is particularly evident during the initial stage of the encounter. Typically the approach is businesslike and civil. But where the officer perceives potential danger and hostility, he is apt to be aggressive, domineering, suspicious, and brusque.[6] Concerned with possible danger from active resistance and outright attack, and sensitive about his low status and lack of respect, the policeman seeks to establish his dominance during the initial seconds.[7] Acquiescence and respectful behavior on the part of the citizen reduces his anxiety and satisfies his desire for respect and status.

A patrolman's behavior after the initial seconds is also shaped in large part by the citizen's reaction.[8] A calm, civil response to the policeman's approach by a sober citizen is likely to elicit businesslike or even good-humored behavior from him. The citizen who is agitated or overly detached, under the influence of alcohol, or antagonistic is likely to receive continued brusque, hostile, or authoritarian treatment. The student who lowers his head and says "Yes, sir" fares better than the one who flashes a peace sign and mutters "Pig."

[6] For a description of this phenomenon, see Jerome Skolnick, *Justice Without Trial* (New York: Wiley, 1966), p. 105.

[7] William Westly, in *Violence and the Police* (Cambridge, Mass.: Harvard University Press, 1970), p. 98, quotes one officer as follows: "In the south side the only way to walk into a tavern is to walk in swaggering as if you own the place and if somebody is standing in your way give him an elbow and push him aside."

[8] The discussion of police response that follows is based on Donald J. Black and Albert J. Reiss, Jr.'s report, "Patterns of Behavior in Police and Citizen Transactions," pp. 1-139 in The President's Commission on Law Enforcement and Administration of Justice, *Studies in Crime and Law Enforcement in Major Metropolitan Areas, Field Survey III, Vol. 2* (Washington, D.C.: U.S. Government Printing Office, undated).

Although they are infrequent, antagonistic encounters between police and citizen have assumed considerable symbolic significance. They demonstrate what happens when a patrolman concerned about his physical safety, prestige, and respect encounters an unfriendly citizen. The following scenario is but one of a dozen variations of the same theme. Police on patrol stop a young black male for "routine questioning." A hostile and disrespectful response prompts the officer to frisk and begin abusive questioning. The young black responds in kind, perhaps muttering insults, pulling away. One or the other strikes a blow. The result is a scuffle and an arrest for disorderly conduct, resisting arrest, or felonious assault.[9] Of course, officers are unjustly assaulted at times; legitimately arrested suspects resist arrest. But at times arrests on these charges are an excuse to take action against the behavior that really prompted the episode—*contempt of cop.*[10]

Whether the behavior of one or both parties is justified is immaterial here. The fact that police sometimes react to contempt of cop does not so much discredit them as it illustrates the awesome power that police have. Objectively legal behavior for all practical purposes becomes illegal if the citizen spends 30 days in jail awaiting trial on such a charge because he cannot make bail. He is little comforted by the fact that in an objective sense he committed no crime. The formal coercive power of the state has been invoked against him to his detriment.

---

[9] For a description of a number of specific instances of police misconduct, including improper arrests on these charges, see Paul Chevigney, *Police Power: Police Abuses in New York City* (New York: Pantheon, 1969).

[10] Westley, *Violence and the Police*, p. 122, provides supporting empirical evidence. When he asked his sample of policemen, "When do you think a policeman is justified in roughing a man up?" the reason *most frequently* given (by 37 percent of those questioned) was disrespect for the police.

Discretion in Law Enforcement

Theoretically, law-enforcement activities involve situations where there is little doubt about whether a crime has been committed and no question about the appropriateness of police intervention. Once the basic decision to enforce the law against the particular crime has been made, there should be little room for differential enforcement. In reality things are not so simple. Many of the opportunities to exercise discretion that are found in order maintenance are found here too.

As in order maintenance, it is not always clear whether a crime has been committed. We have already alluded to the difficulties that can arise in ascertaining whether rape has occurred. Assaults resulting in serious injuries may prompt well-substantiated claims of self-defense, forcing the police (though often in close consultation with the prosecutor) to decide whether to institute criminal proceedings at all.

Even when a crime has been committed, discretion remains. The policeman decides who to question, who to hold, who to arrest. Indeed, he decides whether any serious effort at all will be made to solve the crime. Anyone familiar with the social history of the South knows that murders of blacks by whites went largely unpunished. A number of observers of police behavior have remarked that violence between members of the same minority group frequently is not considered to be serious.[11] Such violence is said to be commonplace, and, it is claimed, the victim would not cooperate if a serious investigation were attempted.

Some law-enforcement activities require detectives to decide what laws they will enforce. This is particularly true for crimes without victims, since the police act as complaining witnesses. How they decide to spend their time largely determines what crimes they complain about. Vice-squad detectives might decide to concentrate on developing informers in narcotics and gambling, arresting prostitutes and homosexu-

---

[11] See, for example, La Fave, *Arrest*, p. 492.

als, or cracking down on after-hours drinking clubs, to list a few alternatives.[12]

At higher levels of the police bureaucracy, discretionary decisions are made involving the assignment of tasks to detectives. These have profound effects. Witness the difference between the ways abortion and narcotics statutes were enforced. Until the early 1970s, nearly all abortions in the United States were illegal. Anyone performing or undergoing an illegal abortion was committing a serious felony. The enforcement potential was enormous; violations were commonplace. Most estimates placed the number of illegal abortions at a million or more each year. Obviously, pregnant women had little difficulty finding abortionists. Developing informants and making purchases of abortions would not have been significantly more difficult than in the area of narcotics. Yet practically no arrests were made for abortion. The possession, sale, and use of narcotic drugs was no more illegal objectively. As a *practical* matter, however, selling or using drugs was treated as a criminal act. Abortion was not.

U.S. attorneys told the author how difficult it was to get the FBI to assign men to investigate security frauds and violations of antitrust laws by local merchants. At the same time, they expended considerable effort in apprehending youths who took stolen cars across state lines. Though designed to break up interstate professional theft rings, the statute (the Dyer Act) was being put to a very different use by the way the FBI chose to enforce it.

Most departments assign only a token number of detectives to investigate housing code violations, organized crime activities, and fraud by door-to-door salesmen. Yet these acts are as illegal, objectively, as those of muggers, robbers, and child molesters.

---

[12] An excellent description of this sort of discretion can be found in Joseph Wambaugh's novel, *The New Centurions* (Boston: Little, Brown, 1970), which, though technically a work of fiction, appears to describe rather closely the experiences of its policeman author. See especially Chapters 12 and 14.

Often, law enforcement directed against vice crimes is not designed to eliminate such activities at all. Rather it is an attempt to exercise some control over how they are conducted. Selective arrests may be used to discipline those who violate implicit rules governing the conduct of the illicit activity. Sometimes, such arrests are really directed against other activities. Arrested prostitutes, for instance, may be released in return for their agreement to act as informers in narcotics investigations.[13]

It is not surprising that enforcement efforts designed to regulate illegal activities often involve an element of illicit licensing.[14] Given the lucrative returns from pornography, prostitution, narcotics, and gambling, the impossibility of eliminating such activities entirely, the low visibility of interaction between those providing such services and the police, and the feeling of policemen that they are underpaid, police tolerance in return for cash payments is a natural development.

Systematic and reliable information on the extent of graft and payoffs is as difficult to obtain as are facts on how many students cheat on exams. The President's Commission on Law Enforcement and Administration of Justice said relatively little about the problem except to classify the types of police dishonesty and to acknowledge their existence.[15] Im-

---

[13] Jerome Skolnick, in *Justice Without Trial*, p. 109, has an excellent description of this. Evidently, the police at times harrass such activities solely for the purpose of harrassment. Wambaugh, in *The New Centurions*, Chapter 5, includes an episode where prostitutes are arbitrarily picked up, given an aimless but bumpy ride around the city for a few hours, and then released without being charged.

[14] For a fascinating analysis along these lines, see "Gamblers Links to Police Lead to Virtual Licensing," *The New York Times*, April 26, 1970.

[15] Said the Commission: "The most common [forms of dishonesty] are improper political influence; acceptance of gratuities or bribes in exchange for nonenforcement of laws, particularly those relating to gambling, prostitution, and liquor offenses, which are often extensively interconnected with organized crime; the 'fixing' of traffic tickets,

pressionistic evidence suggests that in some cities, at least, corruption reaches significant levels. Several long articles in *The New York Times*, for example, suggested that payoffs to police from narcotics dealers, businessmen, and gamblers were so commonplace that they amounted to millions of dollars each year. In addition to payoffs from operators of illicit enterprises, owners of small shops provide free food, liquor, and small payments to avoid harrassment on minor charges and builders pay from $40 to $400 per month at each construction site.[16]

Other Aspects of Police Discretion and Impact

The assignment of law-enforcement tasks to detectives is but one of several allocative decisions made by police executives. They also determine what proportion of their total manpower is assigned to uniformed patrol as opposed to detective work. They decide how many uniformed men are to be engaged in *aggressive preventive patrol* and how many are assigned to respond to citizen complaints. They decide to what areas of the community patrolmen are assigned.

Important consequences flow from such choices. Assigning fewer men to detective work means law-enforcement activities involving burglaries and vice are sacrificed to put more uniformed men in the field. By emphasizing aggressive preventive patrols, street crime will more often be detected and the number of *on-view* (i.e., police-initiated) police-citizen encounters increased. The total discretion enjoyed by patrolmen is greater, since the visibility of such encounters is lower than when radio-patrol cars are dispatched from police headquarters in response to citizen calls. As the number of radio-

---

minor thefts, and occasional burglaries." President's Commission on Law Enforcement and Administration of Justice, *Task Force Report: The Police*, p. 208. Brief discussions of police graft can also be found in Arthur Neiderhoffer, *Behind the Shield: The Police in Urban Society* (New York: Anchor, 1969), pp. 69-75, and pp. 176-177; and in Westley, *Violence and the Police*.

[16] See especially David Burnham, "Graft Paid to Police Here Said to Run Into Millions," *The New York Times*, April 25, 1970.

dispatched cars answering citizen calls declines, the police can respond only to the more serious incidents reported. The level of purely *service* activities performed by the police therefore will decline as well. [17]

The significance of the service function is easily overlooked because of its routine and undramatic character. Yet such activities account for a substantial portion of the total effort of many departments. [18] While the impact of rescuing cats from trees is not especially profound, the police also provide many needed emergency social services. They are frequently called when serious illness occurs. [19] Often it is the policeman who makes the decision to call an ambulance when others

---

[17] The following table, modified slightly from its original form as it appears in Wilson, in *Varieties of Police Behavior*, p. 85, summarizes the alternative activities affected by decisions on the detective:patrolman ratio and the dispatched radio-car:aggressive preventive patrol ratio.

	Basis of Police Response	
	Police invoked ("on view")	Citizen invoked (dispatched)
Law enforcement (detectives, mostly)	Crimes without victims (prostitution, gambling, etc.)	Crimes against property; murder
Order maintenance (patrolmen, mostly)	Aggressive preventive patrol; drunkenness; street quarrels	Sick calls; family disputes; other service activities

[18] A study of a West Side Manhattan precinct by the Rand Corporation found "More than half of the specific tasks performed ... were not directly related to crime but involved problems such as taking care of the sick, settling family disputes and freeing passengers from stuck elevators" ("Noncrime Jobs Dominate Police Time," *The New York Times*, August 3, 1970). Wilson, in *Varieties of Police Behavior*, p. 18, reported that 37.5 percent of the citizen complaints dispatched to radio patrol cars in Syracuse during a one week period involved service.

[19] *The New York Times* article cited above found the single specific task taking most of a patrolman's time (15 percent) when he is not riding in his car is on "sick calls."

have failed to do so.[20] Their intervention in bitter family disputes often goes beyond order maintenance to attempts at mediation and reconciliation. Interestingly, police often serve as the vehicle for bringing certain social services to segments of society that cannot or will not obtain them through other means.

Decisions on where to assign patrolmen within a community affect both the total level of crime and where it occurs. James Q. Wilson has identified two competing strategies for the assignment of police protection that illustrate the significance of such decisions well.

One is the 'crime minimization' criterion: allocate patrolmen so that the last one assigned would deter an equal amount of crime no matter where in the city he was placed. This criterion would produce the smallest total amount of crime in the city, but because the deterrence value of a patrolman varies by the type of neighborhood, some neighborhoods would have more crime than others. The other rule is the 'crime equalization' one: allocate patrolmen so that the probability of being victimized is the same in all parts of the city... equalizing victimization rates may be achieved by concentrating police in the most crime-prone areas to drive down those rates while allowing the rates in relatively crime-free areas to rise.[21]

Another important consequence of police discretion is the ability to affect the outcome of cases after an arrest has been made. For minor offenses such as traffic violations, vagrancy, and drunkenness, their initial decision is usually final. Additional, formal legal steps leading to conviction merely ratify as a matter of routine the policeman's initial decision. The sentence is sometimes predetermined, and the police officer affects what penalties are imposed when he decides what to charge. Moving traffic violations, for instance, often carry set

---

[20] David H. Bayley and Harold Mendelsohn, *Minorities and the Police* (New York: Free Press, 1969), p. 64.

[21] Wilson, *Varieties of Police Behavior*, pp. 61–62.

penalties. Where judges do impose sentences at their discretion, the arresting officer nonetheless may be able to influence what it will be.[22]

In more serious cases, police can affect the final disposition in several ways. Since bail is customarily determined by the seriousness of the offense, poorer suspects can be kept in jail by lodging more serious charges. When the normal bail is felt to be insufficient, police sometimes intercede with the judge or prosecutor to have it raised. They may also play important roles in plea bargaining. In some jurisdictions, defense lawyers bargain with the policemen concerned. If an agreement is reached, the prosecutor usually accepts it.[23] Elsewhere, police only infrequently suggest when to go easy and when to throw the book. A number of patterns in between these two extremes are also found. For crimes where arrests and convictions depend upon the use of informers, it is essential that detectives be permitted to make bargains with suspects.[24]

In the few but symbolically important cases that go to trial, police have much to do with whether convictions are obtained. The amount and quality of investigative work devoted to a case is crucial. The police are responsible for getting prosecution witnesses to appear on the day of trial. The nature of police testimony can also be decisive.

---

[22] In his description of the enforcement of vagrancy laws in Philadelphia, for instance, Caleb Foote notes that magistrates often rely upon suggestions of the police in imposing sentence. Thus, a policeman may say to the judge when a case is called, "Judge, this man's in here all the time. He's a regular pest." See "Vagrancy-Type Law and Its Administration," in William Chambliss, ed., *Crime and the Legal Process* (New York: McGraw-Hill, 1969), p. 316.

[23] The President's Commission on Law Enforcement and Administration of Justice, *Task Force Report: The Courts* (Washington, D.C.: U.S. Government Printing Office, 1968), p. 135. Jerome Skolnick found one defense attorney in the community he studied was able to make deals with vice-squad detectives. See "Social Control in the Adversary System," *Journal of Conflict Resolution* 11 (1967), pp. 63-64.

[24] Skolnick, *Justice Without Trial*, has an especially good description of this process in Chapter 6.

Sometimes police testimony helps the prosecutor's case more than it should. Lying and selective recall of the truth are not uncommon human characteristics. This is particularly true when the witness is convinced the defendant is guilty and knows truthful testimony will lead to his acquittal. One such circumstance that has received some public attention involves illegal street searches for narcotics. By claiming the narcotics were discovered when the suspect "dropped" them carelessly, the real possibility of having the case thrown out because evidence was seized through an illegal search is avoided. The practice is so widespread in New York City that such cases are now commonly called "dropsies."[25] Reliable estimates of the frequency of lying, however, do not exist.

No discussion of police discretion and impact can ignore the highly charged topic of police use of unnecessary force. The President's Commission reached several interesting tentative conclusions.[26] Although the commission admitted it could not accurately measure the frequency of unnecessary force, its limited information suggested that it is less of a problem than in the past. Aside from some areas of the South, major complaints about police behavior in surveys center more on use of insulting language, unnecessary searches, and harrassment. Observation of over five thousand police-citizen encounters by the commission revealed that

---

[25] A former assistant district attorney, law school professor, and eventually New York City criminal court judge is one of the few to speak publicly of "dropsies" and police lying in general. See "Judge Says Police Frequently Lie in Drug Cases," *The New York Times*, September 19, 1970; and Irving Younger, "The Perjury Routine," *The Nation*, May 8, 1967, pp. 596-97. Younger observed in the *Nation* article: "Every lawyer who practices in the criminal courts knows that police perjury is commonplace.... All's fair in this war, including the use of perjury to subvert 'liberal' rules of law that might free those who 'ought' to be jailed."

[26] President's Commission on Law Enforcement and Administration of Justice, *Task Force Report: The Police*. This discussion is based on pp. 181-183.

some instances of excessive force still occur, though only in less than one half of a percent of all encounters.[27]

When "rough stuff" is used, it is more likely to be in response to disrespect shown the police, particularly if it is in public.[28] Police feel challenged when a "wise guy" mocks them before a crowd. Their ability to control the situation, the ability of all police to command respect in the future, and their toughness are perceived to be at stake. Unnecessary violence may also be used when the police feel a guilty suspect is unlikely to be punished by anyone else (sex crimes fall into this category because victims are reluctant to testify) or a serious felony can be solved.[29]

Whatever the actual level of excessive force, it cannot be dismissed entirely. The problem is difficult to control since norms of secrecy and police solidarity inhibit officers who disapprove of such tactics from reporting its use by fellow officers.[30]

The Police in Crowd Control and Riots

The now famous Walker report on the disturbances during the Democratic National Convention in Chicago in 1968 concluded that the Chicago police engaged in a "police riot"

---

[27] For descriptions of specific instances of police brutality, see Paul Chevigny, *Police Power*; and Ed Cray, *The Big Blue Line* (New York: Coward-McCann, 1967). Bayley and Mendelsohn, *Minorities and the Police*, p. 126, found over 60 percent of blacks and Mexican-Americans surveyed in Denver claimed they or a member of their family had experienced physical brutality.

[28] As noted previously, Westley, *Violence and the Police*, found that the most frequent reason given for the use of force was disrespect for the police (37 percent), confirming his earlier conclusions regarding the importance of the doctrine "You gotta make them respect you" among police. A total of 66 percent of the men Westley questioned on the matter used an illegal basis as their primary reason for using force. See Table 4.3, p. 122.

[29] *Ibid.*

[30] This is beginning to change in some urban departments as newly recruited black officers strongly object to mistreatment of black prisoners by white officers.

in response to extreme provocation.[31] The report describes a vicious counterreaction by police which led to indiscriminate beatings and clubbings of everyone in sight—tourists, hippies, demonstrators, photographers and newsmen, innocent bystanders, and neighborhood residents.

There is nothing inherently improper about police use of force. It may legitimately be required in the performance of duty. What is distressing to many people is the use of more than necessary force. We can use this notion to define a police riot as any instance where police engaged in crowd control overreact to provocation by doing more than necessary to maintain control.

Under this definition, do the police riot? Unfortunately, there is rather conclusive evidence that they do. How often do they riot? Unfortunately, we don't know. Many incidents are handled beautifully by the police. The "counter-inauguration" was attended by many of the same people who were involved in the confrontations at the Democratic Convention in Chicago several months before. A report of the National Commission on the Causes and Prevention of Violence praised the restraint of the police in refusing to be goaded into a violent confrontation.[32] We never hear about most incidents that are handled well. However, an unknown number of police riots likely occur that also never receive public attention.

What happens to cause police riots? There are several elements common to situations that lead to them. First, the police are confronted with people who dislike them. These same blacks, young "hippies", and war protestors are regarded, in turn, with extreme distaste by the police. Second, a period of confrontation and provocation precedes police action. The police are subjected to a milling and growing

---

[31] Daniel Walker, *Rights in Conflict: A Report to the National Commission on the Causes and Prevention of Violence* (New York: Dutton, 1968).

[32] "Capital Report Finds Police Restraint," *The New York Times*, June 1, 1969.

crowd's verbal abuse. Physical danger from thrown objects exists and begins to increase. It does not take much imagination to guess what the emotional state of a man is when he must stand his ground while he is taunted and in danger of being felled by a rock or bottle. Third, there is a police charge. Restraints are cast aside. The highly negative and strong emotions of the police toward the crowd take control, pushing aside discipline and notions of minimal necessary force. Although it is difficult to condone such behavior, we can at least understand its roots when we recall the content of police attitudes toward politics, their status in society, and the dangers inherent in their work.

Police behavior in physical confrontations with rioters, peace demonstrators, and student protesters have obvious though limited implications for material politics. Police are subjected to verbal abuse and occasional physical danger. Their opponents face the possibility of official punishment through arrest and conviction as well as unofficial physical punishment.

The real significance of such encounters probably lies more in the realm of symbolic politics, however. Millions of people participate emotionally in them when they see, hear, or read news reports. Those who identify with protesting groups are reassured by evidence that like-minded people exist; they are threatened by the police response. Opinion surveys demonstrate that the large majority of people have the opposite reaction. They disapprove of and are frightened by riots and demonstrations, and both support and feel relieved by their suppression. Although many students find it difficult to believe, a majority approved of the behavior of law-enforcement officials during the 1968 Democratic Convention and at Kent State University. Even people who were doves on the Vietnam war in 1968 disapproved of war-protest demonstrations.[33] Although we can only speculate on the psychologi-

---

[33] Philip E. Converse, Warren E. Miller, Jerrold G. Rusk, and Arthur C. Wolfe, "Continuity and Change in American Politics: Parties and Issues in the 1968 Election," *American Political Science Review* 63 (1969), p. 1087. Nearly 40 percent of the doves felt the police had not used enough force at the Chicago convention.

cal reaction of these people, it is plausible that they are relieved to see police use force vigorously. It is a signal to them that threatening people and movements are being dealt with effectively.

THE CRIMINAL PROCESS AS A SCREENING DEVICE

As a consequence of underenforcement and selective enforcement by the police, only a fraction of all those who conceivably could be arrested actually find themselves at the station house. The postarrest disposition process displays the same winnowing features. At every successive step on the road to trial, some defendants are dropped out.

A study of New York City's criminal court for 1967 clearly demonstrated this screening function.[34] Only about 8 percent of those arrested (25,000 of 330,000) had their cases go to trial. In fact, nearly one in four (23 percent) had their cases dismissed by the prosecutor or thrown out by the grand jury. And although 60 percent were convicted, only 10 percent actually went to jail. The vast majority merely paid fines.

Many of the offenses included in these figures were relatively minor. But the general picture for more serious crimes is not substantially different. Figures on the disposition of felony arrests in Brooklyn for 1960–1962 show that one defendant in four had his case dismissed before indictment, less than 2 percent actually had a trial, and somewhere around 60 percent were eventually convicted of something.[35]

The extensive screening out that occurs is a far cry from the naïve view that people committing violations are typically arrested, tried, and imprisoned. The criminal disposition pro-

---

[34] "Criminal Courts: Statistical Profile," *The New York Times*, March 28, 1970.

[35] Abraham Blumberg, *Criminal Justice* (Chicago: Quadrangle Books, 1967), p. 54. Over half of the felony charges were reduced to misdemeanors. No figures are given on how many of these cases resulted in convictions. The 60-percent conviction rate is an estimate. Blumberg does not have data on the number receiving prison sentences.

cess more resembles a gigantic elimination process which selects out a very small minority for the booby prize of imprisonment. It is essential to keep in mind this characteristic of the criminal process. The full significance of any single step can only be understood if its place in the entire process is acknowledged. Studying sentencing, the conduct of trials, or the setting of bail, while important in themselves, must not obscure the fact that many who are arrested never reach these stages.

THE IMPACT OF THE BAIL SYSTEM

We generally pay little attention to the operation of bail. In spite of its low visibility, however, the bail system has a profound impact on those arrested for more serious crimes. Whether the arrested suspect spends his time awaiting trial at liberty or confined in a pretrial detention facility, after all, depends on whether he can make bail. A less obvious consequence of the bail system is its impact on the final disposition of the case.

Historically, the bail system developed as a technique for giving untried defendants their freedom.[36] Bail can be thought of as ransom. The accused supposedly puts up a sum of money he stands to lose if he does not appear for trial.

Although the amount of bail required for release is formally set by a judge or magistrate, in many jurisdictions they delegate the decision by consistently accepting the recommendation of the prosecutor or arresting officer.[37] Since the

[36] Daniel Freed and Patricia Wald, *Bail in the United States: 1964*, Report to the National Conference on Bail and Criminal Justice (Washington, D.C.: 1964) have a brief history of the development of bail. This is the best single source of the bail system's operation.

[37] Lee Silverstein, "Bail in the State Courts—A Field Study and Report," *Minnesota Law Review* 50 (1966), pp. 622–623. See also Freed and Wald, *Bail*, pp. 11, 14, 16; and Frederic Suffett, "Bail Setting: A Study of Courtroom Interaction," in Richard Quinney, ed., *Crime and Justice in Society* (Boston: Little, Brown, 1969). Suffett found that in the jurisdiction he studied, the judge most often determined the amount of bail. The prosecutor also played an important role, and was more influential than defense counsel when a dispute over the amount arose.

purpose of bail is to insure that the defendant does not flee the jurisdiction, presumably the level of bail should be influenced by factors affecting the likelihood that he will appear. These include the seriousness of charges, the likelihood of conviction, the defendant's prior criminal record, his financial resources, and the strength of his ties to the local community.

In practice, only seriousness of the offense and prior record are usually considered. In many jurisdictions, standard amounts are imposed depending on the crime.[38] These serve as minimums, and are raised for defendants with long records. Elsewhere, the determination of bail levels are individualized. But only rarely are such factors as the strength of the evidence, the defendant's ties to the community, or his ability to make bail taken into account. Though unemployed drifters are more likely to leave town than a life-long resident with a steady job and family, in most jurisdictions their bail will be set at the same level.

Few generalizations can be made about the bail level for a given crime. Those charged with forgery, for example, are most often required to post $1,000 bail, but the typical amount in some jurisdictions varies from $500 to $5,000.[39] There are also differences in the types of offenses that are bailable. No absolute right to bail exists in capital cases, though even the most serious crimes are often bailable at the discretion of the judge.

The specifics of how one obtains his release also vary. It is possible to deposit a fraction (often 10 percent) of the bail amount in cash with the court in a few states. The defendant then receives 90 percent of his deposit when he appears. Most jurisdictions will accept payment of the full amount of bail in cash or other property. But the most common technique is to hire a professional bail bondsman to post a bond with the court on behalf of the defendant. The court supposedly

---

[38] Freed and Wald, *Bail*, p. 16, report the findings of a study conducted in Washington, D.C. that found the minimum bail for *any* felony was $1,000.

[39] Silverstein, "Bail in the State Courts," p. 623.

requires the bondsman to forfeit the amount of the bond if the defendant does not appear.

Bondsmen are private entrepreneurs (though often backed by large insurance companies in urban areas). They are in business to make money. Their fees vary considerably from city to city. A flat rate of 10 percent of the face value of the bond is charged in many cities, but fees range from a low of 5 percent on the first $1,000, 4 percent on the next $1,000, and 3 percent on the balance in New York, to a high of 20 percent for some crimes in Birmingham, Alabama.[40] In addition to the regular fee, some bondsmen charge a service fee. A few apparently extract illegal supplementary payments from their clients as well.[41]

The discretion of bondsmen is substantial. For the overwhelming majority of defendants who cannot meet requirements for posting their own bail, bondsmen in effect hold the keys to the jailhouse in their pockets. They can require collateral in the full amount of the bond (title to a house or car, indeed anything of value) before writing a bond.[42] They can demand their full commission or extend credit and permit installment payments. They can even refuse to write a bond when the defendant has full collateral. They may cancel a client's bond at any time by surrendering him to the court, but are allowed to keep their fees nonetheless.

Ironically, bondsmen use many of the criteria that predict the likelihood of appearance (ties to the community, employment) that are ignored by the court. It is also somewhat ironic that when bondsmen do not require collateral of the defendant, the basic rationale for bail disappears. If he does not appear, the defendant does not lose money, the bonds-

---

[40] Freed and Wald, *Bail*, pp. 23-24.

[41] *Ibid.*

[42] "If a person comes in and I don't know him or his lawyer," observed a New York City bondsman, "we look for collateral; if they don't have it we don't bother with them." Quoted from a *New York Times* article by Freed and Wald in *Bail*, p. 27.

man does.[43] The defendant has already lost his money through the nonreturnable bondsman's fee. Although nonappearance is a crime, it has nothing to do with the amount of bail forfeited.

Since fees are based on the amount of bail, many people are unable to afford the bondsman's services. Figures from Washington, D.C. for 1963 found that 26 percent of those with $500 bail could not post it; at $1,000, it was 46 percent; at $3,000, 79 percent; and at $7,500, 96 percent.[44] Overall, 52 percent of defendants who had a bail level set could not obtain their release.[45] A study of 11,000 felony cases in 190 counties throughout the country found a similar pattern.[46] It also uncovered wide variation in release rates. Only 25 percent of all defendants made bail in Chicago, for example, while in Philadelphia, 86 percent did.[47]

Those who cannot afford bail obviously spend some time in jail. In New York City, nearly 60 thousand did so in 1962.[48] Nationwide, between 30 and 70 percent of inmates of city and county jails are pretrial detainees who cannot afford bail.[49] The amount of time they spend there is often substantial. Though it varies from city to city, stays of a month are not uncommon. In Los Angeles, for instance, the average was 78 days in 1963; in St. Louis, it was six weeks.[50]

[43] Many bondsmen are themselves insured against such loss by major insurance companies. In practice, courts are very lenient, granting extensive grace periods before forfeiting a bond, reducing the amount forfeited, and returning forfeited bonds if the defendant is subsequently apprehended. Freed and Wald, *Bail*, pp. 28-30.

[44] David J. McCarthy, Jr., and Jeanne J. Wahl, "The District of Columbia Bail Project: An Illustration of Experimentation and a Brief For Change," *Georgetown Law Journal* 53 (1965), p. 684.

[45] *Ibid.*, p. 685.

[46] Silverstein, "Bail in the State Courts," p. 624.

[47] *Ibid.*

[48] Patricia Wald, "Pretrial Detention and Ultimate Freedom: A Statistical Study," *New York University Law Review* 39 (1964), p. 634.

[49] *Ibid.*

[50] Freed and Wald, *Bail*, p. 40.

The only way to fully understand the impact of pretrial detention is to experience it, though the descriptions of the quality of detention facilities in Chapter 9 can convey its flavor. The impact is all the more dramatic when the detained defendant is never convicted. Place yourself in the shoes of the man described by President Johnson in signing the Bail Reform Act of 1966: "A man was jailed on a serious charge brought last Christmas Eve. He could not afford bail and spent 101 days in jail until a hearing. Then the complainant admitted the charge was false."[51] Such incidents do not appear to be isolated. One out of every four felony defendants unable to make bail in Washington, D.C. had their cases dismissed or informally dropped.[52] Well over half of them spent a month or more in jail before release.

Perhaps most startling, however, is the apparent effect of pretrial detention on the outcome of cases. Nearly every study of bail practices has found that jailed defendants are more likely to be convicted and more likely to get additional prison sentences than defendants out on bail. The figures from a study of bail in New York City are both typical and striking:[53]

	Out on bail (N=374)	In jail (unable to raise bail) (N=358)
Imprisoned	17%	64%
Convicted, but not imprisoned	36%	9%
Not convicted	47%	27%
Total	100%	100%

[51] President's Commission on Law Enforcement and Administration of Justice, *Task Force Report: The Courts*, p. 38.

[52] McCarthy and Wahl, "The District of Columbia Bail Project," p. 687.

[53] This table is based on figures presented in Ann Rankin, "Effects of Pretrial Detention," *New York University Law Review* 39 (1964), p. 642. Table 1. Freed and Wald, in *Bail* cite a number of studies with similar findings: In Washington, D.C., 25 percent of a group out on bail were given probation, compared to only 6 percent of those in jail; In Philadelphia, 82 percent of jailed defendants were convicted compared to 52 percent out on bail; and among convicted bailed defendants, 22 percent were given prison terms compared to 59 percent of convicted defendants not out on bail (see pp. 46–47).

Of course, it is possible that there is something about defendants and the crimes with which they are charged that causes them both to be released on bail *and* to receive fewer convictions and sentences. Those who cannot make bail may be charged with more serious crimes (leading to harsher sentences) and find they cannot afford the higher bail such crimes produce. However, if we examine defendants in jail and on bail who are charged with the *same* crimes, the differences remain: [54]

	On bail		In jail	
Crime	Percentage convicted	Percentage given prison	Percentage convicted	Percentage given prison
Assault	23	58	59	94
Robbery	51	78	58	97
Dangerous weapons	43	70	57	91

Alternatively, men with no criminal record, whose bail may be less, may be more often acquitted and prove to be better candidates for probation if convicted. One study found those with no criminal records were convicted 61 percent of the time; those with records had an 82 percent conviction rate. The difference in whether prison sentences were imposed or not was more dramatic, 29 percent and 63 percent, respectively. [55] Further analysis showed, however, that being free or in jail still had an independent effect on the outcome. Some defendants with no criminal records nevertheless could not make bail. Seventy-six percent of these were convicted compared to only 52 percent of their counterparts who did make bail. Differences in the number going to prison were even greater. Only 10 percent of those with no records who

---

[54] This table was compiled from data presented in Charles Ares, Ann Rankin, and Herbert Sturz, "The Manhattan Bail Project: An Interim Report on the Use of Pre-trial Parole," *New York University Law Review* 38 (1963), pp. 84–85.

[55] Rankin, "Effects of Pretrial Detention," p. 645.

made bail ended up in prison; 59 percent with no records who stayed in jail got additional prison terms. Similar differences were found when bailed and jailed defendants who did have prior records were compared.[56] Whether the defendant had appointed or privately retained counsel also affected the conviction rate and prison rate, but being out on bail still had an independent effect.

This independent effect of bail was most convincingly demonstrated by an experiment conducted by the Vera Foundation's Bail Project. Briefly, the project used volunteers to interview recently arrested suspects to determine if their ties to the community were strong enough to make them good risks for release on their own recognizance (i.e., outright release without any bail required).[57] Their success was dramatic—the number of defendants released without bail increased fourfold without any increase in the number who did not appear.[58] The experiment consisted of randomly dividing all those who met the project's standards for a recommendation of a no-bail release into two groups. Those in the first group were recommended to the court for release on their own recognizance; those in the second, equally qualified for release, were not. While 59 percent of the first

---

[56] Rankin, "Effects of Pretrial Detention," p. 647. Here is a table summarizing these findings:

	Defendants with no prior record		Defendants with prior record	
	Out on bail	In jail unable to make bail	Out on bail	In jail unable to make bail
Prison	10%	59%	36%	81%
Convicted, but no prison	42%	17%	43%	4%
Not convicted	48%	24%	21%	15%
	100%	100%	100%	100%

[57] The project is described in Ares, Rankin, and Sturz, "The Manhattan Bail Project."

[58] Ibid., p. 86.

group were released without bail, only 16 percent in the second (control) group were. Differences in the outcomes of their cases were dramatic. Sixty percent of the first group were acquitted or had their cases dismissed, but only 23 percent of the control group received such a favorable disposition. And nearly all those convicted in the control group (96 percent) were sentenced to prison, compared to only about 16 percent of those convicted from the first group.[59]

The evidence is fairly compelling. The inability to make bail significantly decreases a defendant's chances of obtaining a dismissal or acquittal and avoiding a prison sentence in the event he is convicted. Reasonable explanations exist of why this is so. A man at liberty can help his lawyer in the preparation of his case in a number of ways: He is readily available to the lawyer; he can locate witnesses and evidence; he can persuade witnesses to testify.[60] His case becomes stronger, making acquittal after trial more likely. Meanwhile, this strengthens the hand of the lawyer in arguing for dismissal of the case.

Judges are more likely to give suspended sentences or probation to defendants who have been free on bail. Patricia Wald sets forth the reasons for this:

... a detained defendant can no longer be a jobholder or the operating head of his household. Indeed, his family may well be on relief. His social life has probably disintegrated; his psychological makeup at the moment is likely to be a mixture of anxiety, depression, hostility, and bitterness. ... how do the rehabilitative prospects of such a man compare objectively with an at-large defendant who has remained a functioning economic and social unit in society, who has proved his capacity for responsible behavior by voluntarily presenting himself in court and staying out of trouble between arrest and sentence?[61]

---

[59] This description of the experiment is drawn from Freed and Wald, *Bail*, p. 63.
[60] Wald, "Pretrial Detention," p. 637.
[61] *Ibid.*, p. 632.

Is bail often set excessively high—that is, higher than necessary to insure the defendant appears? The results of the bail project experiments conducted by the Vera Foundation in New York (and similar projects elsewhere) suggest that it is. Many defendants can be released on their own recognizance without any increase in the nonappearance rate.[62] In Connecticut, a statewide bail-reform program increased the proportion of defendants released without bail from 21 percent to 61 percent with no rise in the nonappearance rate.[63]

If more defendants could be released without bail, with all of the benefits that go along with pretrial freedom, why aren't they? Inertia is part of the explanation. Established procedures that set bail within existing time and resource constraints are not readily abandoned. But other considerations reinforce simple inertia. Prosecutors and judges feel they have little to lose if some defendants who could be released are detained. But if a released defendant commits a serious and highly publicized crime, they feel vulnerable to criticism. Some judges set bail high enough to insure incarceration because they feel the defendant (particularly if he is young or likely to be acquitted) deserves "a taste of jail." And prosecutors evidently do not object to the fact that bailed defendants are more likely to receive a conviction. Finally, bail bondsmen, who frequently have close interpersonal and political ties to other members of the criminal court community, benefit from high bail levels.[64]

Some factors operate to limit bail levels, of course. If bail is

---

[62] Ares, Rankin, and Sturz, "The Manhattan Bail Project."

[63] Thomas O'Rourke and Robert F. Carter, "The Connecticut Bail Commission," *Yale Law Journal* 79 (1970), pp. 513-530. Unfortunately, the program was terminated by the legislature shortly after it was instituted. The proportion of no-bail releases immediately dropped from 61 percent to 35 percent.

[64] A fascinating example of the leverage of bondsmen with the rest of the court community is the bail bondsmen's "strike." By refusing to write any bonds, detention facilities rapidly reach the saturation point. New York bondsmen have used this technique in the past to protest overzealousness on the part of district attorneys in pressing for forfeiture of bonds. See Freed and Wald, *Bail*, pp. 27-28.

too high, few defendants will be able to afford it. This is not good for the bondsmen. Nor do wardens of overcrowded prisons relish the prospect of even more inmates. The number that can be accommodated is limited, making the release of some defendants inevitable.

GENERAL OBSERVATIONS ON THE CRIMINAL PROCESS AT THE STATE LEVEL

Descriptions of the police and bail systems have provided indirect glimpses at the importance of prosecutors, defense attorneys, and judges in the criminal process. Here we shall examine their impact in summary fashion by describing the patterns that emerge in the way their decisions are made.

"Guilty, Please!" The Conviction of Criminal Suspects

In many jurisdictions, preindictment screening of arrestees results in the dismissal of significant numbers of cases.[65] But once the decision to proceed with prosecution is made, the overwhelming majority result in guilty pleas. As noted in Chapter 6, acquittals are extremely rare, and upward of 90 percent of all convictions are obtained by guilty pleas. The practice is so widespread, and the pressures on defendants so compelling that the criminal process can fairly be described by the phrase "Guilty, please." The defendant is in effect told to plead guilty. Formal steps in the process leading to the plea amount to a procedural, perfunctory, "please."

Several important consequences flow from this:

1. Experienced defendants often display considerable skill in bargaining, with the result that they may obtain a lesser sentence to a

---

[65] In Los Angeles, 50 percent of all arrests are rejected by the prosecutor and leave the criminal process. In Detroit the figure is 30 percent and in Houston, 25 percent. Donald M. McIntyre and David Lippman, "Prosecutors and Early Disposition of Felony Cases," *American Bar Association Journal* 56 (1970), p. 1156. This is not universally true, however. In fact, differences in the disposition process between cities as revealed in this article are striking.

lesser charge than inexperienced defendants who have committed the same acts.[66]
2. The determination of guilt and the imposition of sentence are based not upon examination of evidence, but on the bargaining skill of the accused or his official bargaining representative.[67]
3. Important decisions that are the formal responsibility of judges and juries (appropriate sentences, guilt and innocence) are made instead by prosecutors and defense lawyers who take other factors (case load, conviction rate, receiving profitable fees for time spent) into account.[68]
4. Prosecutors may offer particularly attractive bargains in order to prevent the exposure of potentially damaging or embarrassing aspects of a case. A blatantly illegal search by the police, the use of unnecessary force, or the identity of a key informer all remain invisible if a trial can be avoided.[69]
5. The weaker the evidence, the stronger the pressure on the defendant to plead guilty.[70] Because prosecutors seek to obtain convictions and avoid defeats, they are willing to offer very attractive deals (reduced charges and probation) in serious crimes when conviction is doubtful but not impossible. The defendant is presented with an agonizing choice of pleading guilty and obtaining his freedom or going to trial. At best, he will be acquitted and

---

[66] Donald J. Newman, "Pleading Guilty for Considerations: A Study of Bargain Justice," *Journal of Criminal Law, Criminology, and Police Science* 46 (1956), p. 790.

[67] *Ibid.*

[68] One defendant's attorney has argued that he has a duty to bargain since prosecutors charge more than the defendant's actions warrant. Not to bargain runs the risk of conviction on the "wrong" offense and leads to an unfair sentence. The lawyer, then, must make judgments on the fairness of sentences before agreeing to plead guilty. Robert Polstein, "How to 'Settle' a Criminal Case," *Practical Lawyer* 8 (1962), p. 35.

[69] Arthur Rosett, "The Negotiated Guilty Plea," *The Annals of the American Academy of Political Science* 374 (1967), p. 74. See also Albert W. Alschuler, "The Prosecutor's Role in Plea Bargaining," *University of Chicago Law Review* 36 (1968), pp. 82–83.

[70] For an insightful discussion of this, see Alschuler, "The Prosecutor's Role in Plea Bargaining," p. 62.

freed. But there is some possibility that he will be convicted on the serious charge and receive a substantial sentence.
6. Some defendants are embittered by their experience, particularly when they discover men in prison who committed the same crime but who received a lighter sentence than theirs.

Patterns of Decision-making in the Criminal Process

Many of these attributes of the "Guilty, please" system characterize the criminal process at the state level as a whole:

1. The location of effective decision-making has been displaced from where legal theory says it ought to be.

    Police (and prosecutors) decide what is illegal as a practical matter: Decisions on guilt often are not made by judges or juries; frequently, neither are the sentences. Instead, police, prosecutors, and defense attorneys make them. Those who have an influence on bail levels affect whether (and how much) an individual will be punished before final disposition of his case.

2. Many important decisions are routinized, and made informally rather than in a formal, legalistic manner.

    State criminal courts are bureaucratic structures in which various actors cooperate to process large numbers of clients while satisfying basic needs of their own.

3. Consequently, criteria in making these decisions stray from strictly legal criteria.

    Economic and administrative pressures on the major actors lead to the "Guilty, please" system. Low visibility and discretion in the decisions of police make their personal values and prejudices important in deciding what laws will be enforced in what ways and against whom. Prosecutors affect the length of sentences by taking into account such factors as their case backlog, the ability of the defense attorney, and the strength of the evidence. Penological considerations are secondary.

4. In practice there is a presumption of guilt, not a presumption of innocence.

    The underlying assumption beneath police treatment of the young, black, and poor, the impact of the bail system, and the pressure for guilty pleas is that the suspect is guilty as charged.

5. Considerable disparities exist in the disposition of cases even though the crimes committed are identical. Defendants who cannot afford the bondsman's fee are more likely to be convicted and more likely to be imprisoned after conviction. Prison sentences for the same crimes vary substantially.[71] The defendant's prior criminal record, whether he was out on bail, and the individual proclivities of judges have all been found to affect sentences.[72]

The Impact of the Criminal Process on Who Gets What

A major function of the criminal process is to attach formally the label *criminal* to individuals who engage in certain types of behavior and are brought into the criminal process. Whether such labeling is just or unjust is irrelevant to the fact that consequences flow from it. In addition to the possibility of imprisonment, individuals so labeled are affected in several other important ways. Convicted felons can lose a number of legal rights and obligations (such as the right to vote, the obligation to serve in the armed forces). Their future career chances are jeopardized. Felony convictions can preclude the practice of law or medicine. Getting any kind of legitimate employment is more difficult for a man with a record.[73] The

---

[71] Julian C. D'Esposito, Jr., in "Sentencing Disparity: Causes and Cures," *Journal of Criminal Law, Criminology, and Police Science* 60 (1969), p. 183, compares the average sentence for the same crime in adjoining federal judicial districts. Narcotics violators in North Carolina received an average 77.6-month sentence; in South Carolina it was 56.3. Forgery convictions resulted in a 43-month average in the Western District of Texas; in the Southern District, it was 27.2. The same offense in northern Indiana brought 36 months, but in southern Indiana it was 19.6 months. See also Frederic J. Gaudet, "Individual Differences in the Sentencing Tendencies of Judges," *Archives of Psychology* 32 (1938), pp. 5–55.

[72] Edward Green, *Judicial Attitudes in Sentencing* (New York: St. Martins Press, 1961), pp. 97–103; Albert Somit, Joseph Tanenhaus, and Walter Wilke, "Aspects of Judicial Sentencing Behavior," *University of Pittsburgh Law Review* 21 (1960), pp. 613–621, also reprinted in Glendon Schubert, ed., *Judicial Behavior* (Chicago: Rand McNally, 1964).

[73] Richard Schwartz and Jerome Skolnick, "Two Studies of Legal Stigma," *Social Problems* 10 (1962), pp. 133–142.

police naturally tend to focus their attention on known criminals. This probably increases the likelihood of their getting caught when new crimes are committed. But it also means greater harrassment (i.e., being picked up and questioned as a suspect when innocent, being stopped for routine questioning). Finally, the experience of first offenders in the criminal process and in prison can dispose them to commit crimes in the future. Considerable resentment and bitterness are generated by arrest and pretrial detention. A common explanation for the high recidivism rate of prison inmates is that prison socializes and educates them in criminal behavior patterns. Claude Brown's matter-of-fact description of the consequences of his stay in a juvenile facility makes the point well: "We all came out of Warwick better criminals. Other guys were better for the things I could teach them, and I was better for the things they could teach me." [74]

A GLIMPSE AT THE JUVENILE JUSTICE SYSTEM

The juvenile justice system is important both for the number of people it affects and its impact on their lives. Approximately one out of every four arrests for nontraffic offenses involves someone under 18. [75] This means that close to two million youths are arrested, and the number of encounters with police that do not result in arrest is probably even greater. Though many arrested juveniles are not referred to juvenile court, the majority probably are. [76] Somewhere be-

---

[74] Claude Brown, *Manchild in the Promised Land* (New York: Signet, 1965), p. 146.

[75] U.S. Department of Justice, Federal Bureau of Investigation, *Uniform Crime Reports: 1969* (Washington, D.C.: U.S. Government Printing Office, 1970), p. 33.

[76] *Ibid.*, Table 18. FBI statistics from jurisdictions with an estimated population of 106,775,000 show that 51 percent of arrested juveniles were referred to juvenile court. Most of the rest were handled within the police departments and then released.

tween 750,000 and one million find themselves in juvenile court each year to face charges.[77]

Juveniles charged with standard adult crimes are not the only ones who come under the jurisdiction of the juvenile court. Many are there for acts that would not be criminal if engaged in by an adult—drinking, staying out late at night (curfew violation), truancy, running away. In addition, neglected and dependent children—those who have been grossly mistreated, or sometimes simply abandoned by their parents —fall within the jurisdiction and responsibility of juvenile courts. Both categories account for a significant proportion of the matters handled. In 1967, nearly half of the cases heard in Cook County (Chicago) Juvenile Court involved minors in need of supervision (runaways, truants, ungovernables), dependent children, and victims of neglect.[78]

Some form of probation is the typical disposition of the delinquency cases. But significant numbers of youths are sent to state training schools, juvenile homes, and the like. The daily average population in these institutions was nearly 63 thousand in 1965.[79] As the quote from Claude Brown cited earlier suggests, these institutions do more to train their inmates as criminals than to rehabilitate them. Conditions in many of them are likely to stir the anger and outrage of anyone sympathetic to the problems of juveniles. A journalist who spent a year examining these institutions throughout the country found most were overcrowded, old, lacking in adequate recreational and educational facilities, and staffed by underpaid, untrained, and sometimes brutal, guards and ad-

---

[77] Peter G. Garabedian and Don C. Gibbons, eds., *Becoming Delinquent* (Chicago: Aldine, 1970), cite figures for 1967 from the U.S. Children's Bureau which places the number at 811,000. See p. 3.

[78] These figures are cited in Norval Morris and Gordon Hawkins, *The Honest Politician's Guide to Crime Control* (Chicago: University of Chicago Press, 1970), p. 160.

[79] Garabedian and Gibbons, *Becoming Delinquent*, p. 3. Another source suggests that anywhere from 30 to 48 percent of juvenile inmates have not engaged in acts that would be criminal for an adult. William H. Sheridan, "Delinquents Without Crimes," in Paul Lerman, ed., *Delinquency and Social Policy* (New York: Praeger, 1970), p. 70.

ministrators.[80] The fact that nondelinquents (runaways, victims of neglect, and abandoned children) are sometimes held in local jails and juvenile detention centers, often mixed with criminal offenders, while awaiting the court's decision on what should be done with them particularly shocked this reporter.[81]

Less dramatic but probably more important in the long run is the apparent tendency of the juvenile justice system to transform youths into delinquents and eventually into criminals as a result of their contacts with the police, juvenile court judges, probation officers, and detention facilities. Most children engage in acts that qualify them as delinquent or potentially delinquent at one time or another.[82] Discretionary police decisions on where to patrol and what complaints to respond to, and what to do once a youth has been apprehended result in some becoming known to the police as troublemakers while others are not.[83] Once the process of identification as a delinquent begins, the likelihood of further contact with the police increases. Many juveniles respond by further modifying their behavior to conform with their new status and self-image as "no good" and "delinquent."[84]

---

[80] Howard James, *Children in Trouble* (New York: McKay, 1970).

[81] *Ibid.*, especially Chapter 2.

[82] James Short, Jr., and F. Ivan Nye, "Extent of Unrecorded Juvenile Delinquency: Tentative Conclusions," *Journal of Criminal Law, Criminology, and Police Science* 49 (1958), p. 301.

[83] Irving Piliavin and Scott Briar, in "Police Encounters with Juveniles," *American Journal of Sociology* 70 (1964), pp. 206-214, describe factors shaping the discretionary decisions of police when they are dealing with juveniles. The demeanor and attitude of the youth prove to be crucial.

[84] Edwin M. Lemert, "The Juvenile Court—Quest and Realities," in The President's Commission on Law Enforcement and Administration of Justice, *Task Force Report: Juvenile Deliquency and Youth Crime* (Washington, D.C.: U.S. Government Printing Office, 1967), pp. 91-106. Lemert observes that "the juvenile court may become a connecting or intervening link of a serious circle in which delinquency causes delinquency," and later that "The conclusion that the court processing rather than the behavior in some way helps to fix and perpetuate delinquency in many cases is hard to escape."

The juvenile justice system resembles the criminal process generally in the impact imprisonment has and in its functioning as a screening process. Other similarities exist. Like adult criminal courts, juvenile courts have a number of bureaucratic features. Large numbers of cases must be disposed of with limited resources. Like lower criminal courts, the legal training, ability, and dedication of judges and other court personnel often matches their low salary and prestige.[85] And, like lower criminal courts for adults, the decisions of juvenile courts are not visible to those outside of the inner circle of regulars. Requirements that the names of juveniles remain secret and that hearings be closed to the public and press guarantee low visibility.

Much has been written on the theory behind separate courts for juveniles.[86] Unlike adult courts, juvenile courts are supposed to be largely treatment oriented. Dispositions are to follow the principle of "treatment according to need, rather than punishment for the offense."[87] In line with the treatment theory, records and proceedings are kept secret to "protect" the child, procedures followed are informal, and (until recently) attorneys were rarely if ever present. Recent Supreme Court decisions, *In re Gault*[88] in particular, have stated that many rights afforded adult defendants (being informed of the charges brought, right to counsel, prohibition against self-incrimination, right to confront and to cross-examine witnesses) must be extended to juveniles as well. It is not likely, however, that the overall operation of juvenile courts would be affected by faithful implementation of these rights any more than adult criminal courts are affected by them.

[85] Mason P. Thomas, "Juvenile Delinquency and the Juvenile Court," in Elmer R. Oettinger, ed., *Administration of Criminal Justice* (Chapel Hill, N.C.: Institute of Government, 1967), p. 97.

[86] See Lemert, "The Juvenile Court," for a good discussion of the rationales offered for juvenile courts.

[87] Thomas, "Juvenile Delinquency," p. 93.

[88] 387 U.S. 1 (1967).

THE IMPACT OF THE FEDERAL CRIMINAL PROCESS

In terms of the number of defendants involved, the federal criminal process is dwarfed by state criminal systems. Each year, some 30 to 35 thousand criminal prosecutions are initiated by the federal government in district courts. Many are routine. There is little conflict over the desirability and necessity of devoting investigative and prosecutorial resources to them. They are routinely investigated and prosecuted, and rarely raise significant policy questions.[89] Of course, the impact of prosecution is profound on the defendants routinely prosecuted, their families, and sometimes even the victims of their crimes.[90] Also, unexamined decisions on what crimes will be investigated, as the previous discussion on police noted, can have important implications for policy.

There are some criminal prosecutions, however, which assume special significance. Conscious policy decisions of the Department of Justice, which in turn may be related to the general policies of a national administration, account for some prosecutions. The Nixon administration's drive against organized crime and its prosecution of the Chicago 7 and other radical dissidents can be traced in part to the president's rhetoric in the 1968 election campaign and his ensuing policies consistent with it. Even the conduct of foreign policy

---

[89] There are exceptions, however. For instance, a criminal prosecution for draft evasion led to a decision declaring unconstitutional the portion of the Selective Service Act requiring conscientious objectors to be opposed to all wars. See "Some District Judges Establish Precedents on Tough Social Issues," *The Wall Street Journal*, December 14, 1970.

[90] Some understanding of the shape the impact of such prosecutions take can be gained from the relative frequencies of prosecutions for different offenses. The most important ones, with their percentage contribution to total federal prosecutions between 1964 and 1968 include: auto theft (15.4 percent), forgery and counterfeiting (11.3 percent), narcotics (9.3 percent), larceny and theft (8.6 percent), immigration offenses (8.5 percent), liquor and internal revenue (6.3 percent), fraud (6.1 percent), selective service violations (5.9 percent). Sheldon Goldman and Thomas Jahnige, *The Federal Courts as a Political System* (New York: Harper & Row, 1971), p. 103.

may lead an administration to rely upon federal district courts. When *The New York Times* began publishing its series on the "Pentagon Papers," the administration sought and obtained an injunction in federal district court against their publication. Although ultimately reversed by the U.S. Supreme Court, the injunction effectively prevented further publication until the Supreme Court's decision.

Other criminal prosecutions of special significance result from the initiatives of local U.S. attorneys in the various districts. Aggressive and innovative U.S. attorneys are able to bring a variety of cases which have a significant impact. Examples of important cases brought at the initiative of U.S. attorneys include: [91] prosecution of officers of a politically potent local union; prosecution of a jewelry firm which relied upon sewer service to obtain default judgments from its customers; prosecution of fraudulent "debt consolidation firms"; prosecution of wealthy citizens for income tax evasion through the use of illegal Swiss bank accounts; prosecution of local construction unions for discriminatory hiring practices. Much of the considerable impact U.S. attorneys have is realized through litigation in the federal district courts.

AUXILIARY LAW ENFORCEMENT AND PUBLIC POLICY

The analysis of the criminal process throughout this chapter has assumed that the participants are primarily interested in performing their assigned tasks in the law-enforcement process. Laws are enforced for their own sake without ulterior motives on the part of the enforcer. Disturbances of public order are handled, violent crimes investigated, regulations enforced. But law-enforcement activities may also be motivated by ulterior considerations as a means of implementing

---

[91] These examples are drawn from the author's research. See James Eisenstein, *Counsel for the United States: An Empirical Analysis of the Office of United States Attorney* (Ph.D. diss., Yale University, 1968), especially Chapter VI.

policies designed to accomplish ends only incidentally related to law enforcement.

Although it is not always easy to determine whether someone's actions constitute primary or auxiliary law enforcement, there is little question that participants in the legal process engage in such auxiliary behavior. After all, it must be very tempting to those who control the mechanisms of the criminal process to invoke its sanctions to achieve other ends. Prosecutors, police, judges, and others find the criminal process readily available, and its sanctions are potent. The indictment and trial of an individual, even if an acquittal results, can have a significant impact on his life. Because use of the criminal process carries with it the image of legality, the real reasons for which action is being taken can easily be cloaked.

A variety of officials can utilize the criminal process to further external goals. Prosecutors are perhaps the most obvious officials to do so. Journalistic views of prosecutors emphasize their opportunities to bring cases that embarrass the other political party, that bring them extensive publicity, or that relieve pressures from police, press, and the public to do something about notorious crimes or crime waves.

Broader policy considerations may underlie decisions to prosecute what some refer to as "political trials." Of course, whether a particular case is political or merely impartial law enforcement depends upon the personal values of the speaker. For our purposes, it makes little difference whether the label *political trial* is attached to the prosecution of Dr. Spock, the Chicago 7, Daniel Ellsberg, or anyone else. What is relevant are the calculations of prosecutors in deciding whether to proceed or not. Generally, prosecutors are keenly aware of the political ramifications such cases are likely to involve. [92]

---

[92] In the case of the Chicago 7, the Justice Department reportedly decided not to prosecute, but the new Republican administration evidently reversed the decision and asked the U.S. attorney to bring the matter before the grand jury. See Richard Harris, "The Annals of Justice," *The New Yorker*, November 22, 1969, p. 112. Others will dispute this view, claiming Johnson's attorney general, Ramsey Clark, had decided to go ahead, fully recognizing its political overtones.

Decisions to prosecute for auxiliary purposes are not confined to questions of symbolic politics on the national level. A study of the practices of Nebraska sheriffs and county attorneys found that individuals who had passed bad checks were often threatened with prosecution to coerce them into making the checks to the merchants good. Much of the activity in this area appears designed to provide a free collection service to local merchants. [93]

The police are in a particularly strong position to be able to harrass. "Troublemakers," persons who file complaints against the police, or opponents of an entrenched political machine may all find they are frequently stopped and searched, ticketed, and even arrested, only to be released shortly afterward. The enforcement of vagrancy laws often has the explicit purpose of controlling the location and movement of those regarded as undesirable. Well-publicized drives are launched to clear out vagrants and beggers from certain parts of a community. [94]

Other examples of auxiliary law enforcement have already been presented in different contexts. Bail is often set at impossibly high levels to give defendants a taste of jail or to insure they commit no additional crimes while awaiting trial. Vice-squad members may make arrests to reassert their regulatory control over the vice operation or to sanction those who fail to come up with bribes and payoffs.

Other public officials, with the cooperation of police or prosecutors, may use the threat of criminal proceedings to

---

[93] Frederick K. Beutel, *Some Potentialities of Experimental Jurisprudence as a New Branch of Social Science* (Lincoln, Neb.: University of Nebraska Press, 1957), pp. 279-298. Beutel asserts that failure to provide this service results in opposition to the reelection of these officials (p. 293).

[94] Caleb Foote, in "Vagrancy-Type Law and its Administration," *University of Pennsylvania Law Review* 104 (1956), pp. 630-650, describes such a drive and its consequences in Philadelphia in the early 1950s. See the earlier discussion of this in Chapter 6 for a more detailed description.

achieve policy goals. Welfare agencies, for example, have threatened to bring child-neglect proceedings against women with illegitimate children to discourage them from applying for welfare. [95] While this by no means exhausts the examples, [96] it is incorrect to assume that all law-enforcement or order-maintenance activities are motivated by such ulterior considerations. Most are not. Yet it is also misleading to take all law-enforcement activities at their face value and ignore any nonlegal motives that may prompt them. Resources for policy-making are in the hands of the officials who make up the machinery of the legal process. This can result in law-in-action embracing areas and policies neither considered nor condoned by legislative enactment.

---

[95] Patricia Wald, *Law and Poverty* (Washington, D.C.: U.S. Government Printing Office, 1965), pp. 8-9. According to Matthew Holden, the Monmouth (New Jersey) Welfare Board announced it would ask the prosecutor to file charges of adultery and fornication against unmarried parents applying for aid to dependent children. See his "Politics, Public Order, and Pluralism," in James Klonoski and Robert Mendelsohn, eds., *The Politics of Local Justice* (Boston: Little, Brown, 1970), p. 240.

[96] Harry Caudill reports on a truant officer's attempt to jail an impoverished unemployed miner who kept his children out of school because he could not clothe them. The truant officer wanted to coerce others in a similar position to send their children back to school. "The Law in a Rural Setting," in William Chambliss, ed., *Crime and the Legal Process* (New York: McGraw-Hill, 1969), pp. 334-336. The activities of grand juries also may be motivated by ulterior political considerations. The report of the local Ohio grand jury which indicated 25 students and faculty members over disturbances that left four Kent State University students dead in the spring of 1970 is a glaring example of this.

CHAPTER 11
THE IMPACT OF THE CIVIL PROCESS

HOW THE CIVIL PROCESS AT THE STATE LEVEL AFFECTS WHO GETS WHAT

THE impact of the criminal process is easily recognized. Criminal cases present a symbolic confrontation between organized society and individuals who transgress against its rules of conduct. This symbolism finds concrete expression in the format of indictments: *People v. John Doe*. Defendants are confronted by prosecutors and judges who have been delegated the power to act in the name of society to enforce its rules.

The civil process is no less involved in shaping who gets what in society than is the criminal process, though its impact is less obvious and rarely acknowledged. Occasionally, the attentive newspaper reader will note that agencies of government are involved in civil litigation concerning the way they perform their functions. The outcomes of such cases have a direct effect on the agencies' subsequent policies. But the impact that large numbers of routine civil cases have on litigants is essentially invisible.

One way to understand the impact of the civil process is from the perspective of the litigant. Three services are provided by civil courts for those who turn to them:[1] They provide a forum where negotiations to resolve disputes can be conducted; they can legitimize settlements arrived at privately (divorces, adoption); and they authorize the use of government power to achieve private goals (collect debts, receive restitution). Unwilling defendants who lose civil actions find themselves coerced into helping the plaintiff accomplish his goals. The mere fact that a lawsuit has been filed can force the defendant to enter into negotiations. But civil litigation provides defendants with an opportunity to resist the claims of the plaintiff or to obtain vindication.

The civil process can also be described by identifying the types of questions with which it deals. They can be divided into four categories: (1) the transfer, exchange, ownership, and use of property and wealth; (2) settlement of claims for damages and restitution; (3) the regulation of human relationships; and (4) the appropriateness and legality of governmental actions, procedures, and policy.

The first category includes the following types of actions: suits for unpaid rent; eviction; claims for unpaid loans and installment purchases; disputes over ownership of property; implementation (and challenges to implementation) of the provisions of wills; distribution of the property of people who die without leaving a will; foreclosures and repossessions; and suits on contracts (including insurance policies).

Actions for damages and restitution most frequently involve automobile accidents, but other forms of injury (e.g., falls on the ice, airplane accidents, faulty appliances, medical malpractice) also give rise to claims. Damages may also be sought to compensate for losses sustained from failure to honor a contract or to perform a service properly. Slander and libel actions also fall within this category. Although wealth may change hands as a result of these actions, the actions themselves seek compensation for alleged improper

---

[1] Herbert Jacob, *Debtors in Court* (Chicago: Rand McNally, 1969), pp. 16–17.

behavior and its consequences. Usually, the compensation takes the form of money.

A variety of human relationships are affected by the civil process. Hearings are held to determine if persons alleged to be mentally ill should be institutionalized. Divorces, separations, adoptions, annulments, and weddings fall within the civil jurisdiction. Occasionally, other types of disputes (suits between neighbors alleging excessive noise, an ugly fence or house color, or unkept appearance of house and lawn) are also heard.

Finally, a variety of actions and policies of governments and their agencies are challenged in civil actions. Particular decisions of zoning boards, tax assessors, or welfare departments may be challenged as violative of statute or administrative procedure. Even general policies themselves (an ordinance regulating commercial signs, rules of eligibility for welfare, techniques of equalizing tax assessments) may be challenged. Plaintiffs may seek reversal of particular decisions, voiding of statutes or injunctions prohibiting continued application of particular policies. And when the actions and decisions of election officials are challenged, courts may be in a position to determine who is the winner.[2]

The first three categories share an important characteristic that the last does not. For the most part, they are routine cases. Their visibility is low and their impact is restricted to the individuals directly involved. The decisions reached involve relatively little discretion and can be thought of as *norm enforcement*.[3] In fact, claims for damages, unpaid bills, and disputes between neighbors are often settled before official courtroom disposition. But civil actions dealing with the activities of government are rarely routine and often highly visible. Frequently, the impact extends beyond the parties

---

[2] For instance, courts in Minnesota determined the winner of the 1962 election for governor. See Herbert Jacob, *Justice in America* (Boston: Little, Brown, 1965), p. 3.

[3] The distinction between "enforcing norms" and "making policy" is made by Herbert Jacob, *Justice in America*, Chapters 2 and 3.

directly involved in the litigation to include all those affected by the particular policy or action in question. They are more likely to establish precedents that shape future behavior of potential litigants and other courts. Put another way, they are more likely to have important policy implications.

There has been a marked tendency for research to emphasize policy-making decisions of state courts (especially state supreme courts) and to ignore the impact of routine decisions. Policy decisions are more visible and dramatic, but routine decisions are far more common, and their cumulative impact is probably substantially greater.[4]

Compared to the criminal process, however, relatively little research has been done on any aspect of the impact of the civil process. In the remainder of this chapter, we can do little more than suggest its overall magnitude by briefly describing an example of impact in each of the four categories identified above.

The Transfer of Wealth: Debt Actions

When a debtor fails to pay his creditor according to the terms of their contract, the standard legal remedy is for the creditor to sue in civil court. The purpose is to establish the legality of the debt and its amount. If he is successful in his suit, the creditor obtains a judgment against the debtor. Once obtained, there are a variety of legal devices available for collecting the judgment, including garnishment, liens, and forced sale of the debtor's property.[5]

---

[4] Kenneth Dolbeare, in *Trial Courts in Urban Politics* (New York: Wiley, 1967), provides information that gives a rough idea of this ratio. In 1963, 3,500 new cases were set for trial in the county studied. A total of 41 cases decided involved questions of public policy. See pp. 34–35.

[5] A garnishment, as noted in Chapter 4, note 53, is a court order directing someone who owes or possesses money due the debtor (such as an employer or bank holding his funds) to pay all or some of that money to the court, which then turns it over to the creditor. A lien establishes a creditor's claim on property (such as a house or car). A forced sale involves seizure and sale at auction of the debtor's property. The proceeds are turned over to the creditor to satisfy the judgment.

Occasionally, dramatic examples of what the process can entail for debtors become visible. In one instance, a man bought a used car ($1,995 purchase price plus finance charges). After paying $1,000 on a total debt of $2,700, he was unable to make further payments. The finance company repossessed the car, sold it for $500, and went to court where it obtained a *deficiency judgment* for the balance. As partial satisfaction (a legal term for payment) of the deficiency judgment, the man's home was sold at a sheriff's sale for $475. Interestingly, the purchase of the home was made by the finance company's attorney.[6]

Garnishment of wages is far more frequent. A study of four Wisconsin cities found the number per 1,000 population ranged from 2.1 all the way to 30.7.[7] Even if the lowest rate is projected nationwide, it means that there are over a million garnishments filed each year. In all likelihood, it is considerably greater.[8] To a man on a tight budget, sudden substantial reductions in his wages are likely to create new problems. Nearly half of a sample of garnisheed debtors in Wisconsin reported they subsequently experienced problems with other creditors as a result of the garnishment.[9] One in 14 was summarily fired.[10] Others are warned that they will be fired if the garnishment is not dismissed or if another is served. There are also psychological costs incurred. Garnishees generally do not tell anyone about the incident.[11] Apparently, a

---

[6] "Mrs. Knauer's Hometown," *The New Republic*, May 17, 1969.

[7] Herbert Jacob, *Debtors in Court*, p. 87. The rates are for Green Bay and Racine, respectively. In Madison, it was 22.6 and in Kenosha, 12.0.

[8] There is some evidence that Jacob's findings are not atypical of the rest of the nation. *Ibid.*, Appendix A, pp. 135-137.

[9] *Ibid.*, p. 101. The discussion of the impact of garnishments is drawn largely from Jacob, pp. 98-106.

[10] *Ibid.*, p. 104. Evidently many large employers in some regions of the country have a policy of immediately firing any garnisheed employee. See Patricia Wald, *Law and Poverty* (Washington, D.C.: U.S. Government Printing Office, 1965), p. 24.

[11] Jacob, *Debtors in Court*, p. 113. Two-thirds of the garnishees interviewed by Jacob said they told no one.

certain stigma is associated with it. A degree of bitterness and resentment also may follow.[12]

In practice, creditors in Wisconsin use garnishments more as a device for prompting the debtor to contact them and make arrangements for voluntary payment than as a coercive collection technique. Creditors frequently will agree to dismiss the garnishment upon payment of an initial sum and a promise to make regular payments subsequently. Seventy percent of garnishments in the four Wisconsin cities studied were dismissed.[13]

The outstanding characteristic of most civil suits for debt is not that plaintiffs nearly always win (though they do), but that they usually win by default. Most defendants are unrepresented by counsel.[14] In fact, they are not even present when their cases are heard. Their absence is treated as an admission of the validity of the claim and a *default* judgment is entered against them.[15] As a result, no evidence on the debt's validity or the accuracy of the alleged balance is presented. Before the U.S. Supreme Court ruled Wisconsin's garnishment law unconstitutional (a creditor did not need a judgment before running a garnishment), nonappearance at the original garnishment hearing had another important effect: debtors could not apply for the standard 60-percent

---

[12] *Ibid.*, p. 105, describes some of the reactions of garnishees.

[13] *Ibid.*, p. 100.

[14] The prevalence of debt actions in lower civil courts is apparent in a study cited by Wald, in *Law and Poverty*, p. 29, note 90, which found that 80 percent of civil cases in California municipal courts involved debt actions brought by businesses. In 90 percent of these cases, the defendants had no lawyers. In another study (Barbara Rubin, "Consumers in Court," a paper delivered at the American Sociological Association, 1968, p. 11), of over a thousand defendants in installment-debt cases, 80 percent were unrepresented. Only 3 percent of Jacob's sample of debtors were represented in garnishment proceedings against them (Jacob, *Debtors in Court*, p. 99).

[15] A number of studies have commented on the high percentage of default judgments. See Wald, *Law and Poverty*, p. 26, note 23; Jerome Carlin, Jan Howard, and Sheldon Messinger, *Civil Justice and the Poor* (New York: Russell Sage Foundation, 1967), pp. 30 and 37; and David Caplovitz, *The Poor Pay More* (New York: Free Press, 1963), p. 161.

exemption they were entitled to by law. This meant that they received even less of their garnished paycheck than they otherwise would have.[16]

There are undoubtedly a number of reasons why so many defendants fail to appear when their cases are called. Some recognize the validity of the creditor's claim and see no point in attempting to contest it. Others may simply find it impossible to leave work (with consequent loss of pay), travel to court, and spend most of the day waiting for their case to be called. The form and wording of summonses in many jurisdictions is so complicated and obtuse that some debtors simply do not grasp what is at stake or that they must appear if they are to avoid a default judgment. But some do not appear because they don't even know they are being sued. Instead of properly serving the summons, process servers in some jurisdictions destroy it ("throw it in the sewer") and claim it has been served. Although accurate statistics on the frequency of such *sewer service* do not exist, it is evidently commonplace in many cities.[17] These hapless defendants learn the hard way about suits against them—when a garnishment or eviction notice is served.

Sewer service is not the only procedural weakness found in lower civil courts. Like lower criminal courts, bureaucratic procedures are used to shortcut legal requirements in an attempt to handle a burdensome case load. Close working relationships develop between the court regulars—judges, court clerks, and creditors' attorneys. A presumption of the validity of the creditor's claim operates. The judges are fre-

---

[16] Jacob, *Debtors in Court*, pp. 99–100. Even when present, however, debtors seldom requested the exemption. Though part of the statute, the exemption provision had practically no impact.

[17] An assistant attorney general in New York reportedly testified that "So-called 'sewer service' virtually permeates the service of legal process in the Civil Court in the City of New York today." "Study Charges Summons Abuses," *The New York Times*, January 14, 1966. See also Carlin, Howard, and Messinger, *Civil Justice*, p. 37. Rubin, "Consumers in Court," pp. 5–7, found 29 percent of installment debtors in Detroit and 47 percent in New York alleged they had received no summons.

quently mediocre men, and sometimes have surprisingly little knowledge of statutes or of proper legal procedure. A study of magistrates in Philadelphia, for example, found that many did not even know what the requirements were for legal service of a summons. Hundreds of default judgments had been entered where service was clearly improper.[18]

Although we have focused on suits for debts, there are a number of other important types of actions.[19] Hundreds of thousands are evicted each year. In 1963, there were nearly 5,300 summary evictions in Boston; a figure of 92 thousand per year has been cited for the District of Columbia.[20] The link between civil actions and formal governmental power is obvious. Not only are suits heard and decided in courts, but agencies of government play an important part in enforcing the courts' decisions. The police are called upon to assist in the seizure of repossessed merchandise and the forceful eviction of those who refuse to vacate their premises. Sheriffs seize property and conduct auctions. Employers who refuse to withhold wages subject to garnishment find themselves liable to court action and officially sanctioned enforcement of subsequent judgments. Such actions undeniably affect who gets what, and they involve the official power of government in a most direct way.

Damages and Restitution: Auto Accident Litigation

The major characteristics of the process used to compensate auto accident victims have already been described. To summarize, it is up to victims to obtain compensation (usually from an insurance company). They may do so on their own

---

[18] Cited in Carlin, Howard, and Messinger, *Civil Justice*, p. 37, note 131.

[19] Bankruptcy may also be thought of as an aspect of the transfer of wealth through the legal process, though technically it results in the cancellation of debts. For a recent survey of bankruptcy in the United States, see David T. Stanley and Marjorie Girth, *Bankruptcy: Problem, Process, Reform* (Washington, D.C.: Brookings, 1971).

[20] Wald, *Law and Poverty*, p. 15, note 44.

or with the assistance of an attorney paid on a contingent-fee basis. When the victim is compensated, it generally takes the form of a negotiated settlement with a claims adjustor or the insurance company's attorney. Negotiations are structured by the realization that a trial is a remote and generally unwelcome but nonetheless real possibility.

There are several consequences for who gets what flowing from this system that would not be present if other techniques were employed to compensate accident victims. *No-fault insurance* plans are one such alternative. Although such plans differ in detail, their central characteristic is a provision for automatic compensation of all those injured in accidents (regardless of who is at fault). The amount paid is determined by a set scale which is based on the extent of loss and injury.

The current system, as suggested in Chapter 9, results in very uneven compensation. Even some of those injured through no fault of their own receive absolutely nothing while others get substantially more than their out-of-pocket costs. The reasons for this are not entirely clear, but a major variable seems to be whether an attorney is retained or not. Those who are less likely to seek the services of an attorney are less likely to receive awards. [21]

A second consequence of the current system results from the tendency of insurance companies to respond favorably to claims pressed by plaintiffs' attorneys who threaten to go to trial. Considerable additional costs are added in the form of attorneys' fees. These range from somewhere around 30 to as high as 50 percent. These costs are met either by victims (who receive less than they deserve) or by everyone who pays

---

[21] H. Lawrence Ross, in *Settled Out of Court* (Chicago: Aldine, 1970), p. 193, found that only 950 of 1,601 unrepresented claimants received compensation (59 percent), whereas 519 of 615 represented claimants (nearly 85 percent) were paid. There is disagreement on whether small claims are paid. Ross finds 92 percent of claims where damages were between $1 and $200 were paid (calculated from Table 5.1, p. 185). Clarence Morris and James Paul, "The Financial Impact of Automobile Accidents," in *Dollars, Delay, and the Automobile Victim* (New York: Bobbs-Merrill, 1960), p. 10, found victims whose out-of-pocket expenses were less than $100 were particularly likely to get nothing.

insurance premiums. (They are boosted to cover higher awards which reflect attorneys' fees. In this regard, it is significant that motorists' insurance premiums were reduced in Massachusetts shortly after the introduction of a no-fault compensation system.) Looked at this way, the entire accident-compensation system can be thought of as a device to collect a "lawyers tax." [22]

Third, negotiations and threats to go to trial consume considerable time. Since many cases are not settled until trial is imminent or actually begun, the delays encountered due to crowded trial dockets mean that many victims must wait years for an award. One study, for instance, found that in serious accidents where the injured party received something, over half had to wait at least a year. [23] The more meager the financial resources of victims, the more serious such delays are. [24]

All three consequences—uneven compensation, added costs to the system arising from attorneys' fees, and long delays in compensation—are a direct product of the current system. Many versions of no-fault insurance plans would substantially eliminate all three. [25]

Regulation of Human Relationships: Civil Commitment

Often the involvement of the civil process in human relationships provides a forum for ratification of independently arrived at arrangements. Thus, few adoptions, marriages, or

---

[22] Critics have also identified the system for disposal of the property of the dead (probate, estate appraisers, guardians) as a maze of needless regulation which redounds to the benefit of lawyers' bank accounts. Whether justified or not, the tasks performed are often routine while the fees are substantial.

[23] Morris and Paul, "The Financial Impact," p. 14.

[24] Ibid.

[25] It is true, however, that those victims who receive very large awards under the current system would probably do less well under a no-fault plan. There may also be other untold consequences of a no-fault system.

divorces occur because of it (though some divorces may be delayed or prevented through the efforts of a mediating judge). But in some areas vitally important decisions are made because of and within civil courts. Child support and child custody are prominent examples. So is civil commitment.

This is not the place to describe in detail the consequences of involuntary commitment to mental institutions. But three brief observations need to be made. First, there is lively debate over how many mental patients are helped how much by hospitalization.[26] Second, regardless of whether their mental well-being is helped or hindered, patients experience profound psychological reactions to it.[27] Third, hospitalizations may jeopardize the legal rights of patients while they are confined and their life-chances after release.[28] Many employment forms ask, "Have you ever been in a mental institution?" Presumably, those who have experience greater difficulty in obtaining such jobs. Thus, hospitalization is not a routine or uneventful life experience. The large numbers of

---

[26] In testimony before a Senate committee, it was claimed that "in most public mental hospitals, the average ward patient comes into person-to-person contact with a physician about fifteen minutes every month." U.S. Senate, Committee on the Judiciary, *Constitutional Rights of the Mentally Ill*, Hearings Before the Subcommittee on Constitutional Rights, 87th Cong. 1st sess., p. 103.

[27] For a fascinating account of the nature of mental institutions and other total institutions from the viewpoint of the inmate, see Erving Goffman, *Asylums* (Garden City, N.Y.: Anchor, 1961).

[28] The impact of hospitalization on a patient's ability to make gifts, deeds, contracts, wills, and the like varies among jurisdictions. While such rights are lost when persons are "incompetent by reason of mental illness," the fact of hospitalization in a mental institution is not necessarily regarded as conclusive evidence of incompetency. For an interesting discussion of the problem, see Hugh A. Ross, "Hospitalizing the Mentally Ill: Emergency and Temporary Commitments," *Current Trends in State Legislation, 1955-56*, (1956), pp. 512-525. A full picture of the extent to which former mental patients have been stigmatized has not yet been drawn. One observer, however, has concluded it is not a serious problem for most. See Walter R. Gove, "Societal Reaction as an Explanation of Mental Illness: An Exploration," *American Sociological Review* 35 (1970), p. 881.

people affected make it significant on a societal as well as on an individual level.

The description of the commitment process in Chapter 6 noted that because of the implicit presumption of insanity, individual private decisions to initiate commitment proceedings were routinely and authoritatively ratified at the hearing stage. This has several significant consequences for who gets committed.

One aspect that has aroused considerable criticism is the practice of committing the elderly. Senile, eccentric, and financially burdensome old folk are committed by relatives who no longer want them and see no other alternatives. The custodial wards of many state mental hospitals thus serve as terminal nursing and old folks homes. [29]

Another consequence is that police serve as a major source of such commitments. The frequency of police use of emergency civil-commitment proceedings for individuals whose behavior is regarded bizarre is largely unrecognized. The findings of a study of this topic conducted in a western city are instructive.

Despite the strong reluctance of the police, emergency apprehensions of mentally ill persons are quite frequent. Indeed, officers of the uniformed patrol make them about as often as they arrest persons for murder, all types of manslaughter, rape, robbery, aggravated assault, and grand theft, taken together; and more than one fifth of all referrals to the receiving psychiatric service of the public hospital come from this source. [30]

Police are more likely to encounter lower-class and minority group members with mental problems than white middle-

---

[29] Fred Cohen, "The Function of the Attorney and the Commitment of the Mentally Ill," *Texas Law Review* 44 (1966), p. 434. Cohen concludes, "Largely because of the absence of other alternatives, the aged and the impoverished constitute a large percentage of patients at any state mental hospital."

[30] Egon Bittner, "Police Discretion in Emergency Apprehension of Mentally-Ill Persons," *Social Problems* 14 (1966–1967), p. 282.

class suburbanites. Furthermore, they are very likely more willing to seek an alternative to taking the middle-class white to the hospital. The result is that segments of the population who have greater contact with the police (the poor, the young, minority groups) are also more often committed upon police initiative.

The use of civil commitment as a device for populating state mental hospitals with the elderly raises one last question about the persons involved. How sick are they really? We can avoid the philosophical and medical quagmire of debate about what mental illness is if we restrict our discussion to the two most common legal grounds for commitment. They are the right of the state to protect its citizens from people who pose a danger to others, and the right of government to help people who are dangerous to themselves.[31] The suspicion that many people caught up in the routinized processes of commitment do not meet either of these criteria is borne out by some empirical research. Reports of psychiatrists examining incoming involuntary patients in one study revealed that 102 of 161 reported on were "not dangerous nor... severely mentally impaired."[32]

Governmental Policy and the Civil Courts

To what extent are the policies pursued by local governmental agencies affected by state civil courts?[33] A casual survey suggests that the lower courts are at least as important in this respect as appellate courts.[34] One reason is that there are simply many more of them. Moreover, most cases are not

---

[31] Thomas Scheff, *Being Mentally Ill* (Chicago: Aldine, 1966). See also Seymour Halleck, "The Reform of Mental Hospitals," *Psychology Today* 2 (1969), pp. 50–51. He observes, "Thousands of patients in mental hospitals probably could be released without harm to themselves or others."

[32] Scheff, *Being Mentally Ill*, p. 132.

[33] The role of the Supreme Court and state supreme courts in shaping policy is discussed separately in Chapter 12.

[34] This discussion is drawn from Dolbeare, *Trial Courts,* p. 203.

appealed; and even fewer are actually reversed.[35] This means that, as a rule, the decision of the lower court is final. When cases are appealed, the outcome is shaped by the record made in the lower court.

Local civil courts can affect the specific content of governmental policy itself when called into question. But they also have an impact by having some say over who will occupy decision-making positions and what their powers and duties will be. Before summarizing the overall impact of local civil courts on policy, we shall examine both of these areas briefly.

As noted earlier, courts have a direct say in who will hold office when elections are disputed. But a number of other decisions that face local courts bear on the electoral process as well. Disputes over the validity of nominating petitions, the appropriateness of local interpretations of registration laws, and the fairness of redistricting plans are all brought to civil courts and have a definite impact upon who is elected.[36]

Disputes over the rules of the game, particularly the powers of various officials, also come to court. One study found the courts more involved with these powers than any other issues of public policy.[37] Some of the questions decided by local courts included disputes over the power of annexation, the right of a county civil service commission to dismiss adherents of the "out" party, and the obligation of the board of supervisors to pay the salary of an appointed official of the other party.[38]

---

[35] *Ibid.* Dolbeare found about one-fourth of cases involving public policy questions were appealed; only 7 percent were decided contrary to the original ruling.

[36] Courts and judges also indirectly affect election outcomes through their activities as providers of patronage and incentives which strengthen party organizations. See especially Wallace Sayre and Herbert Kaufman, *Governing New York City* (New York: Norton, 1960), pp. 538–543.

[37] Dolbeare, *Trial Courts,* p. 98.

[38] *Ibid.,* pp. 45–51. Dolbeare describes court cases involving "Democrats versus Republicans for Power and Influence in County Government."

Dolbeare's study also illustrates the effect local courts can have over the specific content of governmental policy itself.[39] In Nassau County, New York, disputes in several areas of intense conflict came to court. Zoning and land-use cases were by far the most numerous of these public policy cases.[40] While a few decisions were made on the location of public projects, decisions of zoning boards were frequently challenged by businesses attempting to get permits, and builders of homes and commercial projects.[41] Courts also were involved in deciding on the level of assessments, which has profound consequences on the amount of tax revenue generated.

Not every area of intense conflict will be moved to the courts for final resolution, however. Dolbeare found conflicts over education and taxation were intense in Nassau County, but they did not figure prominently in the courts. On the other hand, decisions affecting policy are made by courts that do not appear to have a major impact on the overall direction of policy and are not a result of intense local conflict. These include licensing and regulation, labor relations, Sunday-closing laws, and governmental contracts.[42]

Thus, although local courts can and do have an impact over public policy, this impact is rather limited. In some important areas, issues are never raised in the courts. In Dolbeare's study, the courts were but rarely able to act as the final shaper of policy when issues generated considerable public

---

[39] His definition of public policy is "the substance of rules of conduct or other allocations of burden and benefit regarding subjects of public concern or impact which are principally the products of the local political system." He excludes criminal cases. *Ibid.*, pp. 3-4.

[40] *Ibid.*, p. 94. The number of cases in each area is as follows: Zoning, land use—200; education—25; taxation—9; nominations, elections—16; governmental powers, forms—34. These figures are for the period 1948 to 1963.

[41] *Ibid.*, pp. 36-37, 95.

[42] *Ibid.*, p. 35.

controversy.[43] If one looks at impact in terms of volume of litigation, moreover, only a small percentage of all civil cases can be classified as involving public policy in the broad sense.[44]

In some public policy areas, however, a definite and important role is played by local courts. Zoning and decisions affecting political power stand out. And while the final shape of policy is not very often determined by the courts, litigation can have a significant impact on *when* things happen. Going to court can be particularly effective when small groups want delay or want to defend the status quo.[45] Local courts appear particularly sensitive to protecting property rights.

Finally, the courts provide a forum for what Dolbeare calls "lesser elements" in local politics (businessmen and individuals).[46] They are also attractive to isolated and relatively weak groups who are unable to succeed elsewhere. When courts are called upon to resolve policy disputes at the request of local individuals or groups it enables them to be heard at some effectual level of government. Major organized interest groups and political contestants need not turn to the courts—usually their preferred arena is elsewhere. The types of policy disputes usually decided in this forum mirror the concerns of the types of litigants involved.

[43] *Ibid.*, p. 56.

[44] *Ibid.*, p. 34.

[45] Dolbeare describes how determined citizens held up construction of an incinerator for five years through litigation. *Ibid.*, pp. 51-55. Citizens of the community of Pleasant Ridge, Michigan held up construction of a vital link in the interstate highway system for nearly a decade by using similar techniques.

[46] *Ibid.*, pp. 39-40, 61. He suggests interest-group activity may be more significant at the appellate level. Sayre and Kaufman, *Governing New York City*, come to a similar conclusion. Considerable influence is exerted in determining who will become a judge in New York City, but little influence is directed at affecting the judge's decisions once he is in office. As a result, policy made by judges is largely "an unwitting byproduct of other considerations" (p. 554).

THE IMPACT OF THE FEDERAL CIVIL PROCESS

There are about 70 thousand civil cases begun in federal district courts each year. Approximately 30 percent (some 20 thousand) involve the federal government.

The strategic location of federal district courts accounts for much of their potential impact. Geographical dispersion makes them readily available to litigants. Most cases coming to the Supreme Court from the federal system originate in district courts, presenting these judges with the unavoidable opportunity to rule on the same questions the Supreme Court ultimately does. And the necessary reliance upon them to implement the decisions of higher courts generates additional occasions for them to make significant decisions.

The four categories of civil cases used to analyze the impact of state courts can be used in assessing civil cases in federal district court.

Several types of cases involve the transfer, exchange, ownership, and use of property and wealth. The federal government is involved as plaintiff in suits to acquire land needed for federal projects (highways, dams, parks, buildings) which the acquiring agency is unable to purchase through negotiation, in actions to enforce compliance by private companies with contracts entered into with federal agencies, and in suits brought under the antitrust statutes. Antitrust cases, though relatively few in number, can have profound consequences for the structure of the economy. The government is defendant in taxpayer claims and actions to recover benefits (from the Veterans Administration or Social Security, for example) claimed but not received. A number of suits involving the enforcement of contracts between private individuals and businesses that can meet federal jurisdictional requirements are also heard.[47] Bankruptcies are handled here as well. As noted in Chapter 9, the number is around 200,000 per year.

---

[47] In fiscal year 1968, for example, over 6,500 of the approximately 71,000 civil cases started in district courts were contract actions involving private parties falling within the diversity jurisdiction. Sheldon Goldman and Thomas P. Jahnige, *The Federal Courts as a Political System* (New York: Harper & Row, 1971), Table 4, p. 101.

A substantial proportion (34 percent) of all federal civil suits filed fall into the second category—claims for damages and restitution.[48] The majority of them involve private parties meeting diversity of citizenship requirements, but a number (over 2,200 in fiscal 1968) involve the federal government as defendant in claims arising from injuries sustained on federal property or as the result of the actions of a federal employee.

Cases involving the regulation of human relationships heard in the federal courts differ in substance from those heard in state courts. At the state level, family problems (divorce, separation, child custody) and civil commitment predominate. At the federal level, they involve the protection of civil rights and employee-employer relationships.[49]

The total number of cases involving the fourth category of civil suits—the appropriateness and legality of governmental actions, procedures, and policy—is relatively small with one exception. The exception consists of cases in which convicted defendants serving prison sentences challenge the manner in which the legal process itself has treated them. Approximately 16 percent of all civil cases in fiscal 1968 were petitions from federal or state prisoners alleging violations of federally guaranteed rights.[50]

Aside from prisoner petitions, the remaining cases in this fourth category typically involved a litigant interested more in questions of broad policy than the details of the specific dispute at issue. The American Civil Liberties Union, business and labor groups, civil rights organizations, ecology and conservation groups, public interest lawyers, and similar groups bring cases specifically designed to force or block action by agencies of government.

Few systematic studies of federal district court decisions have been undertaken. One of them is Kenneth Dolbeare's

---

[48] *Ibid.*, Table 4, p. 101.

[49] *Ibid.* In fiscal year 1968, there were over 1,600 civil rights suits and over 3,500 cases involving federal labor laws.

[50] *Ibid.*

examination of cases decided in district courts located in 20 large and medium-sized cities.[51] He was particularly interested in decisions relating to urban problems—law enforcement, civil rights, urban renewal, public housing, pollution, poverty, and transportation. However, only 12 percent of the total of 335 cases identified as dealing with these urban problems involved public housing, urban renewal, slum clearance, city tax and regulatory powers, or other miscellaneous public policy questions. If these courts had a substantial impact in any of these areas, it had to be due to the significance of individual cases rather than sheer numbers. By far the largest category of cases involved criminal law and police practices (58 percent of the total); another 24 percent involved civil rights questions of one sort or another.[52] On the basis of these findings Dolbeare concludes, "District Court public policy actions are relatively narrowly confined to those areas which rest upon constitutional interpretations or statutory extensions of constitutional rights—principally the post-Civil War Civil Rights Acts."[53]

Several other findings are noteworthy. First, most decisions are in effect final. Seventy-eight percent of the cases either were not appealed or were upheld on appeal. Second, the policies of local governments are overturned less than 20 percent of the time in all areas but one—cases involving race relations.[54] Here 43 percent of the cases resulted in reversals.[55]

Although there are many fewer cases in district courts than

---

[51] "The Federal District Courts and Urban Public Policy: An Exploratory Study (1960-1967)," in Joel Grossman and Joseph Tanenhaus, eds., *Frontiers of Judicial Research* (New York: Wiley, 1969). The discussion that follows is drawn from Dolbeare's article, pp. 376-385.

[52] Race relations cases involving education accounted for 7 percent; other cases dealing with race, 6 percent; and other noncriminal due-process questions such as free speech and church-state relations, 11 percent. Dolbeare, "The Federal District Courts," Table 12.3, p. 384.

[53] *Ibid.*, p. 378.

[54] *Ibid.*, p. 400.

[55] *Ibid.*

in state courts, cases at the district court level can have a very wide impact. In late 1971, the state of New York planned to implement changes in its Medicaid program that would have reduced benefits for 660,000 residents, eliminating 165,000 of them from all coverage due to more stringent standards of eligibility.[56] Several health agencies in the City of New York, along with private individuals in the Medicaid program, sought an injunction against the state to prevent it from implementing the cuts. The federal district judge granted the preliminary injunction, effectively preserving original levels of coverage for the 660,000, at least for the time being.

At about the same time, an American Civil Liberties Union lawyer in Virginia succeeded in getting a federal district judge to issue an injunction against the state's prison system to halt a number of practices—bread and water punishment, unnecessary use of various forms of physical force, forced nudity as punishment, overly small solitary confinement cells, and interference with the legal activities of inmates on their own behalf.[57] All of the some 6,000 state prisoners in Virginia were potentially affected in a rather direct way by the decision.

Examples of other cases in which district judges have overturned decisions and practices of agencies of government could be cited at length. They include: a ruling that public schools may not regulate the length of a student's hair; an injunction against use of federal funds to build public housing in an area already all black; and a ruling that California's Welfare Department had to increase the maximum level of benefits in its aid to dependent children program to keep pace with inflation.[58]

---

[56] This description is based on "U.S. Court Here Enjoins State On Medicaid Cut for 660,000," *The New York Times*, November 12, 1971.

[57] "U.S. Judge Bids Virginia Halt Abuse of Prisoners," *The New York Times*, November 1, 1971.

[58] These examples were taken from a newspaper article, "Some District Judges Establish Precedents on Tough Social Issues," *The Wall Street Journal*, December 14, 1970.

This is not to say that decisions like those just described will survive upon appeal. But a certain number of them undoubtedly will; even those that do not have an impact during the period before reversal. Each of these cases would count for but one in a statistical summary of district court decisions, reinforcing the necessity for looking at the actual impact of individual decisions.

CHAPTER 12
THE IMPACT OF HIGHER COURTS

THE mythology surrounding the American legal process reserves a special place for its higher courts, particularly the U.S. Supreme Court. Our survey of the impact of the legal process would not be complete without an examination of the impact of some of these higher courts.

THE IMPACT OF THE SUPREME COURT ON PUBLIC POLICY

Preliminary Considerations

How important is the Supreme Court of the United States in shaping public policy? Traditionally, those who have written about the Court's impact have operated from an unarticulated assumption that if the Supreme Court rendered a decision, it would be implemented and have a significant impact on the real world.[1]

---

[1] One student of the Supreme Court, Joel Grossman, believes Supreme Court justices themselves share in this view. "For official purposes, at least," he observes, "the Justices tend to assume that once the nation's highest court has made a decision, there will be ready and willing compliance from those to whom the decision is directed." See "The Supreme Court and Social Change," *American Behavioral Scientist* 13 (1969–1970), p. 535.

This perspective is congruent with the image many Americans have of the Court. As Jerome Frank put it, we are willing victims of an "upper court myth." In part, the myth rests on the fact that the Supreme Court is afforded equal status in the Constitution with Congress and the president. Consequently, it has taken on much of the aura and sanctity of the Constitution itself. It is charged with interpreting the intent of the founding fathers. Its decisions are often highly visible. The fact that it has been so intensively studied also contributes to its reputation for importance and power. Finally, because it is called the *Supreme* Court and stands at the top of a formal hierarchy of courts, we easily slip into the error of assuming that it must control and direct the decisions of lower tribunals.

Recently, the assumption that the Court's decisions are automatically implemented has been subjected to critical examination. Past scholarship relied largely upon an analysis of the content of written opinions without actually studying their impact. Today, serious efforts are being made to conduct empirical research on the question.[2]

In light of the importance attached to the Supreme Court, one would think we would already have reliable information giving a clear picture of what the Court's impact actually is. The truth is we have neither the full picture nor the information necessary to produce one. It would be misleading to pretend we are ready to offer here anything more than a partial and tentative view of the Court's impact.

One initial problem encountered in studying the impact of the Supreme Court is the ambiguity of the term *compliance*.[3]

---

[2] Much of this research is summarized in a most useful book by Stephen Wasby, *The Impact of the United States Supreme Court* (Homewood, Ill.: Dorsey Press, 1970). Wasby examines the Court's impact in the following policy areas: economic regulation, reapportionment, church-state relations, obscenity, criminal procedure, and school desegregation. The Court's relationship with the president and executive branch, the lower judiciary (both federal and state), various components of state government, and public opinion are also discussed.

[3] For an excellent discussion of this point, see Wasby, *The Impact of the . . . Supreme Court*, pp. 27-42.

A complete analysis of impact must go beyond the question of whether compliance, noncompliance, or some form of *evasion* follows a decision. Behavior of lower-court judges, litigants and potential litigants, interest groups, and government officials may be altered by anticipations of forthcoming decisions or by quiet efforts to adjust behavior to the new ruling. Policies of defiance and compliance are pursued by those not directly involved in the case. Attempts to pass new legislation, changes in public opinion, and the initiation of new litigation also may be part of a decision's impact. Moreover, one encounters rather sticky conceptual problems in assessing impact: just what constitutes compliance or noncompliance; to what extent can behavior following a decision be attributed to it as opposed to other factors? Obviously, acceptable answers to these questions must be found before comprehensive studies of impact can be undertaken. In the meantime, we are forced to rely upon studies of a more limited scope.

Unfortunately, the studies done to date are not only restricted in their treatment of the impact a single decision has. Taken together, they cover only a limited range of the types of decisions the Court has rendered. Nearly all of the empirical studies of impact deal with cases in which the statutes and practices followed by the various states have been declared unconstitutional. These include malapportionment, school desegregation, school prayer, police treatment of criminal suspects, and the right to legal counsel. Since the Court has rarely declared acts of the federal legislative and executive branches unconstitutional in the past 20 years, there have been few opportunities to study such cases. Perhaps most significantly, practically nothing is known about the impact of Supreme Court decisions which interpret the meaning of federal legislation,[4] particularly with respect to their impact on the agencies that administer these statutes.

---

[4] Walter Murphy's *Congress and the Court* (Chicago: University of Chicago Press, 1962) is a partial exception. The book details the reaction in the U.S. Congress to decisions in the 1950s on internal security and criminal procedure.

It is not possible, then, to provide reliable answers to most of the important questions raised about impact. Once we avoid the obvious errors that stem from restricting our examination to cases where there was a substantial impact (or alternatively, very little impact), we are still left with a series of significant unanswered questions: How frequently do what patterns of impact occur? Are there common characteristics of those cases that do (or do not) have a substantial impact? Are those cases that do have significant impact (even though perhaps small in number) *so important* to the functioning of the political system as to be crucial?

But if it is unreasonable to expect any definitive answers to these important questions, it is similarly incorrect to assume we know nothing at all. To begin with, there are several ways of distinguishing between decisions that provide the necessary first step in assessing impact.

Distinguishing Characteristics of Supreme Court Decisions

Scholars who approach the study of the Supreme Court from more traditional perspectives have categorized decisions and their impact by subject area. Henry J. Abraham regards the Court as "the great and ultimate defender of the basic freedoms of the American people."[5] Before the first third of this century, it primarily focused on the "economic-proprietarian sphere," but now has virtually withdrawn from the economic sphere in deference to state and federal legislative and executive action. Abraham finds the Court's current emphasis is on civil liberties and civil rights, and divides its concerns into five broad categories: procedures used in criminal cases; reapportionment, redistricting and voting; civil rights (race); freedom of religion and separation of church and state; and internal security.[6]

Others, including Samuel Krislov, see the Court as a major

---

[5] Henry J. Abraham, *The Judiciary* (Boston: Allyn and Bacon, 1969), p. 37. This discussion is drawn from Chapter II.

[6] *Ibid.*, p. 38.

shaper of the relationship between the federal government and the states and between the branches of the federal government itself. Like Abraham, Krislov points out that the Court has largely taken itself out of the determination of economic policy. In fact, of the three major constitutional powers of the federal government—taxing and spending, waging war, and the commerce power—the Supreme Court plays a role only in the third.[7] Its role here is minor, confined to interpreting statutes involving economic policy. It does, however, limit actions by states that affect interstate commerce and intervenes in disputes between the legislative and executive branches over their respective powers (e.g., who can remove what officials; can the president seize steel mills during a national emergency?)[8]

A second means of classifying decisions examines whether the issue of constitutionality is present. Few Americans are able to escape from our educational system without being exposed to a discussion of the significance of *judicial review*— the power of the Court to declare acts of Congress and the executive unconstitutional. Typically these discussions emphasize the importance of decisions holding an action or statute unconstitutional. The ability of nine men appointed for life to upset the decisions of popularly elected officials naturally attracts considerable philosophical interest in a democratic society. However, a strong argument can be made that the opposite decision—holding a statute or action to be *constitutional*—is more significant. For one thing, acts of Congress have been declared unconstitutional less than a hundred times throughout the history of the Court.[9] Even

---

[7] Samuel Krislov, *The Supreme Court in the Political Process* (New York: Macmillan, 1965), p. 87, quoting Justice Robert Jackson.

[8] *Ibid.*, pp. 89–105. Jay A. Sigler, *An Introduction to the Legal System* (Homewood, Ill.: Dorsey Press, 1968) identifies the following as areas of Supreme Court policy-making: regulating federalism; correcting the Congress; regulating the president; regulating administrative agencies; and property versus individual rights (pp. 197–214).

[9] Abraham, *The Judiciary*, p. 98.

when major legislation has been declared unconstitutional, Congress is frequently able to reverse the effect of the decision through further legislation.[10] But more significantly, the Court's approval of the actions of other branches of government serves to legitimitize those actions. New programs and policies of the political coalitions that dominate American politics at any given time are routinely challenged on constitutional grounds (recent civil rights legislation is a good example). As the recognized guardian of the Constitution, the Supreme Court applies the "seal of constitutionality" to these programs.[11] One student of the Court argues that this legitimizing function is essential to the maintenance of our system of limited government.[12]

If the Court's power to identify unconstitutional acts is significant, it is with respect to state statutes and state constitutional provisions. Since 1870, there have been 650 such cases.[13] However, a significant portion of the Court's impact on policy is produced by decisions that do not deal with the issue of constitutionality at all, but rather with interpretations of federal legislation. As noted previously, it is difficult to describe this aspect of the Court's activity in any detail since it has barely been studied.

A third way of distinguishing among decisions is by the balance between their material (or tangible) and symbolic impact. If only the impact of decisions on the distribution of material goods and benefits is examined, a very incomplete

---

[10] Robert A. Dahl, "Decision-Making in a Democracy: The Supreme Court as a National Policy-Maker," *Journal of Public Law* 6 (1958), pp. 279-295, found that of 15 decisions reversing major congressional legislation within four years of enactment (excluding the New Deal), Congress in turn reversed the Court's decisions in 10, changed its own views in two, and took action that cannot be classified in either of the other two categories in the remaining three.

[11] For an excellent statement of this argument, see Dahl, "Decision-Making."

[12] Charles L. Black, Jr., *The People and the Court* (New York: Macmillan, 1960), p. 66. The views of Dahl and Black are quite close.

[13] Abraham, *The Judiciary*, p. 98.

picture results. Often, a substantial portion of a decision's impact rests in the psychological reactions to the principles and interests supported or struck down. Some are reassured by the Court's affirmation of certain values; others are threatened. Yet except for the parties to the case, frequently nothing of a tangible nature changes. The images in men's minds are more affected than anything else.

The desegregation decisions are an outstanding example. Integrationists, blacks, and those sympathetic to them were elated by the finding that segregated schools were inherently unequal. Segregationists were despondent. Yet, the overwhelming majority of black preschoolers in the South at the time of the decision have now graduated from segregated high schools.[14] It is true that some desegregation occurred almost immediately after the 1954 decision (in Saint Louis and Baltimore, for example), and substantial change occurred in school-attendance patterns, albeit slowly, as a result of decisions in this area. But it is necessary to keep in perspective the time involved. The delay between the decision in 1954 and its implementation in the late 1960s and early 1970s was *lifetime* for the people involved. Mississippi blacks attending inferior segregated schools in the 1950s and 1960s cannot go back now for an integrated education. Thus, it is true that desegregated decisions affected both material and symbolic politics. But for a significant period of time, the mix between the two was heavily weighted on the side of the symbolic.[15]

A fourth significant characteristic of decisions is the *level of arousal* produced in their aftermath. The term *arousal* refers to a variety of processes that may or may not be set in motion in the aftermath of a decision. The publicity a deci-

---

[14] Ten years after the decision, about 3 percent of southern black school children were in integrated schools. See G. Theodore Mitau, *Decade of Decision* (New York: Scribner's, 1967), p. 68.

[15] The Supreme Court's role in legitimizing the policies pursued by other branches of government is achieved largely through the symbolic mode. Legitimacy is, after all, psychologically based.

sion receives, the importance attached to it among those individuals and groups aware of it, the strength of psychological or symbolic reactions to it, and the amount of activity stimulated by it all affect the level of arousal. Some decisions go almost unheeded by everyone but the immediate parties to the case. Others, like the 1954 school desegregation case, achieve high levels of arousal. In between is a whole range of arousal levels.

Finally, when the level of arousal following a decision moves beyond the bare minimum attained by any case decided by the Court, it becomes relevant to raise a number of questions about the interests and groups in society who are aroused. What groups are mobilized by the decision? Do they support or oppose the decision? How strongly do they feel? Are they willing to commit their political resources in a struggle to implement or circumvent the decision? What resources can they command? How much skill do they have in employing them? Perhaps most importantly, what is the balance between the committed resources favoring implementation and those opposing it?

Limitations on Impact Resulting from the Strategic Situation of the Court

The strategic situation of the Supreme Court in the political system provides it with a fragile basis for exerting influence. Ultimately, the Court commands neither money, force, nor votes. Its chief resource is its legitimacy—its ability to command the voluntary compliance and support of those who do control force, money, and votes. If there is a widespread belief that the Court has the right (and duty) to decide certain questions, that it does so competently, and that its decisions ought to be obeyed, its legitimacy is intact and its influence will be felt. If enough people began to regard its decisions as illegitimate (as many southerners did after school segregation was declared unconstitutional), its effectiveness would rapidly erode.

The fragile basis of the Supreme Court's status is also

illustrated by its reliance on other components of government. Its dependence on Congress is substantial.[16] Nearly all the important cases heard by the Court are at the sufferance of Congress, since Congress has the constitutional power to limit the appellate jurisdiction of the Court. Cases falling within the original jurisdiction of the Court are immune from possible congressional attack, but such cases are infrequent and relatively unimportant.[17]

In one instance, Congress actually did withdraw the Court's right to hear an appeal on a case arising from a Reconstruction Act following the Civil War.[18] Attempts to restrict the Court's appellate jurisdiction serve as constant and not so gentle reminders of its vulnerability.[19] A recent example of considerable significance dealt with the issue of busing to achieve racial balance in public schools. A key provision of President Nixon's package of legislative proposals on the issue, offered in the spring of 1972, called for the withdrawal of federal court jurisdiction to hear such cases.

Congress also controls the Court's budget, and while it

---

[16] One writer described the Court as "a tenant at sufferance" with respect to its relationship with Congress. See Charles A. Curtis, *Lions under the Throne* (Boston: Houghton Mifflin, 1947), Chapter 5, which is the basis of the description presented here.

[17] Abraham, *The Judiciary*, p. 2. Only 130 cases heard between 1789 and the mid 1960s came under the Court's original jurisdiction. Original jurisdiction encompasses disputes between the United States and one of the 50 states; cases involving foreign ambassadors or consuls; suits by a state against citizens of another state, aliens, or a foreign country; and disputes between two states. The Court's jurisdiction is exclusive only in the last category.

[18] The case was ex parte McCardle. See Curtis, *Lions*, for a brief description of the episode.

[19] In 1957, for example, Sen. William E. Jenner of Indiana introduced legislation that would have removed the appellate jurisdiction of the Court in five areas, including contempt of Congress, the Federal Loyalty Security Program, and admission requirements to practice law. The bill and its fate are described by Murphy, *Congress and the Court*, Chapter 7. Senator Dirksen's attempt to eliminate the Court's authority to hear reapportionment cases is a more recent example.

cannot cut the justices' salaries, it does determine whether there will be secretaries to answer the telephone, open the mail, and pay the electricity bill. It also has effectively reversed Supreme Court decisions, sometimes by passing new legislation to replace that which the Court had interpreted, sometimes by passing a constitutional amendment.[20] Finally, the Congress can and has changed the number of justices on the Court and the period of time it is in session.

The Supreme Court's dependence on the executive branch is equally great. The Court has no direct control over coercive power, such as the army, police, or even U.S. marshals. If its decisions and decrees are to be enforced, the executive branch has to do it.[21]

Ironically, though it carries the title *Supreme* Court, the Court finds it must rely heavily on the cooperation of both state and lower federal courts to see that its decisions amount to more than empty paper decrees. The Court, like heads of large bureaucratic organizations, finds it is unable to force ostensible subordinates to implement its decisions.[22] Even when it remands cases to lower courts for action not inconsistent with its decision, lower courts occasionally manage to

---

[20] The most notorious example, of course, is the passage of the Sixteenth Amendment authorizing a federal income tax in response to the Court's prior rulings that such a tax was unconstitutional. For a fascinating account of congressional attempts to reverse decisions through legislation, see Murphy, *Congress and the Court*, Part III.

[21] Judicial reliance on executive power is most dramatically demonstrated when federal marshals or troops are used to enforce a federal court order. Federal troops were used at the University of Mississippi in 1963 and at Little Rock High School in 1957 to enforce the orders of lower federal courts which in turn were implementing Supreme Court desegregation decisions. For a brief description of the Little Rock affair, see Richard Neustadt, *Presidential Power* (New York: Wiley, 1960), Chapter 2.

[22] The ability of lower courts to affect the Supreme Court's influence is described by Walter Murphy, "Lower Court Checks on Supreme Court Power," *American Political Science Review* 53 (1959), pp. 1017–1031.

subvert the Supreme Court's decisions.[23] As described previously, the unwillingness of many lower-level federal judges in the South to implement faithfully the 1954 desegregation decision demonstrates this most painfully. But unlike the heads of most bureaucracies, the Supreme Court does not have the automatic right to review decisions made by subordinate bodies. They can only be reviewed if the losing party appeals. The Court's small size relative to the number of inferior courts and cases insures that only a tiny fraction of decisions appealed to it can actually be reviewed closely. Thus, the ability of the Court to control the behavior of lower courts is sharply circumscribed. The Court necessarily must rely upon voluntary compliance by lower courts. Once again, we are brought back to the central importance of legitimacy.

Ultimately, the Supreme Court's legitimacy rests in the attitudes and feelings of the mass public and special publics composed of lawyers, law journals, and litigating interest groups which watch its behavior closely. The reactions of lower courts, Congress, and the executive branch toward the Court are all directly or indirectly conditioned by mass attitudes. When the Court's decisions begin to arouse widespread and active opposition in the normally apathetic mass public, the legitimacy that is at the basis of its effectiveness begins to erode. The old saying that the Supreme Court follows the election returns may be somewhat exaggerated. But the justices are clearly aware of the importance of public reaction to their decisions and to the Court's survival as an effective institution. It is only natural and prudent that they exercise some degree of self-restraint and allow some deci-

---

[23] "Evasion of Supreme Court Mandates in Cases Remanded to State Courts Since 1941," *Harvard Law Review* 67 (1954), pp. 1251-1259, reprinted in Thomas Jahnige and Sheldon Goldman, eds., *The Federal Judicial System* (New York: Holt, Rinehart and Winston, 1968), pp. 313-317.

sions to be shaped by their anticipations of what the public reaction will be.[24]

Some Examples of Impact

Although we can hardly review the literature on the impact of Supreme Court decisions here, something of the nature of the response to these decisions and the factors that help account for it can be conveyed by describing briefly several of them. We will then be in a position to attempt some generalizations leading to a theory of impact.

The impact of decisions on the treatment of accused criminals after apprehension offers an excellent illustration of the point that the material impact of a decision is often substantially less profound than the symbolic rhetoric surrounding the decision and its aftermath would suggest. These decisions, commencing with *Gideon* v. *Wainwright*,[25] progressively broadened the scope of the right of accused criminals to legal counsel and restricted the conditions under which a suspect's confession would be admissible as evidence in court. In *Gideon*, the Court merely held that a man accused of a felony in a state court was entitled to a lawyer at his trial even though he could not afford one himself. The next year, the Court ruled in *Escobedo* v. *Illinois* that when the investigation has begun to focus on a particular suspect and he has been taken into custody, when he has requested to consult with his lawyer and has been denied the opportunity, when the suspect is not effectively warned of his right to remain silent, and when the interrogation he is undergoing results in incriminating information (such as a confession), he has been denied his right to counsel and the confession is inadmissi-

---

[24] A favorite topic of those who study the Supreme Court is the extent to which it ought to exercise judicial self-restraint in cases involving politically hot issues. Most scholars feel that the Court has exerted somewhat less restraint in recent years, and that this has aroused increased opposition to it from a number of groups with an attendant loss in respect and legitimacy.

[25] 372 U.S. 335 (1963).

ble.[26] The decision raised a number of questions. Did all of these conditions have to be met before a confession could be thrown out? What sort of warning of one's constitutional rights was required?

The ambiguity of the decision in *Escobedo* was cleared up in the controversial *Miranda* case.[27] Here, the majority held that before a confession could be used in court, the police had to specifically and explicitly notify an individual in their custody of: the right to remain silent and say nothing; the fact that anything he might say could be used against him; the right to cease talking at any time; the right to have an attorney present; the fact that if he could not afford a lawyer, one would be provided free of charge.

It is clear that the decisions in the confession cases were conscious attempts to set policy of a very broad type. The Court's majority wanted to establish uniform procedures for police agencies throughout the country. How well did they succeed?

If we go by the public reaction to the *Miranda* decision, the answer would have to be that the Court indeed had a major impact. In the aftermath of the decision, both critics and supporters spoke of the tremendous changes that would be wrought. Supporters saw it as a strong blow for individual rights and liberties, and foresaw a revolution in police practices. Law-and-order conservatives attacked the decision as going too far, as placing the rights of the criminal above the rights of the victim and the crime-bedeviled public. Dire predictions came from police officials on the crippling effect the decision would have on their efforts to handle the crime problem. The substance of the decisions even became the topic of political debate as "law-and-order" assumed the status of a major issue in the 1968 presidential campaign.

If we look at what actually happened—at the conviction rate, at the number of people who confessed or requested an

---

[26] 378 U.S. 478 (1964).
[27] Miranda v. Arizona, 384 U.S. 436 (1966).

attorney at the station house—a different picture emerges. The *Miranda* decision in particular stimulated a number of empirical studies designed to measure its impact.[28] The major findings are summarized below.

The impact was necessarily limited since confessions are necessary in obtaining convictions in only about 15 percent of felony arrests.[29] Thus, even if the police complied fully with the Court's decision and even if all suspects so warned said nothing, the conviction rate would not be much affected. Other sources of evidence, including eyewitnesses and the police themselves, are usually good enough.

Although compliance did increase in the months following the decision, the studies suggest that the police do not fully comply with the requirement that warnings be given. The *Yale Law Journal* study found that only 35 of 118 suspects were given all of the warnings, though all but 22 percent received at least some of them.[30] Even when the warnings are given, subtle techniques of subverting them (through tone of voice and manner of delivery) are sometimes employed.[31]

Even when the police do comply, defendants very often do

---

[28] Michael Wald, *et al*, "Interrogations in New Haven: The Impact of *Miranda*," *Yale Law Journal* 76 (1967), p. 1550. Theodore Souris, "Stop and Frisk or Arrest and Search," in Theodore Becker, ed., *The Impact of Supreme Court Decisions* (New York: Oxford University Press, 1969), p. 176; Richard J. Medalie, *et al.*, "Custodial Police Interrogation in Our Nation's Capital: The Attempt to Implement *Miranda*" in Becker, *ibid.*, p. 168; Richard Seeburger and R.S. Wetlik, Jr., "*Miranda* in Pittsburgh: A Statistical Study," *University of Pittsburgh Law Review* 29 (1967), pp. 1-26. See also Wasby's summary of this research. Wasby, *The Impact of the . . . Supreme Court*, pp. 149-162.

[29] The Yale study found interrogation was crucial in only 12 of the 90 cases studied. Wald, "Interrogations in New Haven," p. 1534. A study by a Detroit police detective placed the proportion of cases where confessions were essential at 13.1 percent of the cases examined in 1961 and 11.3 percent in 1965. Souris, "Stop and Frisk," p. 178. Seeburger and Wetlik, "*Miranda* in Pittsburgh," p. 15, estimate the proportion at 20 percent.

[30] Wald, "Interrogations in New Haven," p. 1550.

[31] *Ibid.*

not remain silent, break off questioning, or request a lawyer.[32] In part, this may be due to the manner in which the warnings are given. But other reasons which suggest the difficulty of instituting change also exist.

Defendants do not always understand the meaning of the warnings.[33] Some suspect that any lawyer provided by the police would be in cahoots with them. Even those who understand the right to counsel do not always request a lawyer. In the Washington, D.C. study, 34 percent fell into this category. Forty-one percent in this same study who understood their right to silence talked nonetheless.[34]

The conclusions of the Yale study that not much changed as the result of *Miranda* seem well founded. In only 6 of the 90 cases studied could the *Miranda* decision have resulted in failure to solve a crime that otherwise would have been solved.[35] Convictions do not seem to have declined in frequency; the number of defendants confessing has not changed much.[36] The police are probably more efficient in their investigations, relying less on confessions. Perhaps a few defendants are not convicted who otherwise might be. But the revolution in criminal procedure and the hoardes of crafty criminals that were predicted as a result of *Miranda* simply have not materialized. The major impact of the confession cases seems to have been in the realm of symbolic politics.

The response to this decision forcefully demonstrates that establishing policies on paper that seek to guide the behavior of others does not mean such policies will be followed. In the words of two students of the Court's impact, "What appears

---

[32] Medalie, "Custodial Police Interrogation," p. 168.

[33] *Ibid.*, pp. 171–173.

[34] *Ibid.*, pp. 173–174.

[35] Wald, "Interrogations in New Haven," p. 1591.

[36] Souris, in "Stop and Frisk," shows this by comparing conviction and confession rates for various categories of crime for 1961 (before these decisions were handed down) and 1965. See pp. 179–180.

to be constitutional law at the Supreme Court level becomes in part local politics at the level of community response." [37] We cannot assume the Court's decisions are automatically implemented. Nor can we assume that they make much difference even if they are implemented. Finally, the impact of *Miranda* demonstrates how the symbolic ramifications of a decision can far outweigh the material ones.

We cannot conclude from this case study, however, that decisions are never implemented, even when they become enmeshed in local politics. Nor can we assume that decisions laden with symbolic content do not have any tangible effect.

The impact of decisions dealing with prayer in public schools demonstrate the validity of this observation and offer an interesting contrast to *Miranda*—interesting because there are significant similarities as well as differences.

In *Engel v. Vitale*, [38] the Court ruled unconstitutional the practice of reciting a prayer composed by the New York State Board of Regents. The next year, the Court ruled in the *Schempp* [39] case that all forms of religious practice (including the recitation of the Lord's Prayer) in public schools were unconstitutional. Both were *high-arousal* decisions. They were denounced in Congress, and inspired a serious effort to amend the Constitution to permit school prayer. [40] Furthermore, both dealt with highly potent symbols—God, prayer, and the patriotic functions performed by schools.

The symbolic impact of *Schempp* has been well documented in a study that examined the attitudes of teachers and school administrators both before and after the ruling. [41]

---

[37] James Klonoski and Robert Mendelsohn, eds., *The Politics of Local Justice* (Boston: Little, Brown, 1970), p. 4.

[38] 370 U.S. 421 (1962).

[39] Abington Township School District v. Schempp, 374 U.S. 203 (1963).

[40] For a brief summary of the national political activity following these decisions, see Wasby, *The Impact of the ... Supreme Court*, pp. 129-130.

[41] William K. Muir, Jr., *Prayer In the Public Schools* (Chicago: University of Chicago Press, 1967).

One of the most striking findings was the variety and complexity of psychological reactions.[42] Some (termed *backlashers* reacted to the decision by becoming *more* favorably disposed to religion in public schools. Some did not change their opinions at all. They either maintained their support for school prayer or experienced vindication when the Court affirmed their opposition through its decision. Others experienced a change in attitude, bringing their views more into conformity with the Court's decision (i.e., disapproving of school prayer and other religious practices). Regardless of the specific effect of the decision, however, it is clear that *Schempp* had some impact on nearly everyone interviewed in the study. The issue of school prayer became salient in the friendship and work-life interactions of these school personnel. Changes—from increased tolerance of opposing views on the issue to overt hostility expressed to coreligionists—resulted from the chain of events initiated by the decision.

Unlike *Miranda*, it is not correct to conclude that nothing changed after *Schempp*. The frequency of prayers and other religious observances declined in the public schools in many areas of the country. One study found the number of districts in which all schools had devotional services dropped from over 33 percent in 1960 to only 8 percent in 1966.[43] Another study, which focused on the practices of teachers, found that the proportion conducting classroom prayers dropped from 60 to 28 percent following these decisions.[44]

But it would be equally incorrect to assume full compliance was forthcoming. In some states (Kentucky and Indiana, for example), compliance was low.[45] Tennessee continued to inform its teachers of a state law *requiring* Bible reading; only 51 of 121 districts changed their practices, and most of these did not fully comply.[46] Finally, even when there was official

---

[42] *Ibid.*, Chapter VI.
[43] Cited by Wasby, *The Impact of the . . . Supreme Court*, pp. 131.
[44] *Ibid.*, p. 132.
[45] *Ibid.*, p. 131.
[46] *Ibid.*, p. 134.

compliance, individual teachers sometimes continued to defy the ruling.[47] The interview study of teachers and administrators before and after *Schempp* found that some teachers (backlashers) actually increased religious activities following the decision: "The backlashers surreptitiously introduced religious ceremony into the curriculum through whatever loopholes they could find in the prayer ban—the Christmas skit, the Easter play, the special occasion."[48]

The factors affecting the degree of compliance are not fully evident. On the national level, the balance of political forces taking a stand on the issue was fairly even. Some church groups, especially among Jews but including many Protestants as well, supported the Court, as became clear in the hearings held on the proposed constitutional amendments. Opposition to such an amendment was strong enough to insure its defeat in the House of Representatives. At the local level, the position of local school administrators and school boards apparently proved to be crucial in several communities studied.[49] But where community sentiment was overwhelmingly and strongly in favor of school prayer, and where school officials shared community doubts about the decision, it was not implemented.

Finally, there are cases where compliance is virtually automatic and complete. When the Supreme Court ruled that 18 year olds could not be granted the right to vote in state elections through federal legislation, 18 year olds were nowhere permitted to vote (unless their state had previously made provisions for the practice). The decision did not prevent 18 year olds from voting in state and local elections very long, of course. The decision provided major impetus behind the drive for the ratification of the twenty-sixth Amendment.

---

[47] *Ibid.*, p. 135.

[48] Muir, *Prayer*, p. 84.

[49] *Ibid.* The role of the superintendent apparently was even more important in a small central Illinois school district which had a strong commitment to religious values. Richard M. Johnson, *The Dynamics of Compliance* (Evanston, Ill.: Northwestern University Press, 1967), especially Chapters 7–9.

When the Court ruled in *Gideon* that indigents accused of felonies in state courts were entitled to free legal counsel, most states managed to comply rather quickly. Thus, the impact was rather significant if one looks at whether indigents had counsel or not. The question of whether this has made much difference in the outcomes of their cases, however, is not so easily answered. From this perspective, the impact of *Gideon* is less clear.

Similar reservations can be entered regarding the Steel Seizure case. The Supreme Court ordered President Truman to return the steel mills seized during the Korean War to avert a strike to their corporate owners. This he did, and compliance was complete and immediate. But the transfer of control was largely symbolic, since the operating management of the mills was carried out by the existing corporate structure even during seizure.

Toward a Theory of Impact: Some Preliminary Steps

What conclusions can be drawn about the factors that affect impact? The most comprehensive and systematic analysis of research on impact has been undertaken by Wasby. It is worth examining his conclusions.

We have seen that the decisions of the Court, far from producing uniform impact or automatic compliance, have varying effects—from instances in which no action follows upon them to wide degrees of compliance (usually underreported), resistance, and evasion. These varying effects included increases in the level of political activity and activity within the judicial system itself and changes in governmental structure. Widespread criticism may follow decisions, and often attempts are made to reverse the Court through enactment of statutes or constitutional amendments. Important social interests, both economic and non-economic, may be dislocated or legitimized, and the Court's decisions also often perform an agenda-setting function for other political actors.[50]

---

[50] Wasby, *The Impact of the ... Supreme Court*, p. 243.

There remain, however, crucial questions about the Court's impact that are not answered by this summary, as Wasby later notes. "We are not able to speak of *degree* of impact or the *proportion* of instances in which the Court's rulings have an effect." [51]

But it is possible to identify some of the variables that apparently shape the impact decisions have. Six general categories of variables are suggested by Wasby. [52]

1. Characteristics of the cases (relationship to other cases on similar matters; scope and clarity of the decision; closeness of the vote on the case)
2. Attributes of the political environment into which the decision is "injected" (geographical scope of the impact: degree of controversy surrounding the decision; amount of political support and opposition to it generated)
3. The way the decision is communicated by the mass media and special channels (number of channels reporting the case; salience of reports relative to other cases handed down at the same time or other important contemporary news; accuracy of news accounts of the decision)
4. The nature of efforts to follow up the decision (do groups or individuals seek to comply with or defy the decision; are there groups available to resist or support the decision)
5. The characteristics of those who respond directly to the decision (their status; power; whether they are judicial personnel or others; their motivation for reacting)
6. The beliefs and values regarding both the Court and the subject matter of the decision among the mass public and those directly affected by and concerned with the decision's implementation.

Specifying a set of variables such as these is an important step in the development of a theory of Supreme Court

---

[51] *Ibid.*, p. 244.

[52] *Ibid.*, pp. 246-266. A number of hypotheses (numbering over 125 in all) are offered under each heading. For example, "Ambiguity in Supreme Court rulings decreases compliance" (p. 250).

impact. But it will be necessary to identify even more basic dimensions that subsume the six categories of variables just presented before our understanding can advance further. Specifically, we need to locate one or two crucial characteristics of cases which can help us answer a fundamental question: How important and under what conditions are which characteristics in shaping impact?

Two of the characteristics of decisions presented earlier appear to be promising: the level of arousal and the balance of political forces engaged in the processes initiated in the aftermath of a decision.

Low-arousal decisions are likely to be restricted in both symbolic and material impact, with the primary effects felt by the parties directly involved in the case. Compliance with the decision is also highly probable, particularly if the decision is free from ambiguity. As the levels of arousal and awareness of decisions increase, both the potential for symbolic and material impact and the probability of resistance increase. A decision can have a significant impact even if it does not reach the highest levels of arousal, particularly when there are special interests and individuals significantly affected.

The level of arousal itself depends in part upon the potential significance of a decision. A feedback process may well result in the aftermath of some cases. Groups or individuals who feel affected by the decision take note of it. Their arousal arouses others. As the general arousal level increases over time, the decision's impact is heightened. In discussing high levels of arousal, however, it is important to recognize that the mass public is no more informed or aware of even major Supreme Court decisions than it is of any major element of public policy. Approximately 60 percent of the mass public cannot think of *anything* the Supreme Court has done that they like or dislike.[53] Over one-third admitted that

---

[53] Walter F. Murphy and Joseph Tanenhaus, "Public Opinion and the United States Supreme Court," in Joel Grossman and Joseph Tanenhaus, *Frontiers of Judicial Research* (New York: Wiley, 1969), p. 277.

they had no idea of what the Court's main job in government was.[54] When we speak of high levels of arousal, then, we are referring to the attentive public for Supreme Court decisions, a public far more restricted than the general public.

With this qualification in mind, what can we say about the impact of high-arousal decisions? Like the school desegregation, criminal procedure, and school prayer decisions, they have a strong symbolic component to their impact. The potential for material impact, even if compliance is forthcoming, may well depend upon the nature of the decision. The obvious conclusion is that highly symbolic and controversial decisions would have a substantial tangible impact if implemented. But as the studies of the *Miranda* decision suggest, this may not always be the case. Some would even claim that the tangible impact of the reapportionment decisions were limited. Although the district lines for state legislatures were redrawn to equalize population, it is not clear just what difference this made in the policies initiated and implemented by the states.

Of course, compliance (whatever its tangible significance may be) does not always follow high-arousal decisions. Although a number of specific hypotheses have been suggested, perhaps the most important underlying variable is the balance of political power of the groups and individuals aroused by the decision. If a high-arousal decision is opposed by a number of influential and active opponents and supported by few, it is unlikely to be implemented even though its symbolic impact may be very great. If both opponents and supporters are strong (as was the case with school desegregation), compliance will be difficult but not impossible.

Though it is true that as a general rule the Supreme Court cannot serve as a major innovator of policy unless strong support already exists for its position, there are several subject-matter areas where the Court appears to have the ability to innovate without such support. Support in these areas is

---

[54] *Ibid.*, p. 281.

automatic because the Court is perceived to have a special expertise and legitimacy there. Decisions involving the rights of criminal defendants are a good example. Few organized groups with much political power were willing to support actively their implementation. And while resistance to some of them was intense and fairly effective (e.g., *Miranda*), others (such as *Gideon*) have largely been accepted by the legal profession, lower judiciary, and law-enforcement community.

THE IMPACT OF OTHER HIGHER COURTS

Between the U.S. Supreme Court and the lower state courts lie a number of intermediate tribunals in the judicial hierarchy. Prominent among them are the courts of final appeal in each of the states, known in most states as the state supreme court. Below these there are intermediate appellate courts in 22 states.

In the federal court system, there are the U.S. courts of appeals. There are also various special federal courts (the Court of Claims, the Tax Court, the Court of Military Appeals, etc.).[55]

Even less is known about the impact of these courts than that of the U.S. Supreme Court. The brief descriptions that follow consequently have the modest goal of suggesting the nature and scope of their impact in an impressionistic fashion.

State Supreme Courts

State supreme courts make four types of decisions that are likely to have significant consequences. Not surprisingly, they resemble the types of decisions the U.S. Supreme Court makes since these courts occupy an analogous position in the state political system. In keeping with this analogy, the first category of decisions might be called *state judicial review*.

---

[55] For an excellent description of the organization of the court system, see Henry J. Abraham, *The Judicial Process*, 2nd ed. (New York: Oxford University Press, 1968), Chapter IV.

State laws, executive and administrative actions, and the behavior of lower courts may be judged contrary to the state constitution. The California Supreme Court's 1971 ruling that the use of local property taxes to finance public schools violated the California constitution is an unusually prominent example. State supreme courts also have the power to declare state laws contrary to the U.S. Constitution.

Another type of decision likely to have a significant impact is the interpretation of state statutes. The formal conditions under which other state political institutions operate are shaped by state judicial decisions.[56] Appeals from lower state court decisions on disputes that arise from the interpretation of state statutes can involve a wide variety of issues. In Michigan, a suit filed against the Ann Arbor City Clerk for refusing to register students ultimately resulted in a Michigan Supreme Court decision that permitted college students to register to vote where they attended school. The Supreme Court of Pennsylvania determined the winner of the Democratic senatorial primary by invalidating 5,000 ballots.[57] A study of the Louisiana Supreme Court's decisions dealing with elections, appointment and removal of governmental employees, and conflicts among agencies of state government found 204 such cases.[58] In addition to deciding who had won elections, these cases affected who held non-elective positions, and even the fate of bond issues, capital improvements, and charter elections.

Decisions on a case-by-case basis can have a profound impact on the content of the common law in a number of important areas. These include contract law, torts, state crim-

---

[56] Herbert Jacob and Kenneth Vines, "The Role of the Judiciary in American State Politics," in Glendon Schubert, ed., *Judicial Decision-Making* (New York: Free Press, 1963), p. 252.

[57] Kenneth Vines, "Courts as Political and Governmental Agencies," in Herbert Jacob and Kenneth Vines, *Politics in the American States* (Boston: Little, Brown, 1966), p. 240.

[58] Kenneth Vines, "Political Functions of a State Supreme Court," in Kenneth Vines and Herbert Jacob, *Tulane Studies in Political Science* (New Orleans: Tulane University Press, 1963).

inal procedure, and the standards to be applied in child-custody cases, to name a few. Thus, state supreme courts shape the standards that lower courts apply when rendering decisions on accident claims or judging the fairness of consumers' installment contracts with retail businesses.

Finally, there are several ways in which state supreme courts can affect policy outside of traditional mechanisms. Some states have provisions for advisory opinions. A study of efforts by state supreme court justices to affect policy outside of regular channels found that a number of other techniques were employed.[59] These included discussing policy alternatives in written opinions and sending the opinions to legislators, the governor, and others; conferences with legislators, the governor, or his aides; recommendations made by judicial councils; and testifying at hearings or submitting formal reports. Most often, these attempts to exert influence involve the administration of the state judiciary—its organization, salaries, the regulation of the bar, and court procedure. Some evidence was found of attempts to change criminal laws and procedures and to change the methods for providing indigent defendants with attorneys.[60] Although it is difficult to measure the effectiveness of such efforts, it is here—in matters directly involving the state judiciary—that success is most probable. Of course, the success rates appear to vary from state to state.[61] Finally, some state supreme courts exercise supervisory control over lower courts. In New Jersey, it is evidently customary for lower-level court judges to adhere to Supreme Court recommendations in such matters as sentencing.[62]

---

[59] Henry R. Glick, "Policy-making and State Supreme Courts," *Law and Society Review* 5 (1970), pp. 273–275.

[60] *Ibid.*, pp. 278–279.

[61] *Ibid.*, p. 287.

[62] See "Top Jersey Court Ends Jail Term for First Offense on Marijuana," *The New York Times*, October 27, 1970. According to this article, the Supreme Court's recommendation that first offenders be given suspended sentences makes imposition of suspended sentences "virtually mandatory" by local judges in New Jersey.

Several concluding observations on the impact of state supreme courts can be made. First, in many areas the justices appear to have considerable discretion in deciding cases. But there is some evidence that judges in several courts reject the role of law-maker and attempt to restrict their decisions to strict interpretation of statutes.[63] Hence, it is not clear how frequently the 50 state courts of final appeal sieze opportunities to make innovative decisions. To the extent they do not, of course, their activities would tend to favor the status quo. Second, their discretion is probably enhanced somewhat by the low visibility that generally accompanies most of their decisions. Finally, we should not be surprised if some of the same problems of implementation facing the U.S. Supreme Court are encountered at the state level. Certainly, we cannot assume that state supreme court decisions are automatically and immediately implemented.

State supreme courts, however, do provide a forum for clashes between major social groups and economic interests. Disputes between business and labor,[64] blacks and whites,[65] and consumers and sellers, are played out in state judiciaries. Issues upon which there is strong public sentiment—abortion and aid to parochial schools, for example—also hit the courts. When interests are strong enough and the issue important

[63] Kenneth N. Vines, "The Judicial Role in the American States: An Exploration," in Joel Grossman and Joseph Tanenhaus, ed., *Frontiers of Judicial Research* (New York: Wiley, 1969).

[64] Kenneth Vines, "Courts as Political and Governmental Agencies," found the interplay of economic interests accounted for substantial proportions (from 37 to 59 percent) of cases before the supreme courts of Louisiana, Pennsylvania, and Idaho in 1962 and 1963 (Table ii, p. 272).

[65] See Kenneth Vines, "Southern State Supreme Courts and Race Relations," *Western Political Quarterly* 18 (March, 1965), p. 5. He reports that although generally unfavorable to the claims of blacks (and less favorable than southern federal courts), these courts did rule in their favor in about one-third of the cases. Aside from a large group of appeals by blacks involving procedural claims arising from criminal convictions, most cases represented attempts by local interests to block integration of facilities. The supreme courts were considerably more favorable to blacks in these cases than were the lower courts.

enough, appeals are made up to the court of last resort. Often this is the state supreme court.

U.S. Courts of Appeals

The low visibility of courts of appeals and a failure to recognize their importance has been responsible for a paucity of research on their operating characteristics. There has been a concomitant lack of attention to their impact. Several general characteristics, however, can be identified.

As a practical matter, these courts serve as courts of last resort for most litigants in district courts and parties to disputes before federal regulatory commissions and administrative agencies. Although a fairly large proportion of cases that go to trial in the district courts are appealed, only about 10 percent of courts of appeals cases are reviewed by the Supreme Court.[66]

The scope of the impact of the cases that receive final adjudication here is narrower than at the Supreme Court level. Many of the cases are routine, if not frivolous. If the losing party in the district court or federal regulatory agency proceeding insists on an appeal, it will be heard. Such cases are typically disposed of quickly and have little impact beyond the parties directly involved. A considerably higher proportion of the Supreme Court's cases deal with issues that have general significance. The low visibility of courts of appeals decisions also restricts their impact. If few people know about the decision, the number upon whom the decision will have a symbolic impact will necessarily be limited. In addition, the full potential of these courts is not realized because they are reluctant to rule contrary to Supreme Court precedents. Although the Supreme Court could reverse them on appeal if they consistently ignored precedent, the burden

---

[66] Richard J. Richardson and Kenneth N. Vines, *The Politics of Federal Courts* (Boston: Little, Brown, 1970), p. 114. In 1969, there were 14,397 trials in district courts and 8,903 appeals to the courts of appeals. See U.S. Bureau of the Census, *Statistical Abstract of the United States*, 1970 (Washington, D.C.: U.S. Government Printing Office, 1970), pp. 153-154.

of other pressing claims would not permit it to correct all such errors. Finally, the scope of issues presented in the cases heard and the segments of society represented in them is dependent upon the jurisdiction of federal district courts and administrative agencies. These courts are not normally able to rule upon the types of matters that come to the U.S. Supreme Court on appeal from state supreme courts.

It would be incorrect, however, to discount courts of appeals entirely. There are a number of ways their decisions have a substantial impact. For one thing, the fact that a case has been considered by a court of appeals undoubtedly affects the Supreme Court's decision as to whether it will review the case itself. Less than 20 percent of the cases appealed to the high court from courts of appeals are decided on the merits. [67] Apparently, it also makes a difference to the Supreme Court as to which court of appeals and which judges on it rendered the decision. [68] When such cases are accepted for review, the decision of the court of appeals is a major source of information. Although it is impossible to evaluate the influence of the court of appeals' opinion on the final decision, it is not unreasonable to presume that in many cases it is substantial.

Courts of appeals may also have a substantial impact in effecting the implementation of Supreme Court decisions, particularly when there is opposition to such rulings. Unfortunately, this aspect of their impact has largely been ignored. But studies of the implementation of the desegregation rulings suggest that the Court of Appeals for the Fifth Circuit (which encompasses much of the South) played a

---

[67] Louis S. Loeb, "Judicial Blocs and Judicial Values in Civil Liberties Cases Decided by the Supreme Court and the United States Court of Appeals for the District of Columbia Circuit," *American University Law Review* 13 (1965), p. 147.

[68] Richardson and Vines, in *The Politics of Federal Courts*, p. 130, quote Justice Frankfurter as saying, "When petitions for certiorari from decisions in which Judge Magruder wrote have come before the Court . . . on more than one occasion one has been led to say to his brethren, 'Were we to bring the case here, could we improve on Magruder?' "

crucial role, and succeeded in resisting local pressures when district judges apparently could not.[69]

Finally, among the cases which receive their final judicial hearing in these tribunals are matters of some importance. Because the Supreme Court can decide only a fraction of the cases appealed to it, many significant ones inevitably go no further than a court of appeals.[70] In some of these cases, the nature and importance of the issues involved is transformed. Cases which originally did not pose civil liberties issues were found to contain them when the court of appeals' decision was rendered.[71] Regardless of the eventual outcome or possible transformation of the issues considered, however, review by a court of appeals effectively delays the final decision in a controversy.

Finally, courts of appeals function as a unifying influence for the federal judicial system.[72] They help overcome the influence of local pressures on district courts by establishing uniform procedures and decision guideposts for the district judges in their circuit. To the extent there is uniformity in the decisions and statutory interpretations rendered within a circuit, it is largely a function of the prestige and supervisory activities of the court of appeals there. Second, the possibility of reversal on appeal helps control the behavior of district judges, an important function given the security of tenure and stature of these judges. Though the prospect of reversal has not prevented some southern district judges from handing down clearly erroneous desegregation decisions that

---

[69] See Jack Peltason, *Fifty-eight Lonely Men* (New York: Harcourt, 1961).

[70] For an interesting discussion of the importance of cases denied a hearing in the Supreme Court, see Fowler V. Harper and Alan S. Rosenthal, "What the Supreme Court Did Not Do in the 1949 Term—An Appraisal of Certiorari," *University of Pennsylvania Law Review* 99 (1950), pp. 293-325.

[71] Richardson and Vines, *The Politics of Federal Courts*, pp. 127-129.

[72] This argument is drawn upon material from Herbert Jacob, *Justice in America* (Boston: Little, Brown, 1965), p. 171.

were subsequently summarily reversed, most federal judges regard a reversal as a slap at their professional competence. The prospect of reversal, particularly if the court of appeals has made such reversal a distinct possibility through its previous decisions, thus can serve as a major means for controlling the behavior and shaping the decisions of district judges.

PART FIVE
CONCLUSION: THE LEGAL PROCESS IN THE POLITICAL SYSTEM

THE legal process is the stepchild of political analysis. The ordinary citizen hardly thinks of it as political at all. Professional observers and commentators are attracted to the dramatic events of American politics arising in Congress, the presidency, and even the Supreme Court. The routine operations of police, prosecutors, lower courts, and other components of the legal process are largely ignored. Even political scientists, who more than any group should acknowledge the political significance of its operation, have devoted little thought and even less research to the task of describing and understanding it.

The failure of political analysis to view American politics from the perspective of the legal process has had several significant consequences. For one, insights into the current state of American politics that can be gained from this perspective have not materialized. This is unfortunate. The legal process reflects the major outlines and developments of politics rather faithfully. If there is opposition to a war, the legal process encounters it in a variety of ways. If certain groups face discrimination and deprivation, their status will be mirrored by the nature of their involvement in the legal process. Indeed, as we shall show in some detail, much of the character of the distribution of benefits and deprivations performed by the political system can be discovered by examining the operation of the legal process. Basic questions going to the heart of the stability and health of any political system—the nature of law-in-action, the invocation of legitimacy to gain acceptance of public policy,[1] and both the necessity and effectiveness of the use of coercive force—are revealed in its functioning as well.

The fact that a major component of the process that determines who gets what in American politics has been overlooked is serious. In retrospect, it is astounding that attempts to describe urban politics, to pick one example, pay scant attention to the cumulative impact of landlord-tenant court, drunk court, sewer service, the bail system, civil commitment, and a host of other elements of the legal process. Whether the political scientist attempts to build toward a general theory of American politics or the informed layman strives to understand what is happening in his society, recognition of the role of the legal process is crucial.

In both organization and content, the foregoing chapters have sought to demonstrate the political essence and impact of the legal process. The two final chapters explore several remaining questions relating to its place in the political system. What major characteristics distinguish the performance of the legal process in its political functions? How can we account for patterns found in the outcomes produced by the legal process? Finally, what are the prospects for major reform in its operation?

---

[1] In this regard, James Klonoski and Robert Mendelsohn observe, "The system's basic legal mission is to place the stamp of legitimacy on the allocations of benefits and penalties produced by the operation of the political system." See *The Politics of Local Justice* (Boston: Little, Brown, 1970), p. xix.

CHAPTER 13
WHO GETS WHAT IN THE LEGAL PROCESS: PATTERNS OF OUTPUT

THE SIGNIFICANCE OF LEVEL

In thinking about the political significance of the legal process, it is only natural to borrow conceptual distinctions used widely in other contexts. Such is the case with the distinction between the terms *civil* and *criminal*. The distinction is a useful one in codifying statutes, organizing a law-school curriculum, and establishing administrative procedures for courts. But its use in thinking about the politics of the legal process is unfortunate.[1] It suggests that important differences exist when they do not. For instance, proceedings in lower criminal and civil courts resemble each other very

---

[1] For a thoughtful theoretical discussion of the similarities between criminal law at the police level and civil law, see Albert Reiss and David Bordua, "Environment and Organization: A Perspective on the Police," in Bordua, ed., *The Police: Six Sociological Essays* (New York: Wiley, 1967), pp. 28–32.

closely in a number of respects.[2] In addition, it obscures a more fundamental and useful distinction. For the purposes of political analysis, it is far better to refer to the *level* of the legal process.

When we speak of *lower levels*, we are referring to those participants and institutions normally involved in the initial invocation of the legal process.[3] The first-line participants include the police, bondsmen, local prosecutors, judges and other personnel in misdemeanor courts, and the private citizens who encounter them. The institutions at this level are centered around state courts of limited or special jurisdiction (both civil and criminal). They include the lower courts described in Chapter 6, courts hearing civil commitment proceedings, small claims courts, landlord-tenant courts, divorce courts, and other tribunals with jurisdiction over lesser civil actions. At the upper level, we find the U.S. Supreme Court, state supreme courts, the courts directly below them in the judicial hierarchy (state appellate courts, federal district and courts of appeals), and nonjudicial personnel such as state attorneys general. Normally, the matters they process are first dealt with by a lower level. State courts of general jurisdiction (both civil and criminal) fall somewhere in between.

A major hypothesis of this chapter is that significant characteristics on at least five important dimensions vary with level. Together, they describe many of the features that

---

[2] At the lowest levels, both witness gross violations of elemental standards of due process and procedure. Bureaucratic efficiency, not adherence to legal principles, is the standard of evaluation. Practical pressures (fees, case loads) force reliance upon stereotypes and procedural shortcuts rather than legal criteria. Defendants are frequently presumed guilty (or insane) and determinations of guilt or the entering of a judgment against the defendant become routine. Attorneys, if present, perform only perfunctory duties. Appeals are rare. And proceedings are often incredibly rushed.

[3] This distinction is similar to that made by Jerome Carlin, Jan Howard, and Sheldon Messinger in *Civil Justice and the Poor* (New York: Russell Sage, 1967), pp. 22–23, n. 87.

differentiate the legal process from other components of the political system.

The Balance of Symbolic and Material Outcomes by Level

Throughout this book, reference has been made to the difference between symbolic and material outcomes. Supreme Court decisions on the rights of criminal defendants and highly publicized criminal trials evoke a variety of psychological responses among both the general public and various special publics.[4] As our discussion in Chapter 12 of the school desegregation decision pointed out, the balance between the symbolic and material impact of a Supreme Court decision can change over time. But differences associated with level of the legal process are far more significant.

At the lower levels, outcomes are primarily material in their impact. A fine is levied, a "suspicious person" stopped and searched, a 90-day jail term for drunkenness or vagrancy imposed, an elderly relative committed to the state mental hospital, a tenant evicted. In all, material conditions are altered. Of course, the citizens directly involved react psychologically. Neither new patients nor their relatives are likely to avoid personal reactions following commitment to a mental hospital. But the symbolic impact is likely to stop there. Such cases are so frequent and routine to lawyers, judges, psychiatrists, and other regulars that their individual impact on them is negligible. It is rare for any outsider to be aware of such events at all.

At higher levels of the legal process, as suggested, the symbolic consequences of decisions increase disproportionately. When a state attorney general initiates an investigation, a federal judge rules a major northern metropolis guilty of de jure segregation, or the Supreme Court outlaws a form of discrimination against women, the symbolic ramifications are likely to be substantial. Material consequences may flow

---

[4] Few systematic studies have been concerned directly with the quality, frequency, and depth of such reactions.

from such actions, too. But they are very often far less significant than the symbolic ones.

The relationship appears to be most striking at the bottom levels of the legal process: The low visibility of the decisions made there insures a restricted symbolic impact. At the highest levels, however, some decisions that produce material but few symbolic consequences are found. Though some cases have high symbolic import at the intermediate levels, most do not.

The capacity of the legal process to generate powerful psychological reactions among the general public is substantial. When a decision achieves public visibility, it is likely to involve subject matter particularly susceptible to symbolic conceptualization. The legal process raises to visibility certain types of events (murders, rapes, political crimes). These elicit deep psychological concerns. People become anxious or reassured about violence, the ability of individuals to control hostile impulses, the capacity of government to punish failures of self-control and to demonstrate dangerous forces can be held in check, the vindication (or subjugation) of cherished principles and values.

The Gap Between Myth and Reality by Level

The sharp contrast between the adversary ideal and the bureaucratic reality of state felony courts is symptomatic of a consistent pattern. In one component of the lower levels of the legal process after another—the bail system, the civil commitment process, the trials of men arrested for drunkenness, and the serving of summonses—the law-in-action differs from what public rhetoric, appellate court decisions, and statutes proclaim it ought to be.

Of course, there are exceptions to the generalization that the lower the level the more pronounced the gap between official myth and reality. An occasional justice of the peace court, drunk court, or civil commitment process may operate in a fashion that brings joy to the heart of a civil libertarian. Until more systematic research is done, no definitive conclusions are possible. But on the basis of available impressionistic evidence, such situations are extremely rare.[5]

Because of the widespread lip service paid to myths about the operation of the legal process, the reality of its functioning is highly vulnerable. It is difficult for higher-court judges, leaders of the bar, and elected officials to condone improper practices once they are exposed. We shall return to a discussion of the significance of this vulnerability in Chapter 14.

Status and Prestige of Participants by Level

In Chapter 4, we found a relationship between the level and status of judges. As noted, this finding is consistent with the conclusions of Donald Matthews' study of background of political decision-makers: "[T]he more important the office, the higher the social status of its normal incumbent. Thus incumbents in the top offices are mostly upper and upper middle-class people.[6]

In the legal process, the generalization also applies to decision-makers who do not hold official positions. A study of lawyers in New York City, for example, found striking differences in the social backgrounds and status of lawyers practicing at different levels.[7] Indeed, the social characteristics of all the court regulars at the lower levels more closely resemble those of the general population than do the characteristics of higher-level decision-makers. The same is undoubtedly true of law-enforcement officials. Federal investigative agents are generally well educated and come from middle-

---

[5] Howard James, who spend a year observing the operation of lower courts throughout the nation on assignment for the *Christian Science Monitor*, confirms this conclusion. See *Crisis in the Courts* (New York: McKay, 1967).

[6] Donald R. Matthews, *The Social Background of Political Decision-Makers* (New York: Random House, 1954), p. 32.

[7] At the lower levels, attorneys are more likely to be solo practitioners, to have lower-middle- or working-class origins, to have attended a less prestigious law school, to have poorer and lower-status clients, and to have a lower income. See Jerome Carlin, *Lawyers' Ethics* (New York: Russell Sage, 1966), especially Chapter 2.

class backgrounds; local police rarely have college degrees and have working class or lower middle-class origins.

The relationship between the level of the legal process and the characteristics of citizens involved in it is even more striking. The lower levels are for the less well-off strata of society. It is the poor man, the immigrant, the minority group member who most often encounters the police, landlord-tenant court, civil commitment proceedings, and misdemeanor court. On the infrequent occasions when a middle-class person becomes involved in a criminal proceeding, it is likely to be in state felony court or even federal district court. Corporations, newspapers, universities, labor unions, governmental units, and other institutions and organizations of higher-status people rarely honor the lowest levels of the legal process with their presence.[8]

There are notable exceptions to this relationship between the level and status of citizen participants. Large numbers of middle-class people are potentially active participants in traffic court. Usually, however, it is possible to pay a fine without appearing in court. Likewise, large numbers of convicted defendants bring petitions to higher appellate courts, but they are rarely physically present.

What are the implications of this relationship? First, those aspects of the legal process that higher-status individuals are likely to encounter are more likely to conform to popular beliefs about how it functions. The gap between myth and reality is smallest precisely where the most influential seg-

---

[8] Carlin, Howard, and Messinger, in *Civil Justice*, p. 22, n. 87, summarize the implications of level within the judicial hierarchy (they do not include nonjudicial settings like citizen-police encounters) as follows: "... the lower the level of the court... (1) the lower the jurisdictional amount of claims (which means the more likely it will be used by lower-class persons), (2) the less likely that the parties will be represented by private counsel (reflecting in part the fewer economic resources of parties whose cases are processed through inferior tribunals), (3) the more likely the lawyers who deal with the court will have a low-status clientele ... and (4) the more likely that the court will be processing types of cases reflecting problems that have a higher incidence in the lower than the upper classes."

ments of society are likely to participate. Second, the leaders of the bench and bar are unlikely to have direct knowledge of how the legal process really operates on the lower levels. Officers of local bar associations, particularly in more populous areas, are likely to be higher-status lawyers who either do not appear in court at all or appear only in higher courts. Third, those citizens who are least likely to be effective in changing conditions they encounter are the very people who are subjected to the legal process at its worst—at the lowest levels.

The Shift in the Locus of Effective Decision-making

At the lower levels of the legal process, decisions frequently are not made where they should be. Nor are they made by the people who should be making them. It is the police who often determine what behavior will result in criminal sanctions, not legislatures, prosecutors, or judges. Statutes, case law, tradition, and popular beliefs hold that judges should determine the sentences which convicted defendants receive on the basis of penological considerations. Instead, prosecutors and defense attorneys frequently arrive at negotiated settlements on sentences and leave the judge with the empty choice of formally ratifying their agreements. The same is true with determining guilt. This is the function of juries, but the plea bargaining system leaves few decisions for them to make. Bail bondsmen have no official power, yet the prospects for conviction are sharply increased when they refuse to write a bond. Family members and the family doctor often decide whether to commit an individual to a mental hospital, rather than a judge after careful judicial review. Businessmen or their lawyers decide to invoke the formal powers of government to collect alleged debts, and they secure judgments and enforce collection nearly automatically.

At higher levels, the relocation of effective decision-making becomes progressively less pronounced. Appellate judges, as far as we know, arrive at their own decisions independently. Although other officials (federal prosecutors, federal district judges) may be strongly influenced by other participants, it is unlikely they dissipate their decision-making power to the extent that their counterparts at lower levels do.

The Nature of the Impact of Decisions by Level

At least three varieties of *impact* result from the actions of decision-makers. One is designated by the familiar term *policy*. Roughly defined, policy consists of explicit, broad decision rules that direct others to make particular choices under specified conditions. At times, however, a set of decision-makers will behave as if they were implementing a general policy even though no explicit decision rules exist. Such *implicit policies* (the second variety of impact) produce consistent patterns that permit us to predict behavior just as accurately as when policies are explicit, official, and publicized. Third, there are decisions made on an ad hoc basis that neither implement explicit policies nor contribute to a pattern of implicit policy. Yet such *ad hoc decisions* can have a significant impact. This category includes discretionary decisions made by prosecutors and police as well as court decisions in specific cases.

Compared to other components of the political system, the legal process as a whole generates a relatively small proportion of explicit policies. In part, this flows from the fact that legislatures and executive bodies are formally charged with establishing policies that police and others in the legal process are supposed to implement. In part it is a reflection of the case-by-case character of decision-making in the judiciary. But the concentration of activity in its lower levels, where explicit policies are nonexistent or ignored, is probably the most important reason.

Of course, this is not to imply an absence of explicit policy-making. Far from it. Appellate courts, particularly the U.S. Supreme Court, hand down decisions explicitly designed to guide the decisions of others, and such decisions may appropriately be designated as *policy* in the sense we are using the term. When prosecutors issue directives to their assistants on when to prosecute, or police chiefs order their men to cease using abusive language toward suspects, they too are engaging in policy-making. But as our analysis of the Supreme Court's impact suggests, it is dangerous to predict the significance of a policy from its content. The crucial question with explicit policy is whether it is being implemented.

Although there may be less explicit policy-making in the legal process than elsewhere, what there is is likely to be found at its higher levels, just as in other components of the political system. At its lower levels, the legal process generates *ad hoc decisions* or *implicit* policies.

A related characteristic of the legal process is the directness of impact when decisions are made. Decisions at its lower levels—by police, prosecutors, lower-level judges, and private attorneys—often have immediate and profound consequences for the individual citizens involved. Even though each decision involves only a few people, the accretion of many such decisions affects substantial numbers. Although other bureaucratic-administrative processes affect many people, the legal process is distinctive for the importance of the impact which its decisions have on the lives of those directly affected. Decisions made at higher levels also exhibit these characteristics, but with diminished intensity.

DISCRETION AND VISIBILITY IN THE LEGAL PROCESS

The legal process is distinguished by a unique combination of low visibility and high discretion that surrounds many of the decisions made. This proposition is summarized schematically in Figure 4.[9] Although all components of the legal process do

---

[9] The lower levels of the legal process share the characteristics of high discretion and low visibility with several other street-level bureaucracies, but the list is not terribly long. It includes postmen, various inspectors (for example, fire, housing code, health), welfare workers, license bureau personnel, teachers, and agricultural agents. All deal on a face-to-face basis with clients. While some rival the legal process for low visibility, few can match its breadth of discretion or the importance of the impact its decisions have on the lives of citizens. The close association between the legal process bureaucracy and *law* gives a legitimacy and a sanctity to the official rules that are supposed to govern its conduct not matched by other street level bureaucracies.

Figure 4. Location of some major decision-makers according to discretion and visibility of decisions. Location to position on the visibility and discretion continua.

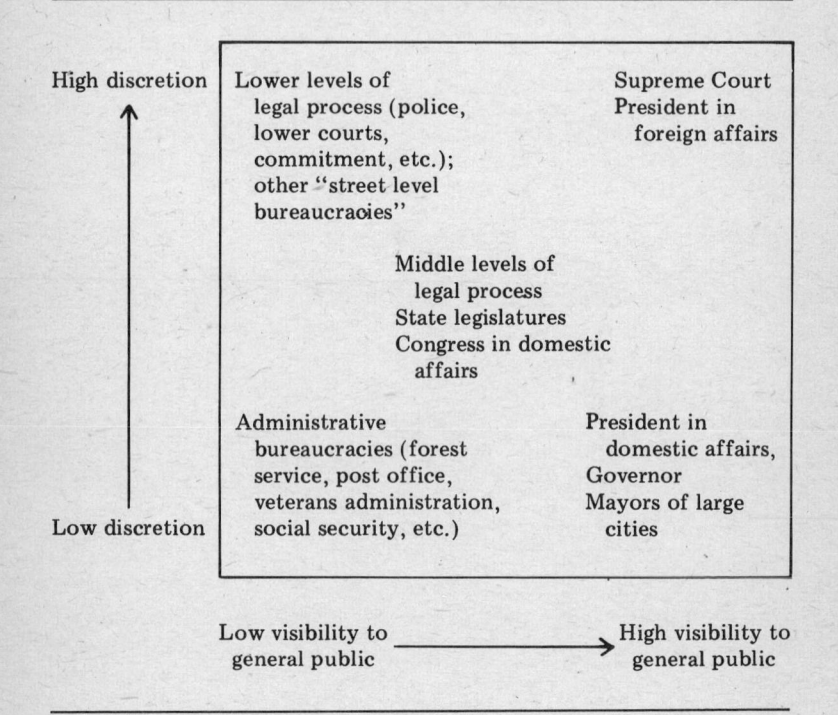

High discretion ↑
 	
Low discretion
	Lower levels of Supreme Court
	  legal process (police, President in
	  lower courts, foreign affairs
	  commitment, etc.);
	other "street level
	  bureaucracies"
	
	          Middle levels of
	            legal process
	          State legislatures
	          Congress in domestic
	            affairs
	
	Administrative President in
	  bureaucracies (forest domestic affairs,
	  service, post office, Governor
	  veterans administration, Mayors of large
	  social security, etc.) cities

Low visibility to ⟶ High visibility to
general public   general public

not fall into the high-discretion—low-visibility region (the Supreme Court is a notable example), on balance the elements of the legal process tend to be concentrated there.

Earlier, we defined discretion as the ability to choose between significant alternatives without encountering severe sanctions. It is also necessary to distinguish between *delegated* and *unauthorized* discretion.[10] When the right to choose between significant alternatives is granted by a higher

---

[10] This distinction is drawn by Jerome Skolnick, *Justice Without Trial* (New York: Wiley, 1967), p. 71.

authority, the discretion exercised is delegated. But when decision-makers are able to choose among alternatives against the express commands of superiors—when they "do it anyway" and get away with it—their discretion is unauthorized.

Any bureaucratic or administrative process exhibits both types of discretion. Decision-makers in the legal process probably enjoy a higher level of discretion than elsewhere; moreover, it is likely that a larger portion of it is unauthorized as opposed to delegated discretion than in other political processes.[11]

The high level of unauthorized discretion can be explained, in turn, by the notion of low visibility. The exercise of unauthorized discretion requires that the officials who are in a position to restrict choices and sanction those who make unauthorized decisions be unaware of what is happening. As long as appellate judges, police chiefs, chief prosecutors, bar association grievance committees, and others charged with enforcing decision-rules do not know what their subordinates are doing, the likelihood of their imposing penalties for unauthorized behavior is remote.

In part, low visibility results from physical obstacles. It is nearly impossible to monitor closely a patrolman's behavior during on-view encounters with citizens. Higher-level judges lack the information, the resources to obtain the information, and the time to analyze it that would be required for them to oversee completely the performance of lower-court judges. Attorneys deal with their clients in private places, and resist outside prying on the grounds that it violates the sanctity of the attorney-client relationship.

But the low visibility of decisions in the legal process cannot be explained by such factors entirely. Lack of interest in discovering what happens at the lowest levels plays a

---

[11] This does not mean, of course, that there are no instances in which discretion is limited or that there is little delegated discretion. Both are found in the legal process. The argument here is that they are overshadowed by the total amount and the prevalence of unauthorized as opposed to delegated discretion.

significant role. After all, if researchers can discover its operating characteristics, so could those with official responsibility. This is especially true for lower courts, where, except for juvenile courts, proceedings are generally open to the public. Could this reticence to investigate partially stem from a desire not to know because of an inkling of what would be found? Certainly no mean role is played by the fact that those in a position to take action are not adversely affected by the current manner of operation. As we shall see, it is the poor, minority group members, the young, and the very old who are disadvantaged by the unauthorized exercise of discretion. The leaders of the organized bar, higher-level judges, and other officials find they can ignore the way the lower levels of the legal process operate without experiencing political pressure or sanctions.

This suggests that when we speak of low visibility, it's important to ask, Low visibility with respect to whom? From the standpoint of the general public and responsible officials, visibility indeed may be low. But to those adversely affected by low-visibility decisions, the impact may be very painfully evident. People are aware that merchandise is seized and sold at auction, that tenants are evicted, and that involuntary commitment to mental institutions exists when these things happen to family members, friends, or neighbors. But those who are aware of such occurrences have little political influence and can do nothing. Those who could do something are neither aware nor particularly concerned.

There is a rough correlation between the level of the legal process and visibility to the general public. At the lowest levels it is unusual for any particular decision or sequence of decisions to acheive notoriety. Civil commitments, garnishments, evictions, default judgments, minor police harrassment, and routine jail sentences for drunkenness and vagrancy occur daily without making a ripple. Even most litigation in state courts of general jurisdiction and federal district courts proceeds with little public recognition. It is the murder trial, a case involving a socially or politically prominent person, or confinement of a middle-class female in a women's pretrial detention facility that is the occasional event visible to the general public.

At higher levels of the legal process, visibility is also restricted, but less so. A higher proportion of Supreme Court decisions attract some attention than the decisions of a county misdemeanor court.[12] Information about proceedings in courts of record, particularly when decisions take the form of written opinions, considerably enhances the potential for visibility.

The significance of relative visibility becomes clearer when it is approached from a different perspective. As we have just pointed out, most of the events and decisions that do achieve some degree of wider visibility originate at the higher levels. And it is precisely at these levels that the gap between myth and reality is smallest. Thus, when the legal process becomes visible to the general public, its beliefs in the myths are reinforced. After all, it is the Supreme Court decision, replete with written opinion, cogently argued briefs, and the sanctity of the Court's legitimacy that accounts for much public awareness of the legal process. The notorious crime, which typically is resolved by a full-fledged jury trial rather than negotiated plea, reinforces the tendency. Notions that all's well in the legal process are perpetuated by the unrepresentativeness of the glimpses the general public sees of its operation.

WHO GETS WHAT FROM THE LEGAL PROCESS—PATTERNS OF IMPACT

Although we have discussed distinct components of the legal process separately throughout this book, their intercon-

---

[12] Nevertheless, many decisions of even the Supreme Court go unnoticed by all but a limited number of lawyers with a particular interest in the subject matter.

nectedness has been evident at a number of points. The Supreme Court, for instance, must rely upon other judicial actors to implement its decisions. Yet clearly its decisions have an effect on these other participants. The elaborate patterns of mutual interaction and dependence found among the regulars in state felony courts demonstrates interrelatedness equally well.

The consequences of interrelatedness are sometimes quite obvious. In an effort to improve police efficiency, two reforms were instituted in New York City—prearraignment processing of criminal suspects and substitution of a court summons for arrest. They were so successful that the police were able to use the time saved to make more arrests. The result was an accelerating backlog of cases in the criminal court. [13] Less obvious relationships also can be found. The size of prison populations and the behavior of police and prosecutors do not at first glance appear to be related. But wardens have been known to telephone judges to warn that prison overcrowding was producing riot conditions. Responding to demands to reduce the number of new prisoners, judges, in turn, pressure prosecutors to be more selective in prosecutions and more lenient in granting probation in plea bargaining. Prosecutors, in turn, indicate to the police to be more selective in making arrests. [14]

Although the uninformed citizen is rarely aware of the extent of such interrelatedness, it is usually a matter of common knowledge to participants, including defendants. In *Manchild in the Promised Land*, Claude Brown provides an example from the perspective of a teenage defendant: "He [the judge] said he was going to give us another chance. We'd expected this: we'd heard that every place they could have sent us was all filled up...." [15] Thus, the legal process

---

[13] "City's Courts Act to Grease Sluggish Wheels of Justice," *The New York Times*, November 11, 1969.

[14] George Cole, "The Decision to Prosecute," paper delivered at the 1968 American Political Science Association Convention, p. 16, reports this sequence of relationships in King County (Seattle), Washington.

[15] Claude Brown, *Manchild in the Promised Land* (New York: Signet, 1965), p. 123.

exhibits one of the prime characteristics of any system; changes in one component produce repercussions in the others.

The legal process as a whole displays a similar relatedness to the general political system. Certainly a major conclusion to draw from Part II is that politics is very much involved in selecting the major participants in the legal process.

But there is another way in which the legal process reflects its ties to the rest of the political system that deserves special emphasis. To a remarkable degree, the impact of its operation parallels that of the rest of the political system. The basic pattern can accurately be summarized in a few words: The poor, the young, the very old (especially if poor), and disadvantaged minority group members receive a disproportionately large share of the sanctions and a correspondingly small share of the benefits allocated by the legal process in comparison to other individuals in society.

A number of people have commented on the existence of this basic pattern. But the assertion that the poor, black, and young suffer at the hands of the legal process is rarely backed by hard evidence. Throughout Part IV, the analysis stopped just short of drawing conclusions about patterns of who gets what. In the pages below, evidence is drawn together to document that the disadvantaged in society do fare poorly in the legal process.

Because it is somewhat awkward to use the phrase "the poor, the elderly, the young, and members of disadvantaged minority groups" repeatedly, we shall use *the Poor* (with a capital "P"), or *the Disadvantaged*, as summary terms to denote all of these groups in the following discussion.

The Police

It is the Poor who most often are the objects of police behavior. Furthermore, they are treated more harshly than members of advantaged groups.

A number of factors contribute to this commonplace but profoundly significant pattern. For one thing, police are more likely to encounter the Poor. Law-enforcement activities tend to be concentrated on behavior more often engaged in by the Disadvantaged. White-collar crimes (consumer fraud, embezzlement, evasion of city taxes) receive little attention. Decisions of police officials on where to assign their patrolmen (who are primarily engaged in order maintenance) usually result in heavy policing of the residential areas of the Disadvantaged. Once in the neighborhood, residents are more visible than elsewhere. Middle-class whites are not forced into the streets to escape crowded, dingy, and dilapidated housing. They can socialize in their homes. But not the Poor. If they get drunk, it is not likely to be in the comfortable home of a friend but in a crowded bar or on the street. If they want to shoot craps or pitch quarters, it frequently must be done in a public place.

Not only is their behavior more visible; but it is also likely to attract order-maintenance responses from the police. Middle-class whites get companionship and kicks from gambling at neighborhood poker games. Though both may involve similar stakes and neither be run for profit, the lower-class dice game is more likely to be discovered and to result in arrests upon discovery. Country clubs that sell drinks after the legal cutoff time are seldom raided; "blind pigs," where blacks can purchase drinks after hours, however, are often the object of vigorous police attention.

Police seem to show less respect for the Disadvantaged. They are typically more polite to an old man than to a teen-ager stopped for speeding, even if a ticket is given to both. They are more likely to believe middle-class victims and to treat them more politely than they do lower-class victims.[16] A well-dressed, substantial-looking drunk may be sent home in a taxi. The derelict gets a ride in a paddy wagon. Pervasive suspiciousness, a conventional morality, and

---

[16] James Q. Wilson, in *Varieties of Police Behavior* (Cambridge, Mass.: Harvard University Press, 1968), reports that police differentiate between the "legitimacy" of victims. A middle-class person claiming a street attack is believed; a lower-class person claiming he was assaulted is treated skeptically. See p. 27.

a deep-seated cynicism combine to determine who they stop, who they believe, who they feel is worthy of respect and who of contempt. Youths with no shirts, long hair, beads, and headbands raise the hackles of most policemen (and most Americans for that matter). The propensity to stop such people is consequently high.

Other elements in the working personality of police have significant consequences. As noted in Chapter 5, suspiciousness, apprehensiveness, and the fear of physical harm force them to search for cues indicating danger. The consequences of such behavior are not neutral. Unfortunately, the appearance and behavior patterns of the Poor produce the very cues that signal possible danger. Encounters with them prompt an aggressive, take-charge approach, and may include abusive language and a quick frisk. This response is likely whenever potential danger is sensed, even if its possibility is low. The consequences of not taking such precautions can be disasterous if a physical attack ensues. The penalties for taking them when they prove to be unnecessary are almost nonexistent. [17] Thus, from the police viewpoint, the policy is quite rational. But the costs are rather high to the Poor. Middle-class blacks, eagle scouts, and the hard-working poor are stopped, frisked, and perhaps verbally abused for no reason they can perceive as legitimate. [18] The situation is exacerbated by the hostile attitudes such people have toward the police. Contempt-of-cop responses are understandably more common among the Disadvantaged.

Since middle-class whites are not perceived as sources of potential danger and disrespect, they can be approached in a more relaxed fashion. Also, police officers respect the ability

---

[17] This point is drawn from Michael Lipsky, "Towards a Theory of Street Level Bureaucracy," unpublished paper, p. 20.

[18] The resentment such episodes produce found articulate expression several years ago on the campus of Yale University. University security guards, responding to increasing thefts from dormitories, began stopping black Yale undergraduates on campus and in their own dorms requesting their student identification cards. The infuriated students raised loud and impassioned objections.

and willingness of such individuals to complain effectively to their superiors.

The behavior of police in encounters with citizens on the street has aptly been described as "unarticulated improvisation."[19] Yet uniformities in the attitudes of both police and citizens and in the situations where they confront each other lead to the familiar patterns just described. Although such patterns result from implicit policies, they arise within the context of certain conscious decisions about where to patrol, what laws to enforce, and so on. The use of *aggressive preventive patrol* to reduce crime, and standing orders to get groups of people on the street to move on contribute to the opportunities for the operation of unarticulated improvisation.

The Bail System

The dramatic consequences flowing from a defendant's inability to make bail were described in some detail in Chapter 10. To summarize, those in pretrial detention are significantly more likely to be convicted, and, if convicted, significantly more likely to be sentenced to prison.

When people do not make bail, it is usually because they cannot afford it. They suffer the consequences of pretrial detention because they are poor. In the words of two critics of the bail system, "Those who go free on bail are released not because they are innocent but because they can buy their liberty. The balance are detained not because they are guilty, but because they are poor."[20]

Discrimination is compounded by the procedures for determining bail levels. To the extent that these procedures result in excessive bail (i.e., bail higher than that which is needed to

---

[19] The President's Commission on Law Enforcement and Administration of Justice, *Task Force Report: The Police* (Washington, D.C.: U.S. Government Printing Office, 1967), p. 18.

[20] Daniel Freed and Patricia Wald, *Bail in the United States: 1964*, Report to the National Conference on Bail and Criminal Justice (Washington, D.C.: 1964), p. vii.

insure the appearance of the accused in court), the situation is even more onerous for the Poor. The effect of this extends beyond a greater probability of conviction and subsequent sentence to prison. Those unable to make bail must endure imprisonment, the most severe sanction imposed by the legal process short of the death penalty, before they are convicted of a crime. As noted previously, many of them never are convicted, and are eventually released.

The prevalence of the Poor in pretrial detention is shocking to anyone who believes in equal justice for all. In New York City, more people are in jail because they could not make bail prior to trial than are sentenced to prison after conviction.[21]

Other Aspects of the Criminal Process

Other important characteristics of the criminal process also contribute to the basic pattern. The behavior of private citizens helps to instigate differential enforcement. One study of the way in which police handle juvenile crimes concludes that black juveniles are more often apprehended for delinquent acts because their black older neighbors are more likely to call the police and urge arrest.[22] A study of shoplifting also revealed department stores' policies lead to differential enforcement.[23] First, they engage in *selective observation*. Store detectives are more likely to watch lower-class and black women. Second, there is *selective prosecution*. Black women shoplifters are more likely to be prosecuted than their white counterparts.

The concentration of the Disadvantaged in lower criminal courts also has its effects. The commitment of the personnel

---

[21] Patricia Wald, "Pretrial Detention and Ultimate Freedom: A Statistical Study," *New York University Law Review* 39 (1964), p. 634.

[22] Donald J. Black and Albert J. Reiss, Jr., "Police Control of Juveniles," *American Sociological Review* 35 (1970), p. 70.

[23] Mary Owen Cameron, "Shoplifters Who Become 'Data'," reprinted in William Chambliss, ed., *Crime and the Legal Process* (New York: McGraw-Hill, 1969), pp. 174–188.

staffing these tribunals to principles of fairness, due process, and equal justice is frequently weak. The training of many judges and other lower-court personnel is so inadequate that they understand little about these principles or the requirement of adhering to them. Furthermore, the attorneys provided the Poor are rarely as effective as the attorneys hired by the well-off.

Finally, although rigorous proof is difficult to obtain, there is probably some truth to the assertion that the content of criminal law tends to fall more heavily on the Poor. The activities the less well-off engage in are more likely to be formally labeled as criminal. Gambling at race tracks is not illegal for those who can leave work, get transportation, and find at least two dollars to bet, but placing a 25-cent bet on the numbers is illegal. The structure of penalties for minor offenses is also stacked against the indigent. It was not until March 1971, that the Supreme Court held it was a violation of equal protection under the Fourteenth Amendment to jail defendants because they could not pay a fine.[24] Although precise figures on the number of people jailed for this reason do not exist, one student of the problem estimates that for at least the last 50 years, between 40 and 60 percent of those in county jails were there for failure to pay their fines.[25] And, as we might expect, the practice did not end when the Supreme Court ruled it unconstitutional.[26]

---

[24] Tate v. Short, 28 L. Ed. 2d 130 (1971). Tate was fined $425 on conviction of nine traffic offenses. Unable to pay, he was sentenced to 85 days in jail—at the rate of five dollars per day.

[25] Derek A. Westin, "Fines, Imprisonment, and the Poor: Thirty Dollars or Thirty Days," *California Law Review* 57 (May, 1969), p. 788.

[26] In Arkansas, the drowning death of a 15-year-old boy exposed conditions on a county penal farm run primarily with the labor of those convicted of misdemeanors and working off their terms at five dollars a day. Eight months after the court's decision in Tate v. Short, the practice was described as being still "common." "Boy's Death on Penal Farm May End Arkansas' Jailing of Poor," *The New York Times*, November 10, 1971.

The Poor as Participants in the Lower Levels of the Civil Process

The Poor as Defendants

An examination of the day-to-day operation of the civil process at its lower levels would show that all segments of society are represented. But no group is so profoundly affected as the Poor.[27] Their relation to the civil process was succinctly summarized by one author: "Poor people are prone to legal trouble. They are often defendants, rarely plaintiffs."[28]

When they are involved in the civil process, the Poor typically find themselves at its lower levels, with all which that entails. They are rarely represented by attorneys. Legal standards and safeguards are often lax or nonexistent. Those safeguards remaining are rarely invoked. Consequently, their interests are sometimes not even represented, and they are practically never well-articulated and fully defended. Instead, the Poor are routinely processed towards an almost inevitable unfavorable disposition.

Default judgments account for the overwhelming proportion of dispositions. Although some result from a tacit acknowledgement of indebtedness, many undoubtedly occur either because the defendant could not understand the import of the summons or because he never received the summons. Process servers are particularly reluctant to go into the neighborhoods of the Poor (especially black neighborhoods). And, relatively speaking, the chances are high that the Poor lack the education needed to understand the summons when it is received.

---

[27] Interestingly, it is not the most impoverished who are typically disadvantaged by being civil defendants. True, they may be subject to eviction. But they find it difficult to get the credit that is a prerequisite to falling into the debtor's spiral. The very poor rarely have the opportunity to be in a position to be sued or garnished.

[28] Patricia Wald, *Law and Poverty* (Washington, D.C.: U.S. Government Printing Office, 1965), p. 6.

At the lower levels, then, the civil process actually operates as an instrument for the commercial and propertied interests to use in dealing with the poor. Landlords and creditors utilize the formal coercive power of the state to evict tenants, repossess merchandise, seize money (garnishments) and conduct forced sales of goods.

The Poor as Plantiffs

Everyone has an equal right to enter the civil process as a plaintiff to seek relief from alleged wrongs. As a practical matter, the Poor do not receive the same benefits from successful civil actions that the better-off do. Their failure to use the civil process as plaintiffs has profound consequences, and it is worthwhile to examine the reasons for it in some detail.

This failure of the Poor to become plaintiffs is well documented. An experimental Judicare system permitted indigents to obtain whatever legal services they wished and was overwhelmed with divorce actions; 84 percent of the cases handled at the start of the program were divorces.[29] This suggests that poverty prevents substantial numbers of people from seeking divorces. A study of automobile accident victims found that those of lower socioeconomic status were less likely to make claims.[30] Since lawyers handling such cases operate on a contingent-fee basis, something more than lack of money is involved.

---

[29] "Eighty-four Percent of Poor Who Get Legal Aid in Wisconsin File Divorce Suits," *The New York Times*, September 2, 1966. The article reports that 80 percent of cases in England's judicare program in its first year were for divorce. The Office of Economic Opportunity neighborhood law offices have been 20 and 30 percent of their case loads in divorce work. Wald, *Law and Poverty*, pp. 7 and 45; and Carlin, Howard, and Messinger, in *Civil Justice*, also point out the poor are unable to obtain desired divorces.

[30] Roger B. Hunting and Gloria S. Neuwirth, *Who Sues in New York City* (New York: Columbia University Press, 1962), p. 98. Only 2 percent of those with a high socioeconomic status failed to take action to recover; 27 percent of those in the lowest socioeconomic status category did nothing.

While marital problems and accidents affect all members of society, the Poor are particularly likely to experience problems with welfare, consumer fraud, and rental housing. Here, too, the Poor seldom initiate legal actions as plaintiffs.[31] Even institutions and procedures designed specifically for the Poor are not used by them. For instance, they do not utilize small claims courts. Established with the intent of providing the indigent with a forum in which small claims could be brought without attorneys, intricate rules, or large fees, these courts in practice provide a convenient and inexpensive way for creditors (collection agencies, businesses, and government) to collect small debts from the poor.[32]

Further evidence of the failure of indigents to initiate civil suits can be found in statistics on how frequently they contact lawyers. Plainly stated, they are less likely to use lawyers.[33] Less than 5 percent of the attorneys in New York City serviced clients with median incomes of less than $5,000 despite the fact that nearly half of the families and unrelated persons in the city were at that income level.[34]

Lack of money is the most obvious explanation for this phenomenon. Litigation requires a lawyer, and lawyers have a fondness for being paid. Programs to provide free legal services alleviate the problem, but they do not solve it. Most programs have strict eligibility requirements, and many people too well-off to meet them nevertheless cannot afford even

---

[31] Both Wald, in *Law and Poverty*, and Jerome Carlin and Jan Howard, in "Legal Representation and Class Justice," *UCLA Law Review* 12 (1965) pp. 381-437, describe and discuss the absence of the poor as plaintiffs in such actions at some length.

[32] Carlin and Howard, "Legal Representation," p. 421, cite research findings that two-thirds of plaintiffs in the Oakland-Piedmont Small Claims Court were business firms or government agencies (collecting tax and hospital bills). See also Comment: "Small Claims Courts as Collection Agencies," *Stanford Law Review* 4 (1952), p. 237.

[33] See Leon Mayhew and Albert J. Reiss, "The Social Organization of Legal Contacts," *American Sociological Review* 34 (June, 1969), pp. 310-311.

[34] Carlin, *Lawyers' Ethics*, pp. 113-116.

modest attorneys' fees. There is not even enough manpower in legal assistance programs to begin to meet fully the needs of those who are eligible. In fact, legal aid bureaus are reluctant to publicize their programs on the realistic assumption that they would be inundated with cases.[35] Legal costs are not confined to attorneys' fees, of course. Various fees (filing fees, fees for serving summonses, fees for printing public notices) are encountered throughout the course of litigation.[36] Appeals are even more expensive; substantial costs are involved in having transcripts of court proceedings reproduced and briefs typed. Again, provisions designed to reduce the obstacles to the poor (for instance, proceeding *in forma pauperis*) have not proved effective.[37]

But the failure of the Poor to use attorneys is not simply a matter of money. The legal profession is organized to deal with problems arising from the ownership of property (along with accidents and divorce), not the problems most frequently encountered by the Poor.[38] The best legal talent is found in law firms located in downtown areas and specializing in corporation law, estates, tax matters, and the like. Few private attorneys specialize in problems of the Poor or locate offices in their neighborhoods. In fact, many attorneys make conscious efforts to avoid lower-class clients.[39] Unless the case involves an accident or divorce, a Poor person may find

---

[35] For discussions of the inability of the legal aid system to meet the legal needs of the poor, see Wald, *Law and Poverty*, pp. 46-52; and Carlin, Howard, and Messinger, *Civil Justice*, pp. 48-51.

[36] Wald, *Law and Poverty*, pp. 59-62. In March 1971, the Supreme Court acknowledged the inherent denial of due process to indigents that the requirement of filing fees in divorce actions imposed. Boddie v. Connecticut, 28 L. Ed. 2d 113 (1971).

[37] Wald, *Law and Poverty*, p. 61.

[38] Mayhew and Reiss, "The Social Organization," p. 317.

[39] Carlin and Howard, in "Legal Representation," p. 428, conclude that "lawyers systematically exclude lower-class clients, and . . . this is based mainly on . . . low expectation of financial gain, a desire to avoid a less prestigeful type of practice and clientele, and perhaps, also conceptions of what merits consideration in the legal arena."

it difficult to locate a lawyer who is willing and able to handle his problems.

Other considerations also enter. The Poor are less likely to recognize that problems which they encounter in their daily lives might have legal remedies. They simply may not think about or know about the possibility of going to court.[40] Furthermore, there is a deep distrust of everything having to do with the law and courts. As Robert F. Kennedy once put it, "The poor man looks upon the law as an enemy, not as a friend. For him the law is always taking something away."[41] Finally, the incentive to go to court is further weakened by the belief that it is not likely to do any good.[42]

The Poor may be quite correct in this belief for a number of reasons. Statutes and precedents in many areas of the civil law operate to their disadvantage.[43] Also, formal procedures are a handicap. They require lawyers and fees. Delays are easy to obtain and they are less easily borne by the poor litigant.[44] Third, the poor litigant may find himself the

---

[40] Wald, *Law and Poverty*, pp. 42-43; Carlin and Howard, "Legal Representation," p. 424.

[41] Quoted by Wald, *Law and Poverty*, p. 6.

[42] Lower-status people are generally found to feel less efficacious in politics. Jacob offers some evidence that this is true of the legal process as well. Those with less income, education, and occupational status score lower on his scale of "judicial efficacy." See Herbert Jacob, *Debtors in Court* (Chicago: Rand McNally, 1969), p. 119. Interestingly, while all auto accident victims who have had prior experience trying to recover are *less* likely to try again than those with no experience, this is even more true of the poor. See Carlin, Howard, and Messinger, *Civil Justice*, p. 75.

[43] Carlin, Howard, and Messinger, *Civil Justice*, pp. 4-18, have an extended discussion of the bias of law against the poor. For instance, they find "the common law has generally promoted the interests of the landlord against the tenant," and that creditors are favored over debtors. See also Wald, *Law and Poverty*, pp. 12-20.

[44] In New York City, commercial cases are given priority, and dockets remain fairly current. This shifts the entire burden of delay on private citizens involved in personal injury cases. See Hans Zeisel, Harry Kalven, Jr., and Bernard Buckholz, *Delay in the Court* (Boston: Little, Brown, 1959), p. 7.

object of retaliation against which there is no effective defense. Tenants who have reported housing violations, for instance, have been summarily (and legally) evicted.[45] Undoubtedly many others do nothing, fearing reprisals. Fourth, unless he has an attorney provided by a legal aid program, the poor plaintiff is likely to have an inferior lawyer. According to two students of the problem, "Lawyers representing lower-class persons tend to be the least competent members of the bar, and those least likely to employ a high level or wide range of technical skills."[46] These lawyers do not expect repeat business from their clients, and are typically more interested in keeping the broker who steered the client to him satisfied than in doing a good job.[47] Finally, many judges and court clerks in lower civil courts appear to be biased against poor litigants. The extent and significance of such bias is unknown and difficult to ascertain, so it must be viewed cautiously. But evidence that it exists in an unknown but significant degree can be found.[48]

The obstacles encountered by the Poor in becoming successful plaintiffs are probably faced in lesser degrees by other groups as well. Large corporations and collection agencies benefit more than do corner grocers.[49]

---

[45] A tenant who drew up a petition protesting conditions in his building was evicted and could not find another suitable apartment. Wald, *Law and Poverty*, p. 15.

[46] Carlin and Howard, "Legal Representation," p. 384.

[47] Carlin, *Lawyers on Their Own*, pp. 135-142.

[48] See Carlin, Howard, and Messinger's *Civil Justice*, p. 38. They cite a study which found dockets in the Philadelphia Magistrate's Court had no space for entering a judgment for the defendant! Court personnel were also found to have financial interests in collection agencies litigating in court. See also Michael Lipsky, *Protest in City Politics* (Chicago: Rand McNally, 1969), p. 113, on the prolandlord bias of New York City's housing court judges.

[49] Jacob, *Debtors in Court*, for instance, finds wide discrepancies in the use creditors make of garnishment proceedings. Finance companies, large retailers, and doctors and hospitals (relying on collection agencies) use them, small businesses do not. See his discussion on pp. 78-86.

Patterns of Who Gets What in
Other Selected Aspects of the Civil Process

Among the many other components of the civil process that operate to the disadvantage of the Poor, several have already been alluded to in previous chapters. In the discussion of automobile accident claims, the importance of hiring an attorney was demonstrated. Naturally, it is the Poor who are least likely to hire attorneys, and, as noted, to make any efforts whatsoever to recover. Furthermore, anyone struggling to make ends meet would find it more difficult to refuse compromise offers in hopes of a bigger settlement later. This weakens his bargaining position. Poverty encourages insurance companies to try to delay settlement even more; there is evidence that the poor wait longer for their settlements than others.[50] Not only is compensation from accidents uneven, but the burden of its unevenness appears to fall most heavily on the Disadvantaged.

The civil commitment process shows a similar pattern: The elderly and the poor are most likely to be committed. Part of the explanation lies in the fact that the police account for a large proportion of those eventually committed. When the police encounter persons displaying bizarre behavior, they are more likely to be persons from disadvantaged groups.[51]

If we examine the impact of the civil process on the functioning of the political system, it is clear that it serves primarily to bolster the status quo. Any ongoing system needs a widely accepted mechanism for resolving disputes

---

[50] Clarence Morris and James Paul, "The Financial Impact of Automobile Accidents," in *Dollars, Delay, and the Automobile Victim* (New York: Bobbs-Merrill, 1968), p. 14, find that in over half of the serious accidents studied where there was an award, more than a year elapsed. A larger proportion of poor people (26 percent) had to wait at least three years.

[51] Another area of the civil law that evidently displays bias against the poor is family law. See Jacobus Tenbroek, "California's Dual System of Family Law: Its Origin, Development, and Present Status," *Stanford Law Review* 16 (1964). He argues that the dual system—one for rich, one for poor—operates over the whole range of family problems.

over the operating rules of the game. Decisions involving election procedures, the powers of governmental officials and agencies, and the political rights of citizens provide such a mechanism. Disputes between the major competing elements that comprise the political elite of a society also must be resolved peacefully. This, too, occurs in the civil process, particularly when the disputes arise from private interpersonal dealings between the politically influential. Finally, political regimes must display flexibility in responding to the demands and aspirations of disadvantaged groups. Groups and interests with at least some political power (for example, the NAACP, a small local business, a newly formed union) often find litigation is their most effective strategy in achieving goals. But the most disadvantaged groups (migrant workers are a good example) are rarely capable of effectively pursuing their interests in the courts.

A similar argument can be made about the impact of civil courts in the economic sphere. As Dolbeare's study of local trial courts concludes, the primary function of these courts is to protect property rights.[52] Businessmen challenge tax assessments, city regulations, and adverse zoning decisions. Retailers and landlords obtain judgments, have evictions served and enforced, garnish wages, and have merchandise repossessed.

A final characteristic of the civil process is its ability to force delays; this tends to support both the political and economic status quo. Opponents of change are frequently able to delay it through costly and involved litigation. The most notable examples occurred at the beginning of this century when opponents of income tax and child labor laws were able to postpone their implementation for years by

---

[52] Kenneth Dolbeare, *Trial Courts in Urban Politics* (New York: Wiley, 1967), p. 127. He observes, "... the property oriented role of trial courts [is] an enduring phenomenon of the urban political context." Later, in ranking the values upheld by these courts, Dolbeare mentions "property rights, the status quo, and openness and regularity of the political process, in that order" (p. 130).

successfully challenging their constitutionality. Far more numerous, however, are efforts at the local level to block construction of highways, incinerators, parks, and other public projects through legal challenges.

Thus, by enforcing property rights, ensuring the smooth functioning of the political status quo, and delaying change, the civil process tends to perpetuate exisiting social and political conditions. Since the Disadvantaged are by definition doing poorly, they certainly do not benefit and probably suffer as a result of its effectiveness in maintaining these conditions.

CHAPTER 14
THE LEGAL PROCESS IN THE POLITICAL SYSTEM: EXPLANATION AND PROSPECTS

TOWARD AN EXPLANATION OF OUTCOME PATTERNS IN THE LEGAL PROCESS

Many citizens believe that the typical mechanisms for translating resources and influence into practical advantage are absent from the legal process. The belief that principles of due process, impartial judgment by judge and jury, equal justice, and the like govern its operation precludes the possibility that politics sticks its sleazy fingers into the legal pie. But if we examine the patterns of who gets what as a result of the operation of the legal process, the inescapable conclusion is that these outcomes reflect the same values and balance of interests that characterize other components of the political system.

On a superficial level, it is quite easy to explain the paradox. There is no paradox when the inaccuracy of conventional myths about the legal process is acknowledged. The real task, however, is not to explain an easily resolved paradox but rather to account for the reality of the pattern of outcomes just described.

The simple answer is that the legal process is merely part of the political system, and as such behaves like the rest of the political system. This response is not completely worthless, particularly to former myth-holders. But it lacks the detail and specificity that we expect from what we normally refer to as an explanation.

A fully satisfactory answer is unlikely. We still lack a general theory of American politics. Until we develop one, we will not produce comprehensive theories describing its component processes. But we can offer several partial explanations that take us somewhat beyond a simple assertion that politics explains outcomes. In the discussion that follows, several explanations, each increasingly substantive and meaningful, will be considered.

The simplest (and least satisfactory) explanation is that the legal process has always displayed these characteristics and continues to do so through simple inertia.[1] How the legal process came to acquire these characteristics in the first place and the mechanisms that perpetuate early patterns is left unanswered. But the *inertia* explanation is useful in two respects. First, it challenges the frequently propounded belief in a golden age of the legal process. This notion, often espoused by critics of current practices, suggests that the legal process has somehow strayed from the high standards and ideals that characterized its operation 50, 100, or even 150 years ago. These critics would probably agree that things are better today if they bothered to inquire how the legal process operated in the past. Second, the inertia theory suggests that we need to examine processes that operate to prevent significant change. They are both strong and pervasive. Given a system that historically has been disadvantageous to the poor, the difficulty of inducing change provides

---

[1] I am assuming without presenting evidence that the English common law, the arrangements for invoking it, and the developments that followed its transplantation to America indeed did favor creditors over debtors, landlords and property owners over tenants, retailers over consumers. For evidence on one aspect of the question, see Allan Silver, "The Demand for Order in Civil Society: A Review of Some Themes in the History of Urban Crime, Police, and Riot," in David Bordua, ed., *The Police: Six Sociological Essays* (New York: Wiley, 1967), pp. 1-24. He finds a major factor leading to the formation of police forces in England was the demand for law and order (protection against street crime and rioting) among the urban propertied classes.

a partially satisfying explanation of why it currently exhibits this characteristic.

A somewhat more sophisticated approach looks to the institutional and procedural environment in which the decision-makers of the legal process operate. In this view, outcomes are determined at least in part by the existing structure and content of civil and criminal law and procedure.

In Chapter 13 we saw how the civil process is structured to protect and enforce middle-class values with respect to property and political relationships. The criminal law to a substantial degree is a mechanism for enforcing middle-class standards of morality. In the words of one writer on the topic, the criminal process "reflects the prevailing customs and prejudices of the established classes in society." [2] Thus, it is not simply a matter of enforcing law and order. The crucial questions are: Whose law? Whose order? [3]

Of course, some behavior is regarded as undesirable by nearly everyone in society, and there is broad consensus that it deserves to be sanctioned. Certain forms of murder, unprovoked assaults resulting in serious bodily injury, and brutal robberies provide several good examples. But the breadth of consensus is considerably more restricted than the average middle-class student, who has not thought about the matter, is likely to realize. Boisterous talking, minor fighting, and sexual relations accompanied by a certain amount of physical force are not uncommon or particularly reprehensible to significant segments of our population. Even more important, however, are forms of behavior that do not produce victims: most forms of gambling, prostitution, drunkenness, vagrancy and loitering, drug use, and sexual acts between consenting adults. A sizable number of people do not consider these unusual, unnatural, or sinful, or think that they deserve

---

[2] William Stringfellow, "Unresolved Issues in the Allocation of Justice, An Existential View," in James Klonoski and Robert Mendelsohn, eds., *The Politics of Local Justice* (Boston: Little, Brown, 1970), p. 235.

[3] See Matthew Holden, Jr., "Politics, Public Order, and Pluralism," in Klonoski and Mendelsohn, *The Politics of Local Justice*, p. 239.

criminal sanctions. If there is any victim when these acts occur, it is the sensibilities of middle-class morality. When such behavior is defined as *criminal* and made the object of enforcement activities and formal sanctions, it represents a clear attempt to impose middle-class standards of behavior on nonmiddle-class members of society.

The importance of such middle-class defined "crimes without victims" is easily overlooked because bank robberies, rape-murders, kidnappings, and the like are continually brought to our attention through the media. If we examine the reality of the criminal process, however, at least half of all arrests are for crimes without victims.[4]

Several other aspects of structure and procedure appear to contribute to outcomes. We have emphasized repeatedly that the Poor are concentrated at the lower levels of the legal process. Neither represented by attorneys nor given helpful advice from official personnel, their difficulties are understandable. Because the legal process and its tangential structures (as, for example, the bargaining process associated with auto accident compensation) makes representation by an attorney almost essential to avoid automatically losing, these people are naturally at a disadvantage.

A third approach to explanation is to determine which factors in the environment of legal process decision-makers lead them to make decisions that result in the outcomes described. In part, the procedural and structural factors just mentioned are responsible. But there are other characteristics of their working environment that are relevant. Some of these have been described in detail in Part III.

As we have seen, important decisions are shaped by partici-

---

[4] The 1965 arrest statistics for jurisdictions serving 134 million people show that excluding traffic offenses, nearly half (2,340,000) of the 4,995,047 arrests were for drunkenness, disorderly conduct, vagrancy, and gambling. Simple assaults totalled 207,000. Arrests for prostitution, drug use, and sexual deviation are not broken down. The President's Commission on Law Enforcement and Administration of Justice, *Task Force Report: Crime and its Impact—An Assessment* (Washington, D.C.: U.S. Government Printing Office, 1969), p. 17, Table 2.

pants who are not formally responsible for making them. Bail bondsmen, for example, decide whether to accept collateral, to extend credit, or even to write a bond in return for cash. Although we do not know how bondsmen make their decisions, we can speculate that considerations of due process and equal treatment are secondary to purely financial considerations. Prosecutors and defense attorneys play important roles in determining sentences in many jurisdictions. In the private offices, corridors, and coffee shops where negotiations are conducted, these attorneys consider their work loads, financial calculations, and the prosecutor's conviction rate.

But the harsh realities of official decision-arenas also affect the choices made. At the lower levels, officials are faced with limited resources, inadequate physical facilities, a poorly trained and underpaid staff, and an oppressive case load. Magistrates coping with the task of processing the 250 drunk arrests made by the police each day understandably ignore the niceties of time-consuming adherence to due process. The pressure to produce results forces prosecutors, civil judges, and police to rely upon similar shortcuts. Those who staff the lower levels of the legal process are forced to function as bureaucrats, not as appliers of traditional legal norms and procedures.

For many decision-makers in the legal process there is also an added element that many bureaucrats do not face: political pressures. In part, these pressures result from the recruitment processes themselves. Where prosecutors and judges are elected, additional channels of access are created.[5] When elected officials hire and fire important decision-makers, policies must be modified to anticipate effective pressures that may be generated and applied to the boss. Little pressure,

---

[5] Abraham Blumberg, in *Criminal Justice* (Chicago: Quadrangle, 1967), p. 105, reports that in the state felony court he studied, criminal lawyers associated with political clubs centered in judges' election districts may be given sympathetic treatment in the disposition of their cases.

however, is likely to come from the clients of the lower levels of the legal process. The vagrant; the evicted tenant; the elderly person committed to a mental institution; the Puerto Rican youth stopped, questioned, frisked, and released; the poor defendant spending 60 days in jail awaiting trial—none of these people are likely to have the political resources, access, skill, or allies required to do anything about their plight.

This suggests the last and most fundamental of our partial explanations for outcome patterns in the legal process. Its basic elements are suggested by Matthew Holden's definition of criminal law as "the regularization of force-and-intimidation on the basis of some presumptive consensus amongst those able to make their wills felt."[6] The key phrase is "able to make their wills felt," suggesting a direct link between the content and application of criminal law and the balance of political influence in society. But the generalization, that outcomes reflect political realities, can be broadened to include the entire operation of the legal process, civil and criminal. In other words, the treatment of the Poor in the legal process results from their lack of political influence generally. Just as they are unable to obtain favorable consideration from legislative and executive institutions, so, to, do they find themselves disadvantaged in the legal process.

Political science has not yet developed an adequate theory to explain and describe the mechanisms that translate resources into political advantage. Inertia in the context of an ongoing system that already favors those who hold influence undoubtedly will be part of such a theory. So will the mechanisms through which myths and notions of legitimacy are created and sustained. The mechanisms that shape the agenda of politics—the questions that capture public interest and official attention—also will be included. Finally, the explicit techniques and processes surrounding day-to-day operations are relevant. Anticipated reactions in particular

---

[6] Holden, "Politics, Public Order, and Pluralism," p. 239.

play a significant role. Police chiefs and prosecutors refrain from enforcing certain laws (country club after-hours drinking, safe but illegal abortions, church bingo), because they anticipate trouble. A sudden crackdown on drunk drivers, with mandatory jail sentences (even for middle-class businessmen and salesmen) is likely to set off a chain of protest.[7]

Until a comprehensive theory is developed, we will have to be content with the sort of partial explanations offered here. Whatever its final shape, however, there is little question about the accuracy of the basic generalization. As elsewhere in politics, those who possess the things that permit one to exercise political power (wealth, education, social standing, good health, and so forth) benefit from the operation of the legal process. Those who do not are its objects and victims. Principles of equal justice and due process are honored mostly in the breach—in the infrequent and highly publicized situation. At the mundane level of its day-to-day operation, the legal process indeed reflects and perhaps exaggerates the inequities found in American society generally.

THE PROSPECTS FOR REFORM

The Varieties of Reform

A number of proposals, some of which are currently being implemented, can best be described as *cosmetic*. Like a matron's make-up, they alter the surface and at times disguise reality, but do nothing to change the basic contours underneath. Much of the money being spent by the federal government's Law Enforcement Assistance Administration funds such projects. They seek to "improve police training", recruit "better" patrolmen, finance the purchase of equipment to make the police more "efficient" (helicopters, riot tanks,

---

[7] The police in Nassau County, New York, began enforcing traffic laws on county highways strictly as a technique to generate pressure for a salary increase. They ticketed *every* violation. The uproar they anticipated dutifully occurred.

antiriot weapons, communications equipment), improve record-keeping and administration in courts of general jurisdiction, and fund research aimed at improving crime detection techniques. Other examples of cosmetic reforms include training sessions for judges to reduce sentence disparities, and the construction of modern prisons.

Middle-gauge reform proposals also leave basic structures, procedures, and assumptions intact. But they are somewhat more far-reaching in their intent and effects. Some are designed to bring operating reality into greater conformity with official myth. Bail-reform projects fall into this category. Also, since the criminal process is predicated on an assumption of competent legal representation for all, steps can be taken to see that such counsel is available. On the civil side, the Neighborhood Legal Services program of the Office of Economic Opportunity (the core of what was once known as the *war on poverty*) has made significant gains in the developing field of poverty law.

A number of other middle-gauge reform proposals have been suggested. Alternatives to prison—work-release programs, weekend sentences, half-way houses, and so forth are prominent examples. Although most proposals to change methods of recruitment are cosmetic (e.g., instituting the Missouri plan for selecting judges), they need not be. For instance, to overcome the mediocrity of judges at the lowest levels of the legal process, all attorneys might be subjected to *judge duty* in much the same way ordinary citizens are subject to jury duty. Even the highest paid partner in the largest firm in town might find himself sitting in drunk court or small claims court under such a system.

Finally, there are a number of theoretically possible changes that involve *fundamental* alteration of procedures, structures, and assumptions without a system-wide social and political revolution. The most widely discussed and perhaps most meaningful would revolutionize criminal law by removing large portions of human behavior now regulated by criminal statutes from the jurisdiction of the legal system entirely. Loitering, prostitution, gambling, drug use, and drunkenness (unless connected with driving) would all be considered legal (though in some instances regulated by government). Crimes without victims would no longer be defined as criminal. Attempts to legislate middle-class morality for all of society would be abandoned. Other public agencies would have to be created in some cases (drug treatment centers, drying-out centers for drunks, publicly operated gambling agencies), but they would not involve the police, courts, or prisons. Presumably, they could do a better job providing services while eliminating the stigma and punishment associated with the criminal process.

Proposals for changing the nature of the political forces operating on various agencies of the legal process would also produce fundamental changes. Many of the schemes for neighborhood or community control of the police fall into this category.

Not all change must necessarily await implementation of a specific proposal, of course. We can think of a number of significant changes that would automatically result from changes in the structure of the legal profession, the values of those who make key decisions in the legal process, or the personnel who make them. This brings us to a consideration of some of the forces that might promote change in the legal process.

Forces and Trends Favoring Change

A basic premise of this book is that the legal process is part of the political process and reflects the balance of interests and influence found in society as a whole. If this is accurate, changes in the relative political power of various groups eventually should be reflected in the structure of outcomes produced by the legal process. Thus, if welfare mothers, blacks, Mexican-Americans, Indians, and poor people become more potent politically, the legal process will be more responsive to their needs. Official decision-makers would be more sympathetic, bail levels reduced, sewer service reduced, and unfair contracts more often overturned. Of course, gains in political influence would not necessarily be fully or promptly translated into more equal treatment. But at least some of the present inequities would be remedied. This has indeed started to occur: the changing treatment toward minority group members by police; recruitment of the Poor into police forces; increases in the number of black judges and other officials in the legal process; and increased concern about prison conditions all stem from the increasing political power of these groups.

Two other groups—neither of which is directly disadvantaged by the current operation of the legal process—are potential supporters of reform. The first consists of certain members of the general public. With increasing education levels and "middle classification" of society has come an expectation that reality should conform to strongly valued principles. As the visibility of the operation of the legal process continues to rise, the extent of the gap between myth and reality will become obvious. Even though the legal process in fact may conform more closely to principles of due process and equal justice today than it did 50 years ago, the awareness of the still substantial gap that remains is much higher. The result may well be at least some moderate pressure for reform. Groups and individuals allied with Ralph Nader and such organizations as Common Cause are prime candidates to provide such pressure.

The second group, somewhat surprisingly, is the legal profession itself. The small but growing group of young lawyers who staff legal aid bureaus, OEO-funded neighborhood legal services projects, and public interest law firms, can make significant contributions, particularly in providing competent representation to the unrepresented, demanding conformity to established procedures and principles (proper service, reasonable bail), and challenging discriminatory law and precedent. Other young lawyers pursuing more traditional careers may also demand time off to practice public interest law. A trend toward such work, even among established Wall Street and Washington firms, had begun in the late 1960s and early 1970s, and could contribute significantly to change if it continues.

But the capacity of these young lawyers to sustain change by themselves is limited. If the higher-status, established members of the profession could be brought to support reform, it would be a significant addition. It is not possible to predict that such support will emerge. But the potential, created by the existence of the gulf between legal ideals and reality, is there. Gaps between ideals and reality are found everywhere in the political system, of course. But nowhere in the American context are ideals so firmly held and yet so consistently violated as in the legal process. The gulf is not only wider here. Its potential for stimulating outrage and a sense of betrayal when exposed is unequaled.

Lawyers are particularly vulnerable. Perhaps more than any other profession, they have a well-articulated set of beliefs that tie their life work to the sanctity of law and the operation of good government. In both public rhetoric and private belief, many lawyers see themselves as servants to society in general, and to the legal system in particular. Who else, they feel, has the knowledge, ability, and motivation to serve as guardians of the cherished principles of due process and equal justice? [8]

As the nature of the gap between the ideal and the real becomes clearer, however, the discomfort and embarrassment of the legal profession is likely to increase substantially. Particularly if they are confronted directly with evidence about the operation of the legal process like that reported throughout this book, a certain number may well try in good faith to institute changes.[9]

Obstacles to Change

If the foregoing analysis is optimistic and naïve, the argument here may well err in the opposite direction. For despite the

---

[8] Not all lawyers take such an exalted view of the functions they perform. Many undoubtedly will acknowledge more than a grain of truth in the description of the practice of law attributed to a founder of a famous New York law firm: "You take money from one rich son-of-a-bitch and give it to another rich son-of-a-bitch."

[9] A similar argument could be made with respect to the political elite generally. Many, particularly elected officials, are lawyers. Even those who are not, however, would find it difficult to condone gross violations of equal justice and due process once their existence is clearly demonstrated and a matter of public knowledge.

forces generating momentum for change in the legal process, there are compelling reasons to be pessimistic.

In the first place, the more meaningful the reforms are, the more difficult they are to implement. Cosmetic reforms are not too difficult to achieve, but they don't result in much change either. Cosmetic reforms do not damage the interests of established groups to any great degree. Middle-level reforms, however, are likely to meet with opposition. Bail bondsmen and their allies are unhappy with bail reform. Marginal members of the bar have led fights in bar associations against neighborhood legal services offices and other forms of legal assistance to the poor because they feared competition. No-fault insurance schemes draw the wrath of personal injury lawyers.

Each of the groups just mentioned oppose middle-gauge change because they fear financial loss. Other reforms are opposed more on symbolic rather than material grounds. Proposals to legalize gambling or to reform any law dealing with crimes without victims elicit the opposition of a colorful assortment of religious, fraternal, and patriotic groups. Proposals for prison reform evoke even more vociferous opposition. Those who seek to reform the criminal law by humanizing punishments or by even largely eliminating punishment fail to recognize one of the functions which punishment performs: the capture, trial, and punishment of criminals satisfies psychological needs based on fears that are not likely to be overcome through rational argument. [10]

Another problem, already alluded to, is that many do not recognize the need for reform even though they share the values of due process and equal treatment. Most people are ill-

---

[10] An indication of the opposition that such reforms are likely to elicit can be found in the politics surrounding the location of prisons, drug treatment centers, and half-way houses. Few oppose them in the abstract, but hardly anyone wants such a facility in *their* neighborhood. Thus for years (and continuing today), prisons like Attica, housing urban residents, are located in rural areas willing to accept them for the economic benefits derived. But visits from family members, recruitment of minority guards, and establishment of work-release programs are stifled by rural locations. For an interesting discussion of the problem, see "Public is Found to Resist Prison Reform Proposals," *The New York Times*, October 26, 1971.

informed about public affairs generally. What they see of the legal process—its most visible and higher-level aspects—conforms rather closely to ideals. Like independent regulatory commissions, the legal process produces the image of effective operation to the public while its operating reality remains concealed.

Third, reforms frequently must be implemented by incumbent decision-makers who are unlikely to be sympathetic to them. Certainly, they are not likely to be sources of innovation themselves. They are products of the status quo and benefit from it. Few who oppose the way things currently operate are able to survive the formal and informal screening mechanisms found in the recruitment process. And as the police reaction to various Supreme Court decisions suggests, enforcing adherence to changes imposed from outside is no easy task. Most proposals for change are regarded as implicit criticisms of past practice, and as such are resented by the practitioners.

Fourth, to the extent that substantial reforms take money (and most do), the legal process is at a disadvantage in the competition for funds. Far-reaching reforms are extremely expensive, and are likely to attract opposition from interests who feel that other more worthy (in their eyes) uses for the money exist.

Finally, several other characteristics of the legal process described earlier make reform difficult. It is highly decentralized. The combination of low visibility and high discretion (both authorized and unauthorized) make it difficult to implement changes. Those at the higher levels do not always select personnel for the lower levels, particularly in the judiciary. Nor can they fire them. They have little control over budgets.[11] Finally, decisions are usually incremental. Sweeping decisions bringing about sweeping changes are the exception.

---

[11] Higher courts do have some say over the procedures used by lower tribunals in some jurisdictions. And they can reverse and review decisions, but only if they are appealed to them.

SUMMARY AND CONCLUSIONS

This book has examined a number of components of the legal process from a political perspective. It is now appropriate to ask what this inquiry reveals about American politics.

One point should be unmistakably clear: The legal process is an integral part of the political process. It not only displays the major characteristics of the political system in recruitment, operation, and impact, but appears to play a particularly crucial role in shaping patterns of who gets what. Because it is intimately bound up in the legitimate use of coercive force in society, it lies at the heart of politics. Because of its role as overseer of the rules of the political game and its profound effect on the way citizens perceive government, the legal process has a major part in shaping the forces that determine stability and change in the political system.

A number of characteristics of the legal process illustrate general propositions about the operation of the political system. Among the lessons of politics suggested, five are particularly noteworthy:

1. The most visible aspects of politics are not necessarily representative. They may tell us more about symbolic politics than material politics. Visible demonstrations of adherence to myths often obscure less visible but far more prevalent violations.
2. Much of the stuff of politics, particularly the allocation of tangible benefits and rewards, occurs at the lower levels and is performed by bureaucratic-like organizations.
3. Decisions at the lower levels use criteria that stray markedly from the ideals proclaimed by highly visible symbolic output. In the legal process, cases are settled by negotiation, not trial. There is, in effect, a presumption of guilt, a presumption of insanity, a presumption of indebtedness. Official goals are displaced by the demands of bureaucratic necessity.
4. Outcomes in politics basically reflect the distribution of political influence. Those with resources and the motivation, knowledge, and skills to invoke them will benefit from the decisions made by the political system. Those without resources assume a dispropor-

tionate share of the burdens. This occurs despite our society's commitment to equal justice, due process, political equality, and democracy.
5. The moral and ethical arguments for substantial change in the operation of the political system (including the legal process) are compelling, particularly if one accepts the proposition that reality ought to conform to cherished principles about what reality should be like. But as worthy and necessary as change may be, the prospects for achieving it are not especially promising.

Change is not impossible, of course. But before meaningful change can come about, there must be a far-broader recognition and understanding of the legal process as it actually operates.

INDEX

Abington Township School District v. *Schempp*, 292-294
Abraham, Henry J., 280-281
Accident litigation, 72-73, 135-142, 209, 212, 214-215, 263-265
Argersinger v. *Hamlin*, 122-123
Attorney general, state, 7, 16-20, 30, 56, 58, 61
Attorney general, U.S., 148
Attorneys, 6-7, 250, 261
  ad litem, 131, 133-134
  defense, 62, 102-125, 228, 243-245, 342
  in federal court, 146, 171-172
  plaintiffs', 73-74, 136-142, 330-335
  public defenders, 101, 105-120
  recruitment of, 55, 70-72
  U.S. attorneys, 35-43, 47-48, 56-59, 144-174, 213, 252

Bail, 103, 109, 121, 127, 215, 228, 234-243, 254, 326-327, 345
Bail bondsmen, 235-237, 242-243, 315, 343, 349
Baker v. *Carr*, 180
Bankruptcy, 72-74, 209, 213, 272

Bar associations, 31, 38, 43, 52, 66-68, 315, 320
Berger, Warren, 187
Blumberg, Abraham, 113, 119-120
Brandeis, Louis, 186-187
Brown, Claude, 141, 247-248
Butler, Pierce, 45

Carlin, Jerome, 71
Carswell, G. Harrold, 45, 48
Certiorari, 178-179, 181
Chase, Harold, 42-43
Civil Commitment, 129-135, 207, 265-268, 314-315, 335
Clark, Charles Edward, 196
Clark, Ramsey, 253
Clearance rate, 50, 95
Constitution, U.S., 143, 278, 300
Conviction rate, 104, 112, 115, 124
Corporation counsel, 20
Courts, state
  appeals, 63-66, 197-203
  circuit, 28-29, 33, 52, 59
  district, 29, 33, 56
  felony, 78-79, 98-123, 170-174, 312, 322
  juvenile, 247-250, 320

353

lower civil, 262-263, 309-310, 320, 334
lower criminal, 121-129, 134, 250, 262, 307-321, 327, 345
probate, 213, 265
recorder's, 30, 67, 121, 125
small claims, 209, 331
supreme, 18-20, 26-29, 52, 69, 197-203, 299-304, 310
Cox, Harold, 153
Creditors, actions by, 72-74, 209, 257-263, 315, 329-331
Criminal record, 75, 235, 239-240, 246-247

Danelski, David, 45
Death penalty, 102, 206
Delay in the legal process, 214-215, 237, 265, 271, 335
Department of Justice, 37-44, 48, 147, 154-157, 160-170, 251, 253
Diversity, 144, 171, 272-273
Divorces, 208, 257-258, 330
Dolbeare, Kenneth, 270-271, 274, 336
Due process, 98-99, 120, 173

Eisenhower, Dwight D., 44
Ellender, Allen, 151
Engel v. *Vitale*, 292
Escobedo v. *Illinois*, 288-289

Fabian, Paul E., 216
FBI, 147-148, 164, 223
Foote, Caleb, 126-128
Fortas, Abraham, 45, 187
Frank, Jerome, 8, 196, 278
Frankfurter, Felix, 186, 196

Garnishment, 74, 209, 259-263

Gideon v. *Wainwright*, 288, 295, 299
Glick, Henry, 200
Goldman, Sheldon, 194-196
Grand juries, 103, 216, 233

Hand, Learned, 190
Hart, Henry, 180-181
Haynsworth, Clement, 44-45, 48
Holden, Matthew, 343
Howard, Woodford, 189-190

In re Gault, 250
Insurance adjustors, 135-142
Investigative agents, 49, 147-148, 173, 313-314

Jackson, Robert, 180
Jacob, Herbert, 21-25, 31, 56, 74
Johnson, Lyndon, 44-45, 187, 238
Judges, 6, 122, 145, 165
appointment of, 42-49, 51-52, 66-69, 198
background, 33, 51, 54-60, 63-66, 128-129, 150, 152, 198-199, 250, 263
bail-setting, 234-235, 242
career ambitions, 48-49, 110
caseload of, 109, 111-112, 119, 140, 144, 158, 165, 172-173, 178-181, 191-192, 209, 322, 342
decision-making by, 61-65, 78-81, 101, 108-110, 122, 124-134, 150, 153-156, 174, 178-179, 181, 203, 234-235, 242-246, 287-288, 302, 304-306, 315-320
election of, 26-34, 59-63, 66-69, 78, 198-199, 342
ideology of, 44-45, 63-66,

79, 152-153, 172, 182-184, 195-197, 328, 334
in plea bargaining, 110-117, 174
and police, 93-96, 110, 128, 228, 234, 322
powers of, 116, 158, 301. *See also* Sentencing
and private attorneys, 62, 102, 106-107, 116-117, 134, 138-142, 262
and prosecutors, 38, 41, 48, 62, 102-104, 109-116, 155, 157-160, 164-172, 234, 322
role perceptions, 200-201, 302
in settlements, 140-141, 266
strategic environment of, 108-111, 128, 146-147, 152, 176-177, 180-181, 190, 197-200, 342
Judicial conference, 146, 172
Judicial review, 281-282, 299-300
Juries, 76-77, 99, 100-101, 109, 110-118, 141, 154, 158, 171, 209-210, 315
Justices of the peace, 122

Kennedy, Robert F., 333
Krislov, Samuel, 280-281

Legal aid, 331-332, 347
Legal realism, 9-10
Levin, Martin A., 78-79
Long, Russell, 151

Magistrates, 126-128, 263
Mason, Alpheus Thomas, 186
Matthews, Donald, 55, 58, 313
Miranda v. *Arizona*, 289-293, 298
Missouri plan, 52-53, 60, 66-68

Mitchell, John, 91
Mize, Sidney, 153
Murphy, Frank, 180

Nader, Ralph, 347
Nagel, Stuart, 63
Narcotics, 95, 222-225, 229
Nixon, Richard, 1, 44-45, 285
No-fault insurance, 264-265, 349

Passman, Otto, 151
Patterson, Edwin W., 5
Peltason, Jack, 152, 175
Plea bargaining, 95, 101-105, 108-121, 173-174, 228, 243-245
Police, 307, 310
attitudes toward, 84-85, 87, 90, 93, 220-221, 230, 233
characteristics of, 88-95
charging by, 101, 113, 227-228
in crowd control, 230-233
detectives, 50, 94-95
discretion of, 77, 86, 92-93, 216-234, 254, 324-326
graft, 103, 224-225, 254
impact of, 216-233, 249, 253-254, 267-268, 315-317, 323-326
interrogation, 290-291
and judges, 93-96, 110, 128, 228, 234, 322
in law enforcement, 10-11, 85-86, 222-224, 323-324
in order maintenance, 77, 85-86, 92, 217-222, 227, 324
organizations, 62, 91, 96
in plea bargaining, 228
and prosecutors, 62, 93, 103-105, 228, 244, 253, 322
recruitment of, 49, 75, 347
strategic environment of, 83-

95, 176, 217, 231-232, 342
tasks of, 86-87, 92, 122, 225-227, 263, 267, 290-291
vice squad, 95, 222-225, 254
as witnesses, 95, 222, 228-229
working personality of, 88-92, 219-221, 230, 232, 324-325
Pretrial conference, 139-140, 173
Pretrial detention, 118, 123, 211, 215, 234-243, 326-327
Prisons, 207, 210-215, 237, 247-249, 275, 322, 349
Probation officers, 49, 144, 148
Prosecutors, local
in bail-setting, 127, 234, 242
careers of, 23-25, 47, 61
characteristics of, 23-25, 56
discretion of, 102-105, 111-113, 173, 253, 254, 316-319
duties of, 20, 122-123, 130
election of, 20-25
impact of, 103, 233, 243-245, 253-254, 316-317
and judges, 62, 102-104, 109-116, 322
in plea bargaining, 101, 105, 110-118, 244-245, 342
and police, *see* Police
strategic environment of, 102-105, 119-121, 172, 342
tenure of, 21-23

Richardson, Richard J., 149, 165
Right to counsel, 99, 106, 121-123, 130-131, 133, 250, 288-291, 295
Roosevelt, Franklin D., 186

Ross, H. Lawrence, 138-139, 142

Schick, Marvin, 190
Schubert, Glendon, 184
Senatorial courtesy, 37-42, 44
Sentencing, 79, 108, 114-119, 121-123, 125-128, 174, 227-228, 238-241, 315, 326-328
Service of process, 262, 329
Sheriffs, 254
Skolnick, Jerome, 50, 120-121
Stone, Harlan Fiske, 186, 196
Symbolic politics, 282-284, 288-293, 297-298, 311-312

Taft, William Howard, 186
Truman, Harry S., 295

U.S. Attorneys. *See* Attorneys
U.S. Court of Appeals, 43-44, 57, 154, 190-197, 299, 303-306
U.S. district courts, 37, 42-44, 143-175, 191, 251-252, 272-276
U.S. Supreme Court, 44-47, 122-123, 176-190, 277-299, 316-317, 318, 321

Vines, Kenneth, 63, 149, 165
Visibility, 2, 20-21, 93, 172, 191, 217, 244-245, 250, 258-259, 302-303, 312, 317-321, 350-351

Wald, Patricia, 241
Waring, J. Waites, 151
Warren, Earl, 44
Wasby, Stephen, 295-296
Wilson, James Q., 97, 227
Wilson, Woodrow, 186
Wright, J. Skelly, 150-151